Emergency Management Planning Handbook

Other McGraw-Hill Chemical Engineering Books of Interest

Emergency Management Planning Handbook

Geary W. Sikich
Logical Management Systems Corporation
Chesterton, Indiana

HV
551.3
555
1996

McGraw-Hill, Inc.
New York   San Francisco   Washington, D.C.   Auckland   Bogotá
Caracas   Lisbon   London   Madrid   Mexico City   Milan
Montreal   New Delhi   San Juan   Singapore
Sydney   Tokyo   Toronto

Library of Congress Cataloging-in-Publication Data

Sikich, Geary W.
    Emergency management planning handbook / by Geary W. Sikich.
        p.   cm.
    ISBN 0-07-057635-1
    1. Emergency management—United States.   2. Crisis management–
United States   I. Title.
HV551.3.S55   1995
363.3'48'0973—dc20   95-10537
                                                                                                CIP

1 2 3 4 5 6 7 8 9 0   DOC/DOC   9 0 0 9 8 7 6 5

ISBN 0-07-057635-1

*The sponsoring editor for this book was Hal Crawford, the editing
supervisor was Bernard Onken, and the production supervisor was
Donald Schmidt. It was set in Century Schoolbook by Donald A.
Feldman of McGraw-Hill's Professional Book Group composition unit.*

Printed and bound by R. R. Donnelley & Sons Company.

This book is dedicated to those who are charged with the responsibility for emergency / crisis management planning. Many of you may oftentimes feel that it is a hopeless and impossible task. Rest assured it is only a task of continuous and unrelenting improvement.

Contents

Preface

Crisis! The mere mention of the word evokes visions of unspeakable affliction and suffering. It seems as if you cannot pick up a newspaper, magazine, or periodical anymore without reading about a crisis somewhere. Television and movies capitalize on crises. Yet, by developing and implementing a well-defined emergency/crisis management system, your organization can mitigate many of the potentially disastrous effects of an incident.

Management systems, no matter at what level, are never put more strongly to the test than in a crisis situation. The objectives are immediate, and so are the results. What you and those around you do or fail to do will have long-lasting implications. Today, individuals responsible for the management of businesses and institutions must have an emergency management system in place that provides the tools to deal effectively with increasingly complex laws, potential crisis situations, and related issues—or face the consequences. This system must become a part of doing business, not an adjunct to the business.

There are many schools of thought about how to effectively manage a crisis. Many of these applications focus on managing the response aspects of an incident or crisis. In doing so, these applications downplay or altogether omit the significance of what may be considered peripheral issues. Such peripheral issues—the involvement of all levels of management, identification of business operations issues, community considerations, and non-incident-related operations—can have an immense impact on the extent of the crisis, the success of the response operation, and the duration and extent of recovery operations. It is not that focusing on response operations is not good, that response applications do not work, or that the response application is flawed. Far from it; today personnel responsible for developing emergency/crisis management plans are faced with a confounding abundance of response-oriented applications. Therein lies the problem—there is no right, or wrong, response application to implement. However, if you omit the broader management portion of the equation, you may be destined for failure or limited in success, at best. You need a management/response application, an *emergency management system*.

Notwithstanding the profusion of emergency response applications, postincident studies suggest that responders do not manage the broader aspects of a crisis very well. Mismanagement is generally cited as one of the main reasons that incident response systems fail. Mismanagement is not the operative word. Rather, misapplication of a response-oriented program to a management/response-oriented situation is the problem. Poor coordination and a general lack of understanding as to how various response and management elements will join to form an integrated management/response team lead to tremendous waste of resources during the response phase. This leads to a lack of confidence in the ability of the management team to support response efforts during an incident. It also leads to management mistrust of response operations due to a lack of understanding (communication and information) of response operations. This in turn leads to public distrust, more government oversight and involvement, and, in general, more potential for confusion, chaos, and panic.

The emergency response application is not the offender. Rather, it is the scapegoat for the poor organization and lack of an integrated management/response system. Few organizations establish, cultivate, and implement a truly effective emergency management system. Ponder the following:

- Emergency response applications are often chosen because the focus of the responsible parties within the organization is limited to response-oriented processes.

- The emergency response application—fight the fire, stop the spill—seldom reflects the organization's structure and true capabilities.

- Once the application has been adopted, there is little or no means in place for preparing personnel with assigned roles for success. This is especially true when you begin to study emergency management functions as part of the overall organization. It is especially true when we analyze the administrative support staff.

- Once selected, personnel are generally given only response-oriented training. They receive little or no orientation, development, or training in how to coordinate the management and response functions required by an emergency management system.

- Once developed, the emergency response application is seldom updated or well maintained.

- The typical emergency response application is restricted in its coverage. That is, the emergency response application generally focuses on incidents that are generated by an internal operational event or a natural disaster. In addition, the few planners who begin to identify externally generated triggering events generally fall short, as they fail to analyze many potential triggering mechanisms.

- The emergency response application, together with expectations for its implementation, is often ill defined.

- Personnel are not forewarned about the chaotic nature of incident-related operations.

- Skills required to perform the expected functions and produce results are often lacking. No effort is made to remedy the situation. Instead, the organization tries to work around the problem.

- Once activated, the emergency response application provides little, if any, feedback to responders, management, external groups, or the population at large.

Response applications of this type ultimately prove to be of limited use, if not totally useless. If little is done to effect changes to the emergency response appliction, when it is implemented during a crisis the resulting chaos and confusion will ensure greater damage, loss of more assets, nonproductive involvement of more entities, substantial negative impacts on business operations and the community, and potentially undesirable regulatory scrutiny.

It is time to do something to integrate management and response functions into an emergency management system that produces acceptable results. Everyone involved in responding to a crisis wants to do his or her best. An integrated approach that brings all the various elements together as a unified front is needed to ensure success.

Purpose of the Book

While there are many acceptable response applications for managing an incident effectively, few comprehensive, integrated emergency management systems are available. Fewer still are available that allow for a universal application of management/response functions regardless of the size of the affected entity. The *Emergency Management Planning Handbook* offers an approach to developing such a system. The examples presented here can be used as a framework of thought for emergency/crisis management planners as they identify, organize, design, and develop their emergency/crisis management systems. Our discussion presents a flexible framework that can be adapted to most organizations and to most circumstances. It can allow you to capitalize on the most precious asset you have during a crisis—time.

The framework in this book is unique in that it begins with a comprehensive assessment of potential initiating events which serves as a basis for the selection of and development of the structure, people, skills, roles, and responsibilities required to address the emerging situation, regardless of the initial triggering event. The framework used here also offers a working model that you can use to design and implement your emergency management system. This framework is also unique in that it distinguishes between the needs of a business-oriented emergency management system and the traditional emergency response applications that are most commonly employed. This is not to say that the traditional emergency response application has been discarded; far from it. The traditional emergency response application provides the basic building blocks for the emergency management system, with the critical difference being the application of emergency management/response functions to the business setting, where the typical organizational structure requires an expansion of management's role in the response to a crisis.

Emergency Management Planning Handbook presents a framework that will allow anyone responsible for emergency/crisis management preparedness planning activities to achieve better results. One note of caution. *You need to apply the concepts presented in this book in the context of your organization's specific setting, current capabilities, ability to fulfill the commitments inherent in the system, and applicable regulatory guidance; and you must have the capability to maintain the system to ensure responsiveness.*

Who Should Read This Book

Emergency Management Planning Handbook is addressed to emergency/crisis management planners, first and foremost. You can use the information contained in this book as a guide to develop a more effective emergency management system. Second, it is addressed to higher-level managers whose responsibility it is to manage and support the emergency response portion of the system, create an emergency/crisis management system that serves the enterprise as a whole, and protect the public. Third, practitioners—consultants, trainers, organizational development specialists—internal and external, can use the concepts presented in this book to organize programs and customize existing emergency/crisis management systems.

Finally, I feel this book is essential for senior executives as a reference manual. It will provide a wealth of information that you should give consideration to, as your decisions will ultimately affect the ability of your organization to carry forward and effectively implement its emergency/crisis management plan in time of crisis.

This book is not meant to provide *the* definitive system for emergency/crisis management, but to be the framework from which you can evolve an effective and responsive system designed to reflect your organization's capabilities. It is hoped that this book will stimulate discussions as to what an effective emergency management system is and will encourage regulators, legislators, and law makers to focus their attention on promulgating laws governing emergency/crisis preparedness, safety, and the environment that are consistent and provide uniform standards for implementation at all levels and by all organizations in a manner suitable to the structure and capabilities of the affected organization.

How This Book Is Organized

I have structured this book in two parts. Part 1, "Planning: Critical Aspects," presents some basic background information useful for moving forward into Part 2. Part 1 consists of three chapters. Chapter 1, "Planning Process of the Emergency Management System" provides an overview and perspective on effective emergency/crisis management applications.

Chapter 2, "Organizing the All-Hazards Emergency Management System," introduces the concept of a standard framework for ensuring the effectiveness of the emergency/crisis management system. Also introduced is the concept of an all-hazards approach to plan development. Key components of the all-hazards emergency management system are presented. Definitions are provided for key concepts.

Chapter 3, "What the All-Hazards Emergency Management System Addresses," introduces a discussion on the preparation and conduct of hazard and vulnerability analyses; audit program concepts are reviewed, as is the composition and selection process for the evaluation team.

Part 2, "All-Hazards Emergency Management Planning System," consists of Chaps. 4 through 15. Each chapter is generally divided into two parts. The first part consists of an introduction and discussion of key aspects in the development of an effective emergency management system. The second part presents practical applications of the material in the form of examples. You can use this information, depicted in figure form, to begin preparing your own unique emergency management system.

As you apply the information contained in this book, you will inevitably modify and improve on the concepts contained here. Please feel free to communicate your experiences, changes, modifications, and applications to me. Sharing information that improves the effectiveness of the system can only facilitate a more dynamic and responsive system.

Geary W. Sikich

Acknowledgments

Books such as this are inevitably the result of experimentation and adaptation. Or, more aptly put, frustration, trial, and error. Countless inputs during many engagements representing a wide spectrum of public- and private-sector entities, each with its own particular needs and requirements, have helped me to test the theories presented in this material. There are many people whose efforts, both direct and indirect, have gone into this book, and many will unfortunately remain nameless. Those who can and should be acknowledged include G. Egan, Professor, Loyola University, Chicago, and Charles L. Webster, former Director of Crisis Management for British Petroleum, America. Many have contributed research, concepts, ideas, thoughts, evaluations, and refinements, although the responsibility for the use and application of these remains solely with the author.

Special thanks to my associate, Stacey L. Simmons, without whose efforts this manuscript would not exist.

Last, thanks to my sons, Aaron and Drake, who continue to provide the inspiration for my efforts.

Planning: Critical Aspects

1

Planning Process of the Emergency Management System

Effective Emergency/Crisis Management: A Perspective

Imagine the following situation. You are assigned the responsibility for emergency planning and crisis management. It is an unfamiliar area for you. You have some concerns about how to go about developing and implementing an effective program. You ask, "What's a crisis for our company?" You begin to review current regulatory requirements. There are many regulations requiring you to have some sort of emergency plan(s). However, you realize that the regulations do not cover all the potential incidents that your company may be faced with. You decide to ask others for their opinions. So, you prepare a few questions and proceed to ask several people for their opinions. They say that they will give you their perspectives and let you decide for yourself. Each goes on to describe what he or she feels a crisis would be. One says, "A crisis for us would be any process-related failure—explosions, fires, material spills, or accidental releases." Another tells you, "A crisis for us would be any sort of product-related issue—contamination, defects, market share loss." Still another tells you, "A crisis for us would be any disruption caused by an employee situation—labor strife, strikes, drug use, sabotage." You begin to realize that your questionnaire is not producing the results you had hoped for. It seems as though everyone has a different concept or opinion as to what a crisis would be, based on her or his perception, expertise, and area of concern.

Undeterred, you put aside the questionnaire and continue the review of regulatory guidance. Federal, state, and local regulations are gathered (the list is impressive), sorted, and reviewed. You begin to wonder, What kind of strategy can we develop to help us comply with all these requirements? Conceivably, you realize that you could write a plan for each regulatory requirement. But you readily realize that some potential incident situations such as those from your brief questionnaire would remain unanswered, for the current regulations do not specifically address these issues. You also realize that if you develop multiple plans, there is a high probability of confusion and chaos during an incident, because there may be different interpretations of which plan to use. After all, look at all the different responses to your simple questionnaire. Someone has to determine which plan to use, and you have to hope that everyone with an emergency role is uniform in the interpretation of the incident, thus ensuring that all parties access the same plan. You remember your experience with the questionnaire and realize that this may not be likely.

Undaunted, you continue the review by looking at the current set of plans. They were designed and developed and are (hopefully) currently being maintained by personnel who are generally chosen, trained, and cultivated in a relatively narrow range of skills. The focus of each plan seems too narrow. You find that the plans generally restate regulatory compliance requirements and are specific to a one-dimensional incident focus. You become uncomfortable.

You ask yourself, "Would I want to be here when the 'big one' occurred?" You conclude, "I do not even want to be close to this place."

You ponder your situation. How can we develop, implement, and maintain an emergency/crisis management program that addresses compliance issues, yet is manageable and provides guidance for non-regulatory concerns? You think and think. *Crisis!* The mere mention of the word evokes visions of unspeakable affliction and suffering for you. It seems as if you cannot pick up a newspaper, magazine, or periodical anymore without reading about a crisis somewhere. You think some more. Television and movies capitalize on crises. Yet, you realize, by developing and implementing a well-defined emergency planning crisis management system, your organization can mitigate many of the potentially disastrous effects of an incident.

Management systems, at no matter what level, are never put more strongly to the test than in a crisis situation. The objectives are immediate and so are the results. What you and those around you do or fail to do will have long-lasting implications. Today, individuals responsible for the management of businesses and institutions must have an emergency management system in place that provides the tools to deal effectively with increasingly complex laws, potential crisis situations, and related issues. This system must become a part of doing business, not an adjunct to the business.

There are many schools of thought about how to effectively manage a crisis. Many of these applications focus on managing the response aspects of an incident or a crisis. In doing so, these applications downplay or altogether omit the significance of what may be considered peripheral issues. Such peripheral issues, the involvement of all levels of management, the identification of business operations issues, community considerations, and non-incident-related operations can have an immense impact on the extent of the crisis, success of the response operation, and length and extent of recovery operations. It is not that focusing on response operations is not good, that response applications do not work, or that the response application is flawed. Far from it; today personnel responsible for developing emergency/crisis management plans are faced with a confounding abundance of response-oriented applications. Therein lies the problem. There is no right, or wrong, response application to implement. However, if you omit the broader management portion of the equation, you may be destined for failure or limited success, at best. You need a management/response application, an *emergency management system (EMS)*.

Not withstanding the profusion of emergency response applications, postincident studies suggest that responders do not manage the broader aspects of a crisis very well. Mismanagement is generally cited as one of the main reasons that incident response systems fail. Mismanagement is not the operative word. Rather, misapplication of a response-oriented program to a management/response-oriented situation is the problem. Poor coordination and a general lack of understanding as to how various response and management elements will join to form an integrated management/response team lead to tremendous waste of resources during the response phase. This leads to a lack of confidence in the ability of the management team to support response efforts during an incident. It also leads to management's mistrust of response operations due to a lack of understanding (communication/information) of response operations. This in turn leads to public distrust, more government oversight and/or involvement, and, in general, greater potential for confusion, chaos, and panic.

The emergency response application is not the offender; rather, it is the scapegoat for poor organization and lack of an integrated management and response system. Few organizations establish, cultivate, and implement a truly effective EMS. Ponder the following:

- Emergency response applications are often chosen because the focus of the responsible parties within the organization is limited to response-oriented processes.

- The emergency response application—fight the fire, stop the spill—seldom reflects the organization's structure and true capabilities.

- Once the emergency response application has been adopted, there is little or no means in place for preparing personnel with assigned roles for success. This is especially true when you begin to study emergency management functions as part of the overall organization. It is especially true when we analyze the administrative support staff.

- Once selected, personnel are generally given only response-oriented training. They receive little or no orientation, development, or training in how to coordinate the management and response functions required by an EMS.

- Once developed, the emergency response application is seldom updated or well maintained.

- The typical emergency response application is restricted in its coverage. That is, the emergency response application generally focuses on incidents that are generated by an internal operational event or a natural disaster. In addition, those few planners who begin to identify externally generated triggering events generally fall short, as they fail to analyze many potential triggering mechanisms.

- The emergency response application, together with expectations for its implementation, is often ill defined.

- Personnel are not forewarned about the chaotic nature of incident-related operations.

- Skills required to perform the expected functions and produce results are often lacking. No effort is made to remedy the situation. Instead, the organization tries to work around the problem.

- Once activated, the emergency response application provides little, if any, feedback to responders, management, external groups, or the population at large.

Response applications of this type ultimately prove to be of limited use, if not totally useless. If little is done to effect changes to the emergency response application, then when it is implemented during a crisis, the resulting chaos and confusion will ensure greater damage, loss of more assets, nonproductive involvement of more entities, and substantial negative impacts on business operations and the community, and potentially undesirable regulatory scrutiny.

It is time to do something to integrate management and response functions into an EMS that produces acceptable results. All those involved in responding to a crisis want to do their best. An integrated approach, which brings all the various elements together as a unified front, is needed to ensure success.

Chapter organizer: What this chapter is about

- *Defining emergency/crisis management.* This chapter discusses an approach to selecting an emergency/crisis management system that can be supported by any organization. It also outlines an effective approach to managing crisis situations.
- *Catastrophe as an opportunity.* Identifying the weaknesses, threats, and strengths that underlie your emergency/crisis management planning process can facilitate a broader range of response and management options.
- *Creating an emergency/crisis management system that adds value.* The role of the emergency/crisis management planner is to create a system that is flexible and responsive and that adds value, i.e., enhances, facilitates, and provides a means for doing things properly. We will investigate how to make the emergency/crisis management system part of the way of doing business, not an adjunct to the business.

Having a framework for developing an effective emergency/crisis management system plays an important part in the planning process. A framework or standardized model for the emergency/crisis management system provides value. It allows for flexibility, standardized terminology, standardized implementing procedures, and clearly defined functions, duties, and tasks; and it can be applied to a variety of situations and organizational structures.

Since a framework spells out a standardized approach to emergency/crisis management planning, it will help those who have to implement it by providing for a shared vision of performance, a systematic viewpoint, and an effective way to manage during the initial chaos and confusion of an incident or crisis; and it will help transform technical competence to managerial expertise. The framework does not have to be prescriptive. You should always consider the value of a component and use or incorporate this information only as it makes sense or fits your situation.

A dilemma: Emergency management system or emergency response application. Just as there are good, bad, and ineffective emergency/crisis management systems, application, plans, etc., there are good, bad, and ineffective regulations. Pointing the finger at emergency/crisis managers for poor management during an incident is, to a large extent, an instance of blaming the victim. Indeed, many, if not most, emergency/crisis managers tend to be scapegoats for an emergency/crisis management system designed with limited perspective that is often poorly executed during an incident.

Several factors contribute to the ineffectiveness of the typical emergency/crisis management system: a tactical response-oriented focus, a response-oriented development strategy, limited scope, lack of trained personnel, and the approach to maintenance.

A response-oriented focus. When the emergency/crisis management focus is primarily on the response aspects of an incident instead of on the management and response aspects, you have utterly limited your capabilities. This limitation can significantly affect the organization's ability to perform well during an actual incident. The reasons for this may be many. First, while the response portion of the organization is busily focusing on mitigation of the incident, the responders fail to communicate critical information to decision makers responsible for supporting the response operation. Second, the decision makers responsible for support of response operations cannot make or implement decisions affecting response operations because they lack a complete and clear picture of what is needed to support the response operation. Third, both responders and the support organization fail to realize the potential impact of decisions and actions made without taking into account all the needed information.

Critical communications are not understood or acted upon because each element has a different perception of what are priority issues. The result is potential panic, chaos, and confusion; ineffective, inefficient operations; public outrage; and loss of credibility.

A response-oriented development strategy. As a result of the response-oriented focus, a narrow strategy is developed that addresses only a particular set of response-oriented issues.

Emergency/crisis management planning techniques and strategies are often an afterthought because of the response orientation of the system. We often commit to developing the kind of emergency/crisis management system that concentrates on meeting some minimal adherence to a regulatory requirement. As additional regulations are promulgated, new plans are developed. Generally, these new plans do not necessarily complement, relate to, or blend with existing plans. They also do not supersede the existing plans. Nor do they support the existing plans.

This example highlights how many, if not most, emergency/crisis management systems are developed. They are adopted not because they are seen as good managerial tools, but because they are good for a specific response orientation or regulatory requirement or have a limited target audience. For example, firefighters, emergency medical technicians, hazardous materials specialists, and civil defense coordinators are often asked to develop, maintain, and manage the emergency/crisis management system because they are skilled at putting out fires, responding to operational disasters, and performing first aid—not because they can perceive the broader implications of a crisis. Good firefighters, emergency medical technicians, hazardous materials specialists, and civil defense coordinators, however, do not necessarily make good emergency/crisis management system managers. They may not possess all the skills necessary to manage the broader implications resulting from an incident.

Limited scope. Few emergency/crisis management systems are developed with a broad range of potential issues in mind. Fewer still receive periodic evaluation, adjustment, and fine-tuning. Once the new emergency/crisis management system is approved, generally it is placed on the shelf where it joins many other programs, to gather dust. Also once developed, the system is generally out of date, as much of the information contained in its pages is subject to frequent change. With the preponderance of literature focusing on emergency response, the operational aspects of a crisis, or the narrow perspective of crisis communications, is it any wonder that the scope of most plans is limited? This means that when the emergency/crisis management system is called upon during an incident, implementation is often a hit-or-miss affair, something left to chance.

Not only are many emergency response management systems limited in scope, but also they are often thrown together just to meet a specific regulatory requirement, without a thorough analysis of what has been committed to. They are then left on the shelf, untouched, to be implemented, under the presence of an incident, by a generally untrained, underdeveloped, and inappropriately staffed organization. And we expect peak performance from them when a crisis occurs!

These inherent deficiencies create a system that is unfair to response personnel, to managers at all levels who must provide support to the response effort, and to the community at large.

No one knows the costs of inadequate and poorly developed, implemented, and maintained emergency/crisis management systems. A number of reasons can be cited:

- New regulations tend to have little or no relationship to previous guidance. For the emergency/crisis management planner to identify lack of compliance would mean risking an audit and potential fines.

- Many companies, communities, and agencies with deficient emergency/crisis management systems think they are doing well because they have never truly validated their systems. When they do attempt to validate their plans, it is generally a response-oriented process, with little done to stress the management decision-making component of the system. Also, they imitate what they saw others in their industry, community, or agency doing. There are no clear standards against which to rate themselves, and there is little or no feedback from others.

- No one is calling attention to the continued deluge of regulations from federal, state, and local government agencies. Further, these agencies cannot seem to provide any consistency for compliance standards, so that an emergency/crisis management system can be uniformly designed, developed, and implemented.

- Government agencies are in the same predicament as many of the regulated entities: They must operate with minimal staff, unclear guidance, and conflicting statutes. Therefore, no one is calling attention to the potential benefits of developing an "all hazards" approach for emergency/crisis management. Neither is government nor industry generally developing emergency/crisis management systems in a cooperative manner. They are choosing and developing emergency/crisis management systems in the same hit-or-miss way, thereby furthering the promulgation of more regulations and more plans of limited scope.

In sum, no one notices how ineffective and inefficient emergency/crisis management systems really are because no one truly comprehends the need for comprehensive systems of broad scope.

An Opportunity

The potential for improving both the quality of emergency/crisis management systems and, in the process, the effectiveness of individuals who develop, implement, and maintain these systems is enormous in most private and public-sector operations. Improving emergency/crisis management systems does not have to be complicated. For example:

- Choose an emergency/crisis management system with the capacity to expand to meet new regulatory initiatives that is easy to use and can be vertically and horizontally integrated.

- Make sure that users really know their job requirements.

- Make it as easy as possible for all levels of management and response to get and exchange information.

- Identify commitments that are achievable, define how they will be attained, and assign the resources needed to fulfill them.

- Develop an EMS that provides ongoing guidance and feedback on performance.

- Establish a culture of collaboration, not confrontation.

Simply put, provide focus, support, and continual development for the emergency/crisis management system.

Another approach to enhancing the viability of the emergency/crisis management system is to review past performance and critique historical data. What went right? What went wrong? Here are some considerations:

- Make sure your personnel are trained and equipped and can perform assigned functions.

- Set an *all-hazards* strategy; ensure its vitality (it should be responsive to changes in regulations, operations, personnel, etc.).

- Stay abreast of changes in applicable regulatory and other guidance.

- Make sure that access to information is universal; that is, personnel in decision-making positions must have quality information in order to make decisions.

- Since organization, time management, and information sharing are crucial, develop and implement a system to manage them well.

Management and response personnel must know what the system or plan consists of, set and enforce higher and higher performance standards, ensure constant constructive innovation, get involved in the substance of the regulatory requirements, and select and develop the right kind of personnel for the organization.

The planning process: Providing a framework. Planning is an ongoing, unrelenting, unforgiving process. Unlike engineering projects or other processes, there is no final completion or end to the project. Planning is a continuous process. Because planning is a continuous process, evaluating the adequacy of your plan is, at best, difficult. What benchmarks do you go by? Is regulatory compliance enough? What about nonregulatory issues?

What is needed is a framework for planning. This framework should be flexible, providing a basis for establishing the plan and any supporting materials. You must establish the planning framework prior to doing any planning or associated activities. As described in the following paragraphs, the planning process is invaluable to achieving a valid working EMS.

The planning process provides a framework for the development of the EMS and establishes the scope requirements for identification and effective use of resources.

This process should apply to each organization within your company that has been assigned responsibility for the development or maintenance of the all-hazards EMS. (See Fig. 1.1.)

Establish planning responsibility. Responsibility for emergency/crisis management planning must be assigned to the appropriate level of management, based on a hazard and vulnerability assessment and the identification of resources to support the plan. Planning responsibilities should transcend organizational boundaries and levels of management, with the goal being the creation of a superior information management system that allows for flexibility, standardization, and mutual support from all elements.

A responsible individual at each level in the organization should be assigned primary accountability for the coordination and attainment of planning goals and objectives. This role should be formally recognized by inclusion in the position holder's job description and performance evaluation criteria. Depending on the size of the operation, the responsible individual may initiate many of the planning tasks directly, or he or she may delegate or coordinate responsibility for some of the planning tasks. The individual should be required, however, to retain ultimate accountability for program development, implementation, and validation. Assignment of emergency/crisis management responsibilities should be based on experience, understanding of broad-based issues, and planning and leadership skills (Fig. 1.2).

A planning team should be established to facilitate the development of the emergency/crisis management program (Fig. 1.3). The importance of the planning team cannot be overestimated. Individuals assigned to the planning team should be selected with the objective of providing integrated multidisciplinary input that results in an all-hazards plan. The planning team will provide the core of

---

Planning for emergency and crisis management is a continuing process, not a one-time event. While the most important product of this process is the establishment of capabilities, the written plans and supporting documents developed during the planning process are critical to effective coordination of the program.

Figure 1.1

THE EMERGENCY/CRISIS MANAGEMENT PLANNER

must be knowledgeable about crisis and emergency programs;

have effective management and communications skills; and

be allocated the necessary time and resources to effectively implement planning responsibilities.

Figure 1.2

A DIVERSE AND EXPERIENCED PLANNING TEAM

Ensures plans and procedures:

- *are consistent with values and desired approach;*
- *accurately reflect management/response capabilities;*
- *consider coordination and cooperation issues;*
- *incorporate actions that have proven effectiveness;*
- *meet regulatory requirements; and*
- *reflect an "all-hazards" approach, that is, they are comprehensive.*

Figure 1.3

expertise from which you should draw on to build the emergency management/response organization. Additionally, the desired end result of the team's effort will be a document that accurately reflects capabilities and commitments. It is sufficient to summarize here that planning team personnel should be selected from an appropriate range of functional areas to ensure that a broad perspective is brought to the planning process.

Planning team personnel should be able to work cooperatively as a group and have the ability, commitment, authority, and resources to address all planning requirements.

Develop planning goals and objectives. Once established, the first goal of the planning team should be to establish planning goals and objectives. It should determine

- *What* needs to be accomplished
- *How* it will be accomplished
- *When* it will be scheduled for completion

Input for setting planning goals and objectives should come from a number of sources. The planning team will need to review applicable regulatory requirements, industry guidance materials, practices, standards, company policy and procedures regarding the operations of the business, and emergency and crisis management issues.

These resource materials and other source documents can provide information on business operations' new or existing technology, performance requirements and/or regulatory requirements, standards, and recent lessons learned within the company and the industry.

Review existing planning documents and regulations. A thorough review of existing emergency/crisis management planning documents is the initial step toward developing a comprehensive program. This review should go beyond the existing emergency planning documents and regulatory criteria applicable to your particular organization. The review should include the following:

- Plans and programs of similar organizations (as available)
- Available literature and case studies
- Plans and procedures from support elements, such as media relations, business resumption planning, security, environmental, and safety
- Potential support sources, such as mutual aid organizations; affected parties, such as neighboring companies; and state and local agencies, hospitals, or other identified facilities in the area
- Other potential responding organizations including government agencies and mutual aid and volunteer organizations such as the Red Cross
- Planning documents not necessarily labeled as emergency or crisis management documents, but that guide related functions or actions
- Existing and proposed regulatory documents

During the review, your planning team should identify critical areas and issues that need to be addressed to improve performance, provide for a comprehensive approach, and define commitments. Creating a matrix or checklist of applicable regulations (federal, state, local), issues, goals, and potential impacts can facilitate the planning process.

Conduct a hazards and vulnerability analysis. To properly plan an organization's response, planners should first fully understand the hazards that their organizations face and the vulnerabilities that those hazards present. Chapter 3, "What the All-Hazards Emergency Management System Addresses," provides an overview of the hazard and vulnerability analysis. Many volumes are available today which detail the conduct of hazard operability studies, process safety management, vulnerability analysis, and risk analysis. All are valuable sources of information. However, a word of caution: Do not become locked into only one form of analysis. Your plan and the EMS must be broad-based enough to address the extensive variety of situations that your company may face.

There is a natural tendency for emergency/crisis management planners to focus on those hazards which stem from operations, products, and processes: fires, explosions, spills, and releases. However, you need to identify, assess, and plan for management and response to hazards that can disrupt business operations. To fully prepare our response capabilities, we should examine a full range of hazards. Figure 1.4 identifies some examples of the potential hazards and issues which industrial corporations typically face today. These haz-

Figure 1.4

TYPICAL HAZARDS AND ISSUES FACED BY COMPANIES

Manufacturing Process Hazards
  Process Failures
  ■ Explosions
  ■ Fires
  ■ Materials Spills/Releases
  Utility Supply Disruption
  ■ Electric
  ■ Water
  Feedstock Supply Disruption
  ■ Due to Accidents
  ■ Due to Market Forces
  Chronic Environmental Contamination

Transportation Hazards
  Accidents
  ■ Explosions
  ■ Fires
  ■ Materials Spills/Releases
  Disruptions
  ■ System
  ■ Political/Economic

Product-Related Hazards
  ■ Product Contamination
  ■ Product Liability
  ■ Product Defect
  ■ Market Loss

Employee-Related Hazards
  ■ Labor Strife
  ■ Operator Error
  ■ Employee Sabotage
  ■ Hostage/Violent Acts
  ■ Contractor Actions
  ■ Litigation
  ■ Employee Drug Use
  ■ Maintenance Oversight

Societal Hazards
  ■ Political Instability/Civil Disorder
  ■ International Conflicts
  ■ Hostage/Terrorist Acts
  ■ Executive Kidnapping
  ■ Consumer Protests/Boycotts
  ■ Product Tampering

(Continued)

Government Regulations
- Manufacturing Process
- Product-Related
- Workplace (Health/Safety)
- Environmental

Financial Hazards
- Hostile Takeover/Leveraged Buyout
- Stock Market/Price Collapse
- Embezzlement
- Executive Misconduct/Fraud

Natural Disasters
- Floods
- Hurricanes
- Tornadoes
- Earthquakes

Miscellaneous Hazards
- Executive Succession
- Computer Failure/Virus

External Hazards
- Neighboring Sites

Figure 1.4

ards may occur internally within the operation, or they may occur externally; all have the potential to affect business operations. Any particular location or operation may well face the hazards included in these examples. Regardless of how or where an incident might occur, if the potential exists to affect your company and its interested parties, the hazards should be identified and addressed in the planning documentation.

At a minimum, you should analyze existing hazard operability and vulnerability studies, examine incidents or other case study examples that have occurred within your industry, examine incidents or situations which have occurred in other industries, and consider a full range of other possible incidents. You should carefully consider and prioritize each type of hazard to determine the extent to which it could occur and affect your operations. You may also want to establish severity thresholds for each hazard to reflect fundamental differences in the level of impact on your operations.

A *vulnerability analysis* continues this process by identifying the specific impacts of the hazards on your operations and defining what your management and response planning options should be. These impacts can vary widely from the immediate emergency situation to longer-term effects on business operations. An effective method to fully identify the range of impacts from particular hazards is to have the planning team work through various hazard scenarios and identify the hazards' impacts at different times (immediate, short term, longer term), on different types of operations (supply, manufacturing operations, administration, security, the environment, etc.), and on different groups both inside and outside the company (suppliers, employees, customers, community, etc.).

The planning team should be able to draw a great deal of the information and data for hazards and vulnerability analysis from ongoing risk management, safety, and hazards reduction programs. A good source of information on risk assessment studies is the insurance industry. Long-standing programs such as hazard operability studies (HAZOPs) and similar prevention and industrial safety programs continue to provide critical information for the planning team.

Because much of the information available will be based on process safety efforts such as those mentioned above, additional effort may be necessary to identify the hazards and related vulnerabilities that do not stem from processing incidents and physical accidents. Prevention of all types of incidents should be a first priority of the emergency/crisis management program.

As a final step, your planning team should prioritize identified hazards based on the potential vulnerabilities that they may create. The higher-priority hazards will provide a focus for the remaining planning steps in the process. Do not overlook low-priority hazards just because they are less likely to occur. These can cause the greatest disruption because of lack of preparedness to deal with them. While practical limits on planning may not allow dealing with all hazards in uniform detail, the management and response capabilities reflected in your planning documents should provide specific capabilities for high-priority hazards and general capabilities that can be adapted to low-priority hazards.

Clarify performance requirements. After assessing the hazards, the planning team should clarify how the organization wants to manage its response to the various hazards facing it. Your organization must look at the full range of hazards and vulnerabilities. Each functional area required to respond to the identified hazards and vulnerabilities should be recognized, along with the required level of response.

All these considerations should be combined into a series of performance standards that can be used to evaluate existing capabilities and further guide development of the EMS.

Regulations, industry practice, public expectations, performance evaluations from exercises and actual responses, and established industry performance standards will provide guidance about desired and expected capabilities.

Evaluate existing capabilities. After performance requirements are defined, the next step is to assess your organization's existing management, response, and postincident recovery capabilities. Comparing desired management and response capacities with existing capabilities will highlight the need for additional resources and/or the integration of existing resources. In assessing capabilities, identify qualified resources available both within the organization and from sources external to the organization. These resources should be quantified as well as qualified. For example, how long will it take to get the resource to your location?

While the resources needed to support an incident are established, consideration should be given to the support required for extended operations (i.e., more than 24 hours) and for support of continuing business operations. Resource burdens should be anticipated and planned for appropriately, with the division of resources factored into the planning process. After available internal resources are identified and measured against desired response options, the next step is to determine whether external and/or specialized resources are needed.

To meet the defined performance requirements, capabilities can sometimes be supplemented from other parts of the organization or by arranging for outside support from such sources as contractors, consultants, industry mutual aid groups, and government agencies. These resources should be carefully assessed and agreements formally executed, before they are included in your inventory of capabilities (Fig. 1.5).

I cannot emphasize too strongly the importance of formalizing agreements for mutual aid and other support. In addition to formalizing them, you should plan on periodically validating these agreements through training, drills, and exercise programs.

Establish additional needs. The planning process may result in the identification of issues for which additional resources are needed to ensure the organization's desired management and response capability. In this way, your planning team can determine where

- Difficulties can be expected in meeting performance standards or objectives.

EXTERNAL RESOURCE CONSIDERATIONS

Ability of available resources to accomplish what is needed when directed.

Reliability of available resources to be there when needed.

Selection of the "best" resources, while maintaining cost-effectiveness.

Figure 1.5

- Additional external resources are needed to supplement existing capabilities.
- Development of new capabilities should be considered.

It is important that your planning team accurately assess existing capabilities. Once the need for additional resources is identified, your planning team should actively seek to determine their availability as well as the process for gaining access to these resources.

Obtain management approval.   Management's concurrence and active participation are critical throughout the planning process. Management's full, continuing support and commitment ensure the necessary authority to develop a dynamic EMS. Management approval and regular, ongoing participation are also critical in providing the leadership to build employee support and involvement in the program, to make it part of the way you do business.

Prepare or revise written plans.   Having completed the steps outlined above, you can now begin developing an *all-hazards* EMS with continued help from the planning team.

One individual should be assigned overall responsibility for preparing the planning documents, drafting material, or assigning portions to planning team members, who have particular expertise, to develop. Each functional representative in the planning team should review and comment on the planning documents. Planning documents should be written in a format that facilitates integration with (internal and external) plans. Implementing procedures in particular should be structured to maximize their use during actual incidents.

The planning documents should reflect only the actual existing capabilities of the organization and those external resources where clear arrangements have been made for support. Additional resources should not be added to plans and incorporated into training until they have been developed and are available.

Planning team review.   The planning team should have periodic review sessions throughout the development process to ensure efforts are on course and integrated. When a complete draft of the planning documents is finished, the planning team should thoroughly review them before they are submitted to management for approval. As part of this review, the planning team should be able to establish that all applicable regulations have been met. An appendix to the basic planning material that cross-references the plan documents to applicable regulatory guidance is helpful. The cross-reference appendix (previously mentioned in the document review phase) of regulations and associated documents will facilitate this review.

Management review and approval. Following the final review by the planning team, the responsible management personnel should be given the opportunity to conduct a formal review and petition for periodic written approval. Informal and formal management input and support should be sought throughout the planning process.

Postplanning activities. After the all-hazards emergency management plan has been developed, analyzed, supplemented, reviewed, and revised, management and response capabilities should be verified to ensure they work as designed. The process for validation consists of training, drills, and exercises. These activities are discussed in Chap. 12, "Training Considerations," and Chap. 13, "Plan Validation (Drills) Considerations."

The planning process, combined with the postplanning education and validation components mentioned above, represents a continuous loop system. Capabilities and planning documents should be regularly validated, assessed, and revised as appropriate to continually improve capabilities and performance.

Role of the emergency/crisis manager. If the basic purpose of the planning cycle is to provide a framework for the EMS, then the primary role of the emergency/crisis manager is to facilitate the viability of the system. The emergency/crisis manager should perform or oversee the performance of the following critical functions:

- Establish the scope of the EMS.

- Provide guidance and support during system development phases.

- Ensure access to a variety of experts, resources, and key decision makers.

- Ensure two-way communications flow (horizontal and vertical).

- Set priorities, establish deadlines, and ensure that focus is maintained.

All-hazards model for emergency/crisis management. Application of the appropriate emergency/crisis management system to your unique situation is critical. A standardized approach that allows for sharing of principles, methods, and skills needs to be embraced and implemented. Establishing an integrated and comprehensive framework for understanding and dealing with myriad regulatory requirements and for ease of use during an incident constitutes a major step toward clarifying the elements of a good emergency/crisis management strategy. A standardized framework for emergency/crisis management contributes to the kind of alignment of resources that facilitates integrated management and response activities.

The EMS framework discussed in subsequent chapters of this book provides a design pattern that organizations of all types and sizes can use to develop a system that will be responsive to their needs.

Continuous-improvement approach to emergency/crisis management. We live in the day of the quick fix. We are bombarded by brochures that promise quick fixes for everything. The all-hazards EMS framework, described here, however, provides the principles and concepts required for effective emergency/crisis management activities. It does not provide a ready-made, fill-in-the-blanks approach to fulfilling regulatory or policy requirements. It is your job to tailor these principles and the examples provided here to your organization's specific needs.

Taking emergency/crisis management seriously, then, means developing a cadre of personnel who have the core competencies, skills, and commitment to make the system work, to continually improve it, and to enlist the efforts of everyone else in these endeavors. It helps to start with a pragmatic model.

Organizing the All-Hazards Emergency Management System

A Standardized Framework = Emergency/Crisis Management Effectiveness

The all-hazards emergency management system (EMS) provides a framework for developing a well-defined and executable emergency/ crisis management system; it is the central theme of this book. It has three major parts: the plan, appendices, and implementing procedures. This chapter provides an overview of the entire model.

An advanced organizer: What this chapter is about

- *Basic requirements of an effective emergency/crisis management system.* A shared framework that outlines the approach to emergency/crisis management.

- *Advantage of a standardized framework.* Management and response personnel need a standardized framework to make the emergency/crisis management system operate in a seamless manner, both vertically and horizontally.

- *All-hazards EMS.* The EMS provides a framework for the design, implementation, maintenance, and continuous improvement of a comprehensive emergency/crisis management system. The desired outcomes achieved by employing this process are standardized structure, common terminology, a template for doing things right, an organized and focused approach, superior information flow and management, and optimization of critical resources (personnel, equipment, time).

Basic requirements of the all-hazards EMS

Responding to an incident is difficult enough, but in many instances it is made even more difficult because there is a gap between response and management. This gap may be a communication gap or a combination of several issues from operations to equipment. This gap can be eliminated by developing a model for effective emergency/ crisis management. It is essential to know what the key components of the all-hazards emergency/crisis management system are, how they are put together, and how changing one (such as organization) affects another (such as concept of operations).

Few entities use a comprehensive and integrated framework to guide their efforts. Many do have some kind of system, but it is often regulation-driven and more response-oriented than management/ response-oriented. Some organizations have systems carried around inside the heads of key personnel that are not generally shared with others. Moreover, this "in-the-head" approach does not facilitate comprehensive or integrated implementation strategy. For instance, it may focus on response operations but ignore broader issues. Or it may focus on spills but ignore the operational processes needed to respond to everything else. To make things worse, personnel tend to forget key parts of their in-the-head working approaches in times of crisis. Or, the individual who possesses this knowledge becomes a casualty or is in some other way incapacitated, thereby rendering the system essentially useless. The lack of a comprehensive, integrated framework makes the response-management relationship a much more erratic process than it need be. Moreover, the lack of a standard framework is one of the things that prevents the members of the *emergency management/response organization (EMRO)* from pulling together as an integrated team.

The basic requirements of the EMS are simple. They are embodied in three volumes, or sections if you prefer:

Volume 1: Basic plan

Volume 2: Supporting materials

Volume 3: Implementing procedures

Volume 1: Basic plan.   The basic plan sets forth the philosophy and key concepts under which the EMRO will operate. The basic plan is developed to ensure stability within the system. That is, it is designed so that it is not subject to frequent change.

Key components of the basic plan are divided into sections, chapters, or topics. Subsequent chapters discuss each of these components in more detail:

- Administrative considerations
- Emergency management/response organization
- Concept of operations
- Communications
- Emergency classification system
- Emergency response facilities
- Public information/outreach programs
- Postincident operations
- Human resources development: training, drills, and exercises
- Audit and evaluation mechanisms

The above ordering is not meant to be prescriptive. How you order the basic plan is secondary. The primary concern is addressing the issues identified above.

Volume 2: Supporting materials.   Often referred to as the appendices, this portion of the all-hazards EMS contains material subject to frequent change. The operative term is *frequent change*. This material supports the basic plan. The appendices may contain information that is proprietary or on a need-to-know basis. They also contain lists of reference material that is too cumbersome to detail in the basic plan.

Key components or topics for consideration include, but are not limited to, the following:

- Letters of agreement/mutual aid considerations
- Cross-references to key components
- List of current implementing procedures and associated plans
- Recognized acronyms, abbreviations, and definitions
- Support resources (internal and external)
- Technical support library
- Chemical information and material safety data sheets (MSDSs)
- Equipment resources (internal and external)
- Community- and location-specific maps and diagrams
- Media information
- Hospitals and health care facilities and organizations: capabilities and services
- Agencies, regulatory and nonregulatory

- EMRO function description
- Master set of forms and checklists
- Hazard and vulnerability analysis
- Cross-reference to regulatory requirements

The above list is not meant to be exhaustive. In some instances, the information contained in some of the appendices can be combined into a single appendix, thereby reducing the need for a large number of separate appendices. Examples are provided in subsequent chapters as appropriate.

Volume 3: Implementing procedures.   Critical to the ability of any organization to effectively and efficiently implement its plan and operate during a crisis is the ability to field a trained, experienced EMRO. To ensure consistency, supplement the basic plan, and provide quick reference material, a set of implementing procedures derived from the basic plan and supporting materials needs to be developed. The primary purpose of the implementing procedures, often referred to as *emergency plan implementing procedures (EPIPs)*, is to provide quick reference for the members of the emergency management/ response organization during a crisis.

The implementing procedures generally take the form of checklists; flowcharts; and function, duty, and task highlights. Examples are provided in the following chapters.

Reasons to adopt a standardized model

Adopting an all-hazards standardized emergency/crisis management program design enables the user to achieve concrete and specific goals efficiently. The all-hazards approach also provides for coverage of areas where specific regulatory requirements do not yet exist. The all-hazards approach also differs from regulation-driven models that merely restate compliance requirements. While regulatory compliance is ultimately necessary, often the requirements set forth can be too abstract or too complicated to be applied directly when immediate action is required.

Three criteria characterize the all-hazards EMS: (1) It provides a flexible platform for compliance, (2) it is simple to use, and (3) it provides for a seamless structure—vertically and horizontally—that is, management and response are integratable.

In summary, the all-hazards EMS, as opposed to regulation-driven or predominately response-oriented plans devised primarily to comply with a specific regulation with limited focus, has the following advantages:

- It provides a means for translating business strategy, response strategy, and compliance requirements into how things really work.

- It constitutes a framework for action.

- It outlines and details the methods, technologies, and skills needed to complete the management/response cycle of activities.

- It is simple without being simplistic.

Some desired outcomes.   Adopting the all-hazards EMS approach provides some readily apparent benefits. Some of these desired outcomes that all emergency/crisis management programs should strive for include quick, effective response; superior information flow; management/response mutual support; regulatory compliance; optimization of critical resources, effective time management, and provision of a standardized template for doing things right.

- Quick, effective response

- Superior information flow

- Management/response mutual support

- Regulatory compliance

- Optimal resource management

- Optimal time management

- Template for doing things right

Achieving the desired outcomes: Essential Elements of Analysis.   What do we need to do to get the desired mix of quick and effective response, superior information flow, management/response mutual support, and the other desired outcomes? The Essential Elements of Analysis or pragmatic guiding principles must be addressed in order to achieve these desired outcomes. There are nine *Essential Elements of Analysis* (*EEAs*): (1) administration, (2) organization, (3) training and retraining, (4) facilities and equipment, (5) implementation procedures, (6) coordination with off-site agencies, (7) program validation: drills and exercises, (8) communications, and (9) hazard identification and evaluation. They are called Essential Elements of Analysis because they are the major tasks that any organization in the pursuit of quality in emergency/crisis management program performance must address. Each EEA includes a number of subtasks or Measure of Effectiveness and Measure of Performance.

As described in my previous book, entitled *It Can't Happen Here: All Hazards Crisis Management Planning* (PennWell Books, 1993), the following definitions will be useful:

An *essential element of analysis (EEA)* is a structure that encompasses a major aspect of the emergency planning and preparedness process. For example, administration is a major area of analysis; i.e., it is not dependent on another structure to define its structure.

A *measure of effectiveness (MOE)* is dependent on the essential element of analysis for structure. Measures of effectiveness form subgroups of information relating to specific areas encompassed by the essential element of analysis. For example, within the EEA administration, a measure of effectiveness might be the assignment of responsibility. Measures of effectiveness are not "stand-alone" structures, however; when grouped, they form an essential element of analysis.

A *measure of performance (MOP)* is a data structure. Measures of performance answer a specific question. Measures of performance are grouped to form measures of effectiveness. Measures of performance are measurable and observable; i.e., they provide a quantitative basis for evaluation of a specific area. For example, a measure of performance might be the question, Is there an individual at the site formally assigned/appointed as the emergency planning coordinator (by job description, job title, or memorandum)?

Essential Elements of Analysis Defined

Administration

This essential element of analysis evaluates the administrative aspects of the emergency/crisis management program. Such things as how the program is structured and managed, assignment of responsibilities, authority, regulatory requirements, and documentation are analyzed.

Emergency management/response organization

This essential element of analysis evaluates the composition, qualifications, support functions, and involvement of various levels of management within the emergency management/response organization.

Emergency management/response training and retraining

This essential element of analysis evaluates the training and retraining of EMRO. Formally developed lesson plans, training program content, and implementation and evaluation of training are analyzed.

Emergency facilities and equipment

This essential element of analysis evaluates the adequacy of facilities and equipment that the EMRO uses during its operations. Facility plans, layouts, equipment type, availability, and operability are analyzed.

Emergency plan implementing procedures

This essential element of analysis evaluates the supporting procedures, their structure and usability, and how functions, duties, and tasks of personnel assigned to the EMRO are defined and supported. I have categorized the EPIPs into four areas: Administrative, Management/Response Organization, Emergency Operations, and Postincident Operations.

Coordination with off-site agencies

This essential element of analysis evaluates community outreach, integration of plans, and procedures for defining the functions, authorities, and relationships with off-site emergency organizations.

Plan validation: Drills and exercises

This essential element of analysis evaluates the drill and exercise program, frequency of drills, types of drills, involvement of all levels of management, and adequacy of scenarios.

Communications

This essential element of analysis evaluates the hardware and non-hardware capabilities, operation, information management/exchange systems, and coordination of the communications function during emergency operations.

Hazard identification and evaluation

This essential element of analysis evaluates with adequacy of the hazard analysis and procedures for determining susceptibility or vulnerability. Areas of analysis include, but are not limited to, hazardous materials, chemical process, physical operations, natural resource damage assessment analysis, equipment design, facility location and layout, and external hazards evaluations. Other categories of hazards that are identified as non-regulation-driven include natural hazards, employee-related hazards, terrorism, ecoterrorism, computer systems, and executive and management issues.

Managing the complexity of the system.   While the nine essential elements of analysis may appear simple and straightforward, each must be addressed in sufficient detail to be entirely successful. Do not let the apparent simplicity of the EEA structures mask the complexity of implementing and managing the response to an actual incident.

One of the most daunting tasks you will face as you move forward to develop your program will be to develop a cadre of knowledgeable, skilled, and ardent supporters to facilitate the initial development and ongoing maintenance of the system. Therefore, it is imperative that you seek to develop leaders, at every level of your organization, who will support the system.

Once you have accomplished the "buy-in" or vesting process of getting people to internalize the system, you can begin to shape and mold the system to serve your entire organization's needs rather than just specific segments or particular regulatory requirements.

In this way, not only can you develop a response system, but also you can bring about innovative change and create an environment of empowerment for members of the EMRO, thereby enabling them to implement decision-making strategies without fear of repercussion or being second-guessed. This can occur because there is a standardized understanding of how to assess and respond to the potential wide variety of hazards. It also occurs because everyone has a vested interest in the success of the system. "It's not my job" is a quote you should never hear or a sentiment that should never underpin your organization's basic philosophy.

Once you have addressed these nine essential elements of analysis, you can begin to get results that exceed expectations. When you begin to hear the organization's rule that producing "ordinary results" is not acceptable, you will have achieved a strategic goal—the embodiment of the all-hazards EMS as a way of doing business, not merely a way of dealing with extraordinary situations.

3

What the All-Hazards Emergency Management System Addresses

Critical to the development of the all-hazards emergency management system (EMS) is a comprehensive, well-conceived, and well-executed hazard analysis/vulnerability assessment. The hazard analysis/vulnerability assessment should not be confused with the hazard operability study (HAZOP) or traditional methods of assessing risk. This is not to say that the information, data, and output from these traditional methods should be discarded or not looked at. Indeed, they should be heavily relied upon to provide a foundation for establishing a viable hazard analysis/vulnerability assessment. You should, however, take into account areas where the traditional methods are not necessarily focused on. There are many hazards and potential areas of vulnerability to be studied. These include, but are not limited to, terrorism issues, employee-related concerns, military-related actions, and other nonoperational issues. You've got to know what you are potentially going to be faced with before you can plan, organize, and train for the appropriate response. It makes little sense to build an elaborate plan chock full of commitments, detailed position descriptions, and other information, if you have no intent to fulfill the commitments, lack the ability to fulfill the commitments, do not have a clear understanding of what has been committed to, and lack an appreciation of potential incidents, situations, or circumstances that could put your organization at risk.

An advanced organizer: What this chapter is about

- *Identifying and quantifying hazards.* Formulate a broad-based strategy that provides for an analysis of operational and nonopera-

tional issues. Components of the hazard analysis involve identifying the risks and threats that underlie the planning effort, determining compliance-related issues and response capabilities, and
establishing and communicating worst-case and most-probable-
case scenarios.

- *Organizational surveys.*   You must combine hazard analysis data
  with a survey of your organization to determine (1) the level of
  awareness within the organization regarding emergency/crisis preparedness and (2) the current capabilities available to respond to
  an incident. This will assist you in determining what the organization perceives as potential areas of concern. It will also help you
  identify its strengths, weaknesses, and level of commitment.

- *Hazard analysis: establishing the basis for the planning effort.*
  When preparing to conduct the hazard analysis, you must establish
  the parameters of your investigation. How much information do
  you want to gather? In what form do you intend to present the
  information? Who is your primary audience? Who are your secondary audiences? How useful is this information during an actual
  incident? All these and many more questions will have to be
  answered.

Many tools are available to aid you in this process. Some are simple; others are complex. Also regulatory statutes guide you through
this process. A word of caution: Carefully evaluate the output from
the hazard analysis process. The documents you create from your
analysis can have a major impact on your organization.

You should begin the hazard analysis process by reviewing current
efforts. Once this is done, review the current regulatory guidance;
then begin to fill in the gaps. What is not currently addressed? What
do the regulations fail to cover?

In my previous book, *It Can't Happen Here: All Hazards Crisis
Management Planning,* I devoted a chapter to hazard analysis assessment. A brief summary of the key points presented in that chapter
follows.

In that chapter I reviewed an approach to the development of an
all-hazards hazards analysis. The focus was less on the detailed, step-
by-step approach for each aspect of the analysis, and more on areas
not normally associated with the typical regulation-mandated,
process safety, or hazard operability type of analysis.

This methodology in conjunction with the hazard operability and
process safety management approach has been used to provide my
clients in the petrochemical, industrial gas, steel, health care, food service, manufacturing, municipality, and government sectors with a
basis for developing their all-hazards EMSs. Note the effectiveness of

this approach in helping to identify potential hazards not covered by a hazard operability or process safety management assessment. Please note, however, that this approach does *not* supplant the process safety management or hazard operability assessment programs approach. Rather, it serves to supplement these assessment tools.

I recommend that you research current literature, experts, and regulators to ensure that the most up-to-date information is available for your use in preparing the hazard analysis.

Briefly, the chapter in my earlier book discussed the following:

1. *Hazard analysis goals.* The primary goal is the reduction of vulnerability.

2. *Hazard analysis team selection.* The primary goal is to engage a team with a broad range of expertise. The team must possess superior communication skills and be able to look at issues from multiple perspectives, thereby enabling the broadest range of assessment of the potential impacts of identified hazards.

3. *Hazard analysis format.* The output of the hazard analysis must be organized into a logical discussion of issues. It should also be pragmatic. That is, you should be able to use the information to reduce vulnerability. All conclusions and the logic behind them need to be appropriately documented. Since the hazard analysis is subject to frequent change due to either the introduction or removal of potential hazards, the format must ensure ease of maintenance. Figure 3.1 shows an outline of key areas for analysis, as described in the chapter from my previous book.

4. *Hazard analysis process.* In the chapter from my previous book, I presented a three-step approach. This includes, but does not have to be limited to, personnel interviews, documentation, reviews, and physical inspections. Since each of these steps is well documented in my previous book, I will not expand upon them further here. Rather, I will attempt to provide some of the tools necessary to accomplish these three steps.

5. *Prioritization of hazards.* Several methods can be used. These should reflect your best analysis of how the prioritization data will be interpreted and to what use they will be put. Caution should be used to discriminate between worst-case situations and most-probable-case situations when hazards are prioritized. Remember to include, as part of the review process before you publish your assessment, a review by someone in your organization who is able to assist you by helping structure the assessment so that it is understandable in lay terms. With the expansion of community outreach programs and regulatory requirements covering process safety and risk management planning, the ability to communicate clearly and in terms easily understood by a wide-ranging audience is essential.

Hazard Analysis - Sample Report Format

- General Site Information

- Assignment of Responsibility/Emergency Planning

- Identification of Hazardous Materials

- Extremely Hazardous Substance List

- Release State of Material (i.e., gas, liquid)

- Release Pathways

- Release History

- Hazard Analysis

    HAZOP Methodology

    Hazard Categories

    Prioritized Hazard List

    Summary of Processes, Storage, Transfer Locations, etc.

- Highly Toxic Materials Handled

- Other Major Risks (including Business Impact Analysis)

- Other Hazards (external to location/company)

- Surface and Groundwaters (including public/private water supply impacts)

- Wildlife and National Resource Damage Assessment

- Worst-Case Scenarios

- Prevention Programs

- Waste Stream Analysis

- Summary

Figure 3.1

Assessment tools. To assist your efforts, the following example shows how to prepare and conduct a hazard analysis. As you review the example, a word of caution is advisable. You should tailor your hazard analysis to your particular situation. Also you should analyze what legal obligations you must comply with for this effort. You will be making documented commitments of your current efforts. How you use this information, or fail to use this information, can be critical to your overall planning efforts and the eventual effectiveness of the all-hazards EMS you create.

The first step in your analysis should be to establish your team. As noted earlier, the team should be composed of personnel (subject matter experts) representing all parts of your operation. Team members may be selectively brought to complete their portion of the analysis. However, when the analysis is complete and in first draft, all team members should review the data for further input concerning their areas of specialization.

The second step consists of identifying the parameters of the analysis. You want to establish the priority of each identified hazard as it relates to the functioning of the whole organization. The output provides a basis for identifying the critical resources required to develop your response and recovery strategies. You will also begin to establish an order or priority for restoring the functions of your organization's operations. Your outputs from this step should include

- A list of hazards prioritized from most likely to least likely
- Identification of critical business functions
- Identification of impacts of disruption to operations over time
- Identification of critical dependencies
- Identification of critical resources

You should also strive to ensure an accurate, consistent, and complete approach to data gathering. One helpful way of doing this is to establish scenario-based analyses. Develop a disaster scenario, evaluate the business unit's mission, primary service objectives, dependencies to other units, and resources required to respond, mitigate, and recover. As an example, you may look at impacts from disruption over time. The discussion topics may include

- Service objectives
- Financial impacts
- Cash flow
- Legal and/or regulatory issues

- Customer service
- Market share and/or competitive edge
- Other functions

For each hazard scenario, you should develop a strategy outline for impact mitigation. Notice that I said *outline*. Your hazard analysis, while detailed, should not be forced on problem solving or elimination. Rather, you should identify potential problems, outline a response impact mitigation strategy, and present the data. You can seek to eliminate the problems after the analysis is complete. Remember, the hazard analysis is not a onetime event. You should be constantly evaluating potential issues and hazards because nothing stays the same for very long. Beware especially of subtle changes that are almost invisible.

The third step in your hazard analysis is to validate the results. This can be accomplished through formal presentations of the data of key decision makers and subject matter experts. At the end of this step, you should be able to prepare a formal document regarding your hazard analysis. This document should highlight the identified, prioritized hazards (internal and external), impacts from disruptions over time, and critical dependencies (internal and external).

The following example is provided from the evaluation program Auditrak™, developed by me and Logical Management Systems, Corp. The program is designed as a tool for evaluation of the all-hazards EMS. It is based on the evaluation of nine *essential elements of analysis (EEAs)*. These EEAs are reflective of the critical components of any well-defined emergency management system. Each EEA contains subelements called *measures of effectiveness (MOEs)*. Each MOE contains further data elements called *measures of performance (MOPs)*. MOPs are presented in question or checklist form.

Using the EEA entitled *hazard evaluation* as an example, I will attempt to walk you through a typical hazard analysis. Where appropriate, I will explain terms and/or contexts.

The EEA called *hazard evaluation* consists of three measures of effectiveness:

Hazard identification and analysis

Evaluation of compliance

Commitment identification, resolution, and tracking

It is defined as follows:

EEA definition. The hazard analysis segment focuses on the identification and analysis of potential hazards, susceptibility, and vulnerability. Areas of analysis include hazardous materials, chemical process, physical operations, equipment design, business impacts, location, and layout evaluations.

Comprehensive evaluations or audits are necessary to verify that the EMS, emergency management/response organization (EMRO), and physical facilities are in compliance with standards prescribed in codes, industry or consensus standards, and applicable regulations. These evaluations measure the performance of the EMS as well as compliance and provide recommendations for corrective actions.

The analysis items are presented in the form of questions. While they generally require a yes/no answer, you should begin to do a further analysis based on the answer provided to each question. For example, under the heading 9.1.

Measure of effectiveness. Hazard identification and analysis, measure of performance 3, asks, Has the hazard analysis identified [followed by a listing of issues, categorized by type of potential hazard]? As you answer yes or no to each item, consider the following. For every yes answer, do you have the documentation to back up the answer? If so, where is it located? And, finally, how comfortable do you feel about the adequacy and accuracy of the data?

For every no response, you should make a determination of applicability of the item. For those items that do not apply and for which a no answer was given, further analysis and assessment are indicated.

Further down the list is item 12. At first glance you might say, "What does this item have to do with hazard analysis?" The answer is, Ask any business executive, employee, customer, vendor, etc., who experienced the Chicago tunnel system flood in April 1992. The flood occurred as a result of a contractor's driving a piling through the roof of the old Chicago freight tunnel system. The subsequent flood, all of which occurred underground in the tunnel system, closed downtown Chicago. A crisis? You bet. It was covered for days on CNN and took weeks to mitigate and begin the recovery process. Many business operations were disrupted as a result. So, I say, it is never too early to begin to assess the adequacy of recovery operations. What if you had to evacuate your facility or location today and reestablish your business at a remote location? Would you think of having the mail service transferred? Or what about all the normal forms, letterhead paper, etc., you require to run your operation effectively? Remember the earlier discussion on impact mitigation. This is part of your hazard analysis!

Conclusion

As you can see, the process of determining what your plan and supporting materials will address is not a simple matter. In addition to the above, you should reference the requirements of applicable regulatory guidance. Compliance with these programs should be readily reflected in your plan. We will discuss the regulatory compliance cross-reference in Part 2 as well as where to put your hazard analysis information in the planning document that you will be developing and/or revising.

Auditrak™
Emergency Management System
Assessment Guide

Sample

The information contained in the following example is excerpted from Auditrak™, an EMS assessment guide developed by Logical Management Systems, Corp. Logical Management Systems, Corp., assumes no liability for injury or loss or damage of any kind resulting directly or indirectly from the use of the information contained in this example, the Auditrak™ assessment guide, and/or related materials.

Essential Element of Analysis 9: Hazard Analysis

Measures of effectiveness

9.1 Hazard identification and analysis

9.2 Evaluation of compliance

9.3 Commitment identification, resolution, and tracking

EEA Definition. The hazard analysis segment of the audit focuses on the identification and analysis of potential hazards, susceptibility, and vulnerability. Areas of analysis include hazardous materials, chemical process, physical operations, equipment design, location, and layout evaluations.

9.1 Measure of Effectiveness: Hazard Identification and Analysis

1. Does the organization attempt to control hazards whenever possible by reducing its inventory of potentially hazardous materials or by using appropriate substitutions and/or reclamation?   Yes/No _____

2. Is the hazard analysis conducted by a team of technical/subject matter experts?   Yes/No _____

3. Has the hazard analysis identified:

Manufacturing process hazards

Process failures
- Explosions   Yes/No _____
- Fires   Yes/No _____
- Materials spills and releases   Yes/No _____

- Mechanical failure   Yes/No _____
- Corrosion, fatigue, erosion   Yes/No _____

Utility supply disruption

- Electric   Yes/No _____
- Water   Yes/No _____
- Fuel (natural gas, fuel oil, etc.)   Yes/No _____

Feedstock supply disruption

- Due to accidents   Yes/No _____
- Due to market forces   Yes/No _____

Chronic environmental contamination

- Due to operating systems   Yes/No _____
- Due to accidents   Yes/No _____
- Externally generated situations   Yes/No _____
- Surface waters   Yes/No _____
- Groundwater   Yes/No _____
- Public water supplies   Yes/No _____
- Public and private wells and springs   Yes/No _____

Transportation hazards

Accidents

- Explosions   Yes/No _____
- Fires   Yes/No _____
- Materials spills and releases   Yes/No _____

Disruptions

- System   Yes/No _____
- Political and economic problems   Yes/No _____

Modes of operation

- Highway   Yes/No _____
- Railway   Yes/No _____
- Pipeline   Yes/No _____
- Fixed site   Yes/No _____
- Air freight   Yes/No _____
- Marine   Yes/No _____

Product-related hazards

- Product contamination   Yes/No _____
- Product liability   Yes/No _____
- Product defect   Yes/No _____
- Market share loss   Yes/No _____

Employee-related hazards

- Labor strife   Yes/No _____
- Human error   Yes/No _____
- Employee sabotage   Yes/No _____
- Hostage violent acts   Yes/No _____
- Contractor actions   Yes/No _____
- Litigation   Yes/No _____
- Employee drug use   Yes/No _____
- Maintenance oversight   Yes/No _____

Societal hazards

- Political instability and civil disorder Yes/No _____
- International conflicts   Yes/No _____
- Hostage/terrorist acts   Yes/No _____
- Executive kidnapping   Yes/No _____
- Consumer protests and boycotts   Yes/No _____
- Product tampering   Yes/No _____

Financial hazards

- Hostile takeover and leveraged buyout   Yes/No _____
- Stock market or price collapse   Yes/No _____
- Embezzlement   Yes/No _____
- Executive misconduct and fraud   Yes/No _____

Natural disaster hazards

- Floods   Yes/No _____
- Hurricanes   Yes/No _____
- Tornadoes   Yes/No _____
- Earthquakes   Yes/No _____
- Severe winter storms   Yes/No _____
- Wildfires   Yes/No _____
- Rainstorms   Yes/No _____

- Electrical storms   Yes/No _____
- Other   Yes/No _____

Miscellaneous hazards

- Executive succession   Yes/No _____
- Computer failure or virus   Yes/No _____
- Organized crime   Yes/No _____

External hazards

- Neighboring sites   Yes/No _____
- Property listed on national register of
  historic places   Yes/No _____
- National register of historic landmarks   Yes/No _____

War-related hazards

- Nuclear war   Yes/No _____
- Terrorist attack   Yes/No _____
- Conventional war   Yes/No _____

Natural resource hazards

- Baseline scientific data   Yes/No _____
- Identification of trustees   Yes/No _____
- Sensitive areas   Yes/No _____
- Potentially injured natural resources   Yes/No _____
- Services adversely affected   Yes/No _____
- Data collection and sampling   Yes/No _____
- Habitats and seasonal variations   Yes/No _____
- State and federal wildlife management areas   Yes/No _____
- Wildlife refuges and sanctuaries   Yes/No _____

4. Are all identified materials categorized as

- Potentially hazardous   Yes/No _____
- Hazardous   Yes/No _____
- Extremely hazardous   Yes/No _____
- Toxic   Yes/No _____
- Extremely toxic   Yes/No _____
- Combustible liquid   Yes/No _____
- Explosive   Yes/No _____
- Organic peroxide   Yes/No _____

- ■ Pyrophoric   Yes/No _____
- ■ Water-reactive   Yes/No _____
- ■ Compressed gas   Yes/No _____
- ■ Flammable   Yes/No _____
- ■ Oxidizer   Yes/No _____
- ■ Unstable (reactive)   Yes/No _____

5. Has the hazard analysis identified and categorized the potential release state for each
   identified material?   Yes/No _____

6. Has the hazard analysis identified the release
   pathways for all identified materials?   Yes/No _____

7. Has the hazard analysis provided guidance for
   establishment of priorities for protection and
   means of protection?   Yes/No _____

8. Have worst-case scenarios been developed for
   all identified hazards?   Yes/No _____

9. Have most-probable-case scenarios been
   developed for all identified hazards?   Yes/No _____

10. Have physical security systems been analyzed
    as follows?

Alarm systems

Is there an intrusion alarm system?   Yes/No _____

Is the intrusion alarm system connected to a
central station or to the local police?   Yes/No _____

Is the alarm tested on a weekly basis?   Yes/No _____

Does the alarm system have battery backup?   Yes/No _____

Perimeter security

Is fencing of acceptable design and construction? Yes/No _____

Is current condition of fencing able to meet
design requirements?   Yes/No _____

Are there any places along the fence where the
ground is eroded, permitting access under
the fence?   Yes/No _____

Are there any trees, poles, or materials in
the clear zone (10 to 15 feet) on both sides
of the fence that could be used to circumvent
the fence?   Yes/No _____

Are "No Trespassing" signs posted?   Yes/No _____

Are all gates and doors into the premises
adequately secured and operating properly?   Yes/No _____

Are gate openings controlled (automated, key-
locked, or controlled by guards)?   Yes/No _____
- During working hours (normal business hours)   Yes/No _____
- During nonworking hours   Yes/No _____
- Are controls working properly   Yes/No _____

Is protective lighting adequate inside the
perimeter? [The minimum is 1 footcandle (fc);
3-fc power is recommended in parking lot areas
at night when employees are present.]   Yes/No _____

Is lighting adequate at entrances and fire exits?   Yes/No _____

Are lighting repairs made promptly?   Yes/No _____

Is there backup or emergency lighting in the
event of power failure?   Yes/No _____

Employee and visitor access control

Are employee entrances controlled by guards,
receptionists, or card access?   Yes/No _____

Are all other entrances controlled by alarms,
locks, or people?   Yes/No _____

Are ID badges issued to employees? (This is
recommended for facilities with 100 or more
employees.)   Yes/No _____

Visitors, contractors, etc.

- Are visitors and contractors issued badges?   Yes/No _____
- Are visitors escorted?   Yes/No _____
- Are visitors required to sign in and out?   Yes/No _____

Are employees allowed to bring in or take out
packages?   Yes/No _____

- If yes, is there a package control procedure?   Yes/No _____
- Are there provisions for inspecting packages?   Yes/No _____

Parking

- Is employee parking allowed near storage
  areas, loading docks, and employee entrances?   Yes/No _____
- Has a contractor parking area been designated?   Yes/No _____
- If yes, is it near any building entrances?   Yes/No _____

Internal security and audits

Are buildings and offices locked after regular
business hours?   Yes/No _____

Are cleaning and janitorial personnel supervised
by company personnel and restricted to non-
critical areas?   Yes/No _____

Are employees required to lock desks and
cabinets at the end of the workday?   Yes/No _____

Is there a locker inspection program?   Yes/No _____

Are bulletin board announcements posted
concerning the search of company lockers?   Yes/No _____

Locks and safe

- Is a key control system in effect?   Yes/No _____
- Are safe combinations and locks changed
  periodically?   Yes/No _____
- Are keys and safe combinations recorded
  and secured so that authorized personnel have
  access in case of emergencies?   Yes/No _____

Is maximum use being made of security
electronics, such as closed-circut TVs, card
access systems, and intrusion alarms?   Yes/No _____

Is the computer room access-controlled?   Yes/No _____

Is office equipment inventoried?   Yes/No _____
- Are serial and asset numbers recorded?   Yes/No _____
- Is equipment without serial numbers marked
  for identification?   Yes/No _____
- Are tools and office supplies charged out?   Yes/No _____
- Is access to tools and nonexpendable supplies
  restricted?   Yes/No _____

Shipping and receiving
- Is there accountability for incoming and
  outgoing shipments?   Yes/No _____
- Is inventory control maintained?   Yes/No _____
- Are seals utilized where appropriate?   Yes/No _____
- Is access to the shipping and receiving
  area restricted?   Yes/No _____

Do you audit cash accounts periodically at
unscheduled times?   Yes/No _____

Are private cameras and other photographic or
video equipment restricted?   Yes/No _____

Security services

If a contract guard agency is used, are they
(A) responsive to company needs, and (B) is
the level of service satisfactory?   A: Yes/No _____

                                                         B: Yes/No _____

Is the frequency of contact between guard
service representatives and company manage-
ment adequate?   Yes/No _____

Are the duties and responsibilities of the guard
force in compliance with local laws and
regulations?   Yes/No _____

Are guards armed?   Yes/No _____

Are written instructions (emergency plan
implementing procedures) available to
the guards?   Yes/No _____

Survey of criminal problem

Has the facility been subject to the following?
- Sabotage   Yes/No _____
- Internal thefts   Yes/No _____
  Tools and supplies   Yes/No _____
  Finished products   Yes/No _____
  Cash   Yes/No _____
- External thefts   Yes/No _____
- Vandalism   Yes/No _____
  Company property   Yes/No _____
  Employee property   Yes/No _____
- Assaults on or by employees   Yes/No _____
- Crimes in parking areas   Yes/No _____
  Auto theft or burglary   Yes/No _____
  Robbery, i.e., holdups, purse-snatching, etc.   Yes/No _____
  Sex crimes   Yes/No _____

Are criminal violations (thefts, larceny,
burglary, etc.) reported to local authorities?   Yes/No _____

Is liaison maintained with local law
enforcement?   Yes/No _____

Have company regulations, where pertinent,
been discussed with local police?   Yes/No _____

Are losses being logged and reported according
to established procedures?   Yes/No _____

Are adequate steps taken to prevent intentional
product tampering and/or contamination?   Yes/No _____

11. Have emergency planning zones (EPZs) been
    established for each location with an emergency
    management plan?   Yes/No _____

12. Does your emergency management plan include the preplanning reentry and recovery operations, as follows?

Facilities recovery plan

Activation procedures   Yes/No _____

Alternate emergency operations center (EOC)   Yes/No _____

Facilities recovery team telephone list   Yes/No _____

General office occupancy list, by floor   Yes/No _____

General office contact list, by floor   Yes/No _____

Assigned recovery sites   Yes/No _____
- Floor-by-floor site assignments and
  requirements   Yes/No _____
- Company and department site assignments   Yes/No _____
- Floor plan of room assignments in
  [RECOVERY SITE]   Yes/No _____
- Building   Yes/No _____

Facilities and services departments   Yes/No _____

Facility recovery requirements, by floor   Yes/No _____

Relocation sites for shared quarters

Assigned relocation sites   Yes/No _____
- Floor-by-floor site assignments and
  requirements   Yes/No _____
- Company and department site assignments   Yes/No _____
- Floor plan of room assignments in
  [RELOCATION SITE]   Yes/No _____
- Building   Yes/No _____

Facilities and services departments   Yes/No _____

Facility relocation requirements, by floor   Yes/No _____

Specialty furniture and equipment requirements

Listing of requirements   Yes/No _____

Special-purpose rooms or areas

Requirements for rooms or areas   Yes/No _____

Requirements for locked rooms or security areas   Yes/No _____

Building documents and records required in emergency

Architectural drawings and blueprints   Yes/No _____

Lease information   Yes/No _____

Floor plans   Yes/No _____

Emergency teams—names of members and designated responsibilities

List of emergency services and responsibilities   Yes/No _____

Facilities recovery plan manager   Yes/No _____

Facilities recovery operations team   Yes/No _____
- Manager leasing   Yes/No _____
- Administration group   Yes/No _____
- Security group   Yes/No _____
- Operations group   Yes/No _____
- Architectural services group   Yes/No _____
- Leasing group   Yes/No _____
- Tape retrieval group   Yes/No _____
- Audiovisual equipment group   Yes/No _____
- Surface transportation group   Yes/No _____
- Aviation group   Yes/No _____
- Performance and cost management group   Yes/No _____
- Information services group   Yes/No _____
- Computer equipment acquisition group   Yes/No _____
- Meeting services group   Yes/No _____
- Executive services facilitator   Yes/No _____

Services

Copy/office machine services	Yes/No _____
Forms design and distribution	Yes/No _____
Inactive records retrieval	Yes/No _____
Library services	Yes/No _____
Lodging and travel arrangements	Yes/No _____
Mail services	Yes/No _____
Photography	Yes/No _____
Real estate	Yes/No _____
Records restoration	Yes/No _____
Reprographics	Yes/No _____
Inactive records retrieval	Yes/No _____
Tape retrieval	Yes/No _____

Critical requirements checklists and questionnaire

Critical requirements questionnaire	Yes/No _____
Departmental business resumption contacts	Yes/No _____

Hazard potential analysis
- Floor-by-floor listing of critical requirements and recovery — Yes/No _____
- Locations for each critical business function — Yes/No _____

Personnel skills requirements

Secretarial and clerical	Yes/No _____
Administrators and analysts	Yes/No _____
Security officers	Yes/No _____

Operations personnel   Yes/No _____
- Building engineers   Yes/No _____
- Maintenance supervisors and carpenters   Yes/No _____
- Electricians   Yes/No _____
- Painters   Yes/No _____
- Laborers   Yes/No _____
- Furniture specialists   Yes/No _____
- Carpet installers   Yes/No _____
- Safety and environmental specialists   Yes/No _____
- Telephone system specialists   Yes/No _____

Architects, designers, CAD technicians   Yes/No _____

Transactional real estate people   Yes/No _____

Restoration contractor list   Yes/No _____

Public sector contacts

City of [LOCATION]   Yes/No _____

[LOCATION] County   Yes/No _____

State of [LOCATION]   Yes/No _____

Federal government   Yes/No _____

Telephone and utility company contacts

Telephone
- Local   Yes/No _____
- Long distance   Yes/No _____
- Other   Yes/No _____

Gas   Yes/No _____

Electric   Yes/No _____

Water   Yes/No _____

Other   Yes/No _____

Forms and supplies

Incident report form   Yes/No _____

EOC activation form   Yes/No _____

EOC emergency situation log   Yes/No _____

Damage assessment form   Yes/No _____

Emergency acquisitions form (purchase order)   Yes/No _____

Insurance claim form   Yes/No _____

Listings of [COMPANY] forms and supplies   Yes/No _____

Associated plans and information

Prefire plan   Yes/No _____

Drawings   Yes/No _____

Environmental, health, and safety manual   Yes/No _____

Humanitarian assistance plan   Yes/No _____

Purchasing acquisition plans   Yes/No _____

Telecommunications plan   Yes/No _____

Crisis communications plan   Yes/No _____

Security communications   Yes/No _____

Law department plan   Yes/No _____

Insurance and risk management plan   Yes/No _____

Treasury contingency cash plan   Yes/No _____

Controller's system for tracking recovery
expenses   Yes/No _____

Community maps   Yes/No _____

Newspapers, radio, and television stations   Yes/No _____

Vendor, supplier, and consultant list   Yes/No _____

Floorspace alternatives outside main office   Yes/No _____

Business recovery center   Yes/No _____

Local hotels   Yes/No _____

Mass transit information   Yes/No _____

Landlords and non-[COMPANY] tenants   Yes/No _____

Stress management and monitoring guidelines   Yes/No _____

Performance and cost management   Yes/No _____

Property operations   Yes/No _____

Building administration   Yes/No _____

Building operations   Yes/No _____

Building protection services   Yes/No _____

Communications facilities and services   Yes/No _____

Design and construction services   Yes/No _____

Tape retrieval   Yes/No _____

Library and information center   Yes/No _____

Meeting and travel services   Yes/No _____

Forms administration   Yes/No _____

Forms and records storage center   Yes/No _____

Graphic services   Yes/No _____

Mail service   Yes/No _____

Records planning, storage, and retrieval   Yes/No _____

9.2 Measure of Effectiveness: Evaluation of Compliance

1. Have appropriate and applicable federal regulatory standards addressing emergency preparedness, safety, etc., been consulted as part of the hazard analysis?   Yes/No _____

2. Are appropriate and applicable federal regulatory standards cross-referenced to the applicable portions of the emergency management plan?   Yes/No _____

3. Have appropriate and applicable state and local regulatory standards addressing emergency preparedness been consulted as part of the hazard analysis?   Yes/No _____

4. Are appropriate and applicable state and local regulatory standards cross-referenced to applicable portions of the emergency management plan?   Yes/No _____

5. Have appropriate and applicable company and organization policies and guidance addressing emergency preparedness been consulted as part of the hazard analysis?   Yes/No _____

6. Are appropriate and applicable company and organization policies and guidance cross-referenced to the applicable portions of the emergency management plan?   Yes/No _____

7. Is there a current file for EMS audits and evaluation?   Yes/No _____

8. If periodic audits are conducted to verify proper implementation, when was this last accomplished?

   _____ Within the last quarter

   _____ Within the last 6 months

   _____ Within the last year

   _____ Over 1 year ago

   _____ Not done

   _____ Do not know

9. How are changes to the emergency management
   plan and affiliated documents accomplished?

   _____

10. Who is responsible for ensuring that changes to
    the emergency management plan and affiliated
    documents are communicated to the appropriate
    elements within the facility and/or company?

    _____

11. Who is to be notified of changes in operations
    and processing procedures and specifications so
    that an appropriate hazard analysis and deter-
    mination may be made?

    _____

12. When did you last review policies and
    procedures for environment, health, and safety?
    _____ Within the last quarter
    _____ Within the last 6 months
    _____ Within the last year
    _____ Over 1 year ago
    _____ Not done

13. Are safety and health hazards identified and
    recorded on job and process hazards safety
    analysis sheets?   Yes/No _____

14. Who is accountable for conducting audits of
    compliance with environmental and occupational
    health standards?

    _____

15. After an audit of compliance with environ-
    mental and occupational health standards, is
    there a structured follow-up system that does
    the following?

    Establishes priorities for follow-up actions   Yes/No _____

    Identifies critical items to be corrected   Yes/No _____

    Establishes time frames for corrections   Yes/No _____

    Assigns responsibility to ensure that corrective
    actions are taken   Yes/No _____

16. Are appropriate employees knowledgeable and current on company policies regarding emergency preparedness?   Yes/No _____

17. Are policies, regulations, and related materials properly filed to assist in periodic review and ensure updating where necessary?   Yes/No _____

18. Has a list of all hazards been compiled and reviewed to determine the need for specialized emergency plan implementing procedures?   Yes/No _____

19. Is there a system for evaluation and revision of hazards at least yearly or when facilities, processes, or equipment are changed?   Yes/No _____

20. Is a written disciplinary policy used as a guide in dealing with violators of emergency preparedness and safety guidance?   Yes/No _____

9.3   Measure of Effectiveness: Commitment Identification, Resolution, and Tracking

1. Has a survey of the EMS been made to determine what commitments have been made?   Yes/No _____

2. Has a survey of EMS users been made to determine if identified commitments can be fulfilled?   Yes/No _____

3. How often is an unbiased evaluation made, with results communicated to related management, to determine the degree of compliance with appropriate regulations, policies, etc., within the organization?

   _____ Semiannually   _____ Annually   _____ Not done

4. How often is an unbiased and statistically valid comprehensive audit conducted of management's compliance with the commitments made in the EMS?

   _____ Semiannually   _____ Annually   _____ Not done

5. Have the personnel conducting the audit of the EMS been trained in program evaluation techniques?   Yes/No _____

6. Are techniques such as random sampling, physical measurement, and actual count used to ensure the statistical validity of these audits?   Yes/No _____

7. Indicate which of the following elements are included in the comprehensive audit of management's compliance with the commitments set forth in the EMS.

Leadership and administration   Yes/No _____

Management training   Yes/No _____

Planned inspections   Yes/No _____

Task analysis and procedures   Yes/No _____

Accident and incident investigation   Yes/No _____

Task observation   Yes/No _____

Emergency preparedness   Yes/No _____

Organizational issues   Yes/No _____

Accident and incident analysis   Yes/No _____

Employee training   Yes/No _____

Personal protective equipment   Yes/No _____

Hazard control   Yes/No _____

Program evaluation system   Yes/No _____

Engineering controls   Yes/No _____

Personal communications   Yes/No _____

Group meetings   Yes/No _____

Community outreach   Yes/No _____

Hiring and placement   Yes/No _____

Purchasing controls   Yes/No _____

Off-the-job safety   Yes/No _____

8. Has an action plan been developed to meet
   identified EMS needs as indicated by the last
   comprehensive program audit?   Yes/No _____

9. Is there a commitment tracking and information
   management system designed to monitor the
   status of crisis management, emergency preparedness, and related commitments?   Yes/No _____

10. Can EMS commitments be categorized as follows?

Item no.

A chronological numeric listing of commitments   Yes/No _____

Responsibility

Identification of the specific individual responsible for completion of the action item or commitment or the individual with overall authority for
ensuring completion of the commitment   Yes/No _____

Commitment date

Lists the month, day, and year that the commit-
ment is anticipated to be completed   Yes/No _____

Status

Open, closed, or recurring   Yes/No _____

Topic

Twelve key planning elements:
- Emergency management plans   Yes/No _____
- Emergency plan implementing procedures   Yes/No _____

- Emergency facilities and equipment   Yes/No _____
- Hazard identification and analysis   Yes/No _____
- Communications systems   Yes/No _____
- Training   Yes/No _____
- Plan validation: drills, proficiency
- Demonstrations   Yes/No _____
- Emergency management/response
  organization   Yes/No _____
- Emergency management system
  administration   Yes/No _____
- Coordination with external entities   Yes/No _____
- Public information   Yes/No _____

Resolution

A brief description outlining the various
deliverables and the resolution of the
commitment   Yes/No _____

Summary

As you can see, there are many resources to draw upon in this area. Choosing the one or ones that fit your particular situation is very important. The review can be used to assist you in developing or expanding your program.

The other EEAs you should consider for evaluation are:

Administration, including assignment of responsibility for program development, implementation, and maintenance; authority; coordination efforts; selection and qualification of personnel; management guidelines; and reference library data

EMRO, including organizational structure, organizational composition, position qualifications, and augmentation of resources

Emergency management/response training and retraining, including instructional systems development, training/retraining programs, certification, documentation, and record keeping

Emergency facilities and equipment, including emergency facilities (mobile and fixed), emergency equipment, expanded support facilities

Emergency plan implementing procedures, including general content and format, control and updating, inventory

Coordination with external agencies, including external agencies (federal, state, local, company), general public, news media

Plan validation (drills and exercises), including establishing the program, implementation, types, evaluation procedures

Communications, including crisis communications program, training in personnel communication techniques, community outreach, program monitoring and evaluation

All-Hazards Emergency Management Planning System

Administrative Considerations

Administration of the all-hazards emergency management system (EMS) is important. This chapter will provide an overview of the key considerations. You will need to adjust the items presented here to your particular situation and circumstances.

Perhaps the best way to get started is to define, in the context of the all-hazards EMS, what *administration* means.

> *Administration* constitutes the day-to-day management portion of the all-hazards EMS. This includes, but is not limited to, setting the framework for the system, controlling the scope of planning activities, developing strategic focus, and creating a forward-thinking vision of how the system will become part of the way you do business.

I have grouped the administrative considerations into three areas:

- Basic administrative considerations
- Legal factors
- Planning factors

Chapter organizer: What this chapter is about

- *Basic administrative considerations.* Key to the organization of an effective all-hazards EMS is guidance on how to administer the various elements or parts of the system. Within this context, you must address issues such as authority for the program, human factors issues, regulatory compliance, and development of internal policy guidance for managing the system.

- *Legal factors.* As you define the system, you must address compliance issues, content of written materials, and protection of materials after the fact; commitment identification and commitment tracking are related administrative considerátions.

- *Planning factors.* The administrative portion of your all-hazards EMS should clearly define the scope and purpose of the plan; set objectives; provide basic preincident information; define planning factors such as mission, business operations description, and associated information; and summarize the hazards analysis results.

Basic Administrative Considerations

"Who's in charge?" It is a common enough question during an incident. It is one that you should think through thoroughly prior to the occurrence of an incident and prior to the completion of the all-hazards EMS.

The person "in charge," i.e., responsible for the administration of the system, may be someone entirely different from the person who exerts authority and is "in charge" at the time of an incident or at the incident scene. Clear delegation of authority for planning, administering, and implementing your all-hazards EMS should be described in the administrative portion of your plan, and other key functions should be identified. From a corporate perspective, the authority for the system should reside at all levels. A corporate officer should be designated to oversee the development and administration of the system. Your system should be designed to ensure an exceptional flow of information upward, downward, and sideways. Thus you should strive to develop a planning standard that exhibits uniformity, common terminology, and efficiency. It also means that the program has support and participation at all levels of management.

Remember, in the aftermath of an incident, the corporate personnel, whether it be the president, chief executive officer, business unit manager, or risk manager, will be in the spotlight. Therefore, they must be part of the team from the beginning, but more about this later when we discuss legal factors.

Once authority for the program has been established, you need to work your way down through the organization. At each management level you should designate a person with appropriate authority for the level of responsibility. This individual or group of individuals should have the ability to view the system in its broadest context. Information sharing is essential to ensure that the system develops along these three guidance points (a planning standard, common terminology, and efficiency of operations). Remember, this is an *all-haz-*

ards approach. You have to look beyond purely operational issues and expand your scope to include other factors such as those addressed in your hazard analysis (Chap. 3). The person who administers the system, regardless of the level within the organization at which the system is developed, must be able to apply the broadest range of thinking to the planning process. And she or he must be able to communicate this thought process to all elements having a role in incident response.

Having a purely operational view will beget a purely operational plan and a purely operationally oriented system. The downside to this is seen when a nonoperational incident occurs, such as the Chicago freight tunnel flood of 1992, and there is no plan to respond to it. You must ensure that the system addresses all potential issues and types of incidents with the appropriate degree of detail. At the end of this chapter, I have provided working examples of an administrative section and some of its supporting materials. These examples can be modified as needed and applied to all levels within an organization.

Legal Factors

As stated earlier, the all-hazards EMS should clearly delegate authority. Many of the decisions made in the early stages of an incident can and will be assessed, analyzed, and utilized by both sides after the incident. Yes, by both sides. By that, I mean the litigants! This is an area of particular concern. And well it should be.

As you develop your all-hazards EMS, regardless of the level within the organization, careful consideration should be given to what is put into the written materials that constitute your all-hazards system components.

Compliance with regulatory mandates is a key driving force. However, blindly regurgitating regulatory requirements in your plan is a sure prescription for disaster during an incident, when it comes to litigation after an incident, or when it is evaluated by regulatory agencies.

You must understand what you are committing to in the plan, and you must be willing to fulfill those commitments. Regulatory compliance and commitment fulfillment are important. But merely being in compliance is, unfortunately, not sufficient. You must have a system in place that provides for documentation of your efforts. And the documentation must be accurate. It is one thing to state in the plan that you will have the local fire department or a hospital respond to assist you. It is quite another to be assured that they have the capability (equipment, facilities, training, etc.) to respond and are willing to do so.

Even closer to home, say you commit to having an *emergency management/response organization* (EMRO). Have you carefully considered the staffing, training, equipment needs, functions, duties, and tasks of the organization? How will you fulfill these resource commitments? Establishing a planning standard, defining the scope of your system, and identifying and addressing commitments will help you to effectively administer the all-hazards EMS.

It is essential to affirm the capabilities and willingness of identified support organizations in your all-hazards EMS. These can be external or internal. Letters of agreement with these parties should be drafted, executed, and included in an appendix to the basic plan.

Corporate and, in some instances, outside counsel should be involved with the administration process. Your counsel should also look for warning signs of potential concern. These include written commitments, letters of agreement, compliance issues, and wording of written documentation and associated documentation from nonemergency programs and policies. These may include securities laws, environmental laws, safety and health laws, civil and criminal laws.

Establishing a Planning Standard

What is a planning standard? Simply, it is a benchmark for the minimum acceptable criterion that your plan or system is judged against. Many regulations provide guidance for emergency planning. Essentially, this guidance serves as the standard against which your plans are judged. Other sources to draw from when you establish planning standards include corporate safety and environmental policy statements, local and state-sponsored regulations, and industry group guidance, such as the Responsible Care program of the Chemical Manufacturers Association (CMA) and the Strategies for Today's Environmental Partnership (STEP) program of the American Petroleum Institute (API).

What you do from the instant an incident occurs will be microscopically scrutinized in the postincident period. It is, therefore, incumbent to have a planning standard that is rigorously adhered to by all elements. You must also ensure the adequacy of your documentation and record-keeping efforts. This includes all available means to protect your records and the documentation generated prior to, during, and after the incident.

Establishing Common Terminology

This may be one of the most difficult and frustrating areas to address. Everyone has his or her own ideas as to terminology. And everyone thinks his or her idea is best and that all others should conform to her or his terminology. Whatever your choice of terminology, do your utmost to standardize it throughout your organization and affiliated entities.

Common terminology is helpful in many ways. It provides meaning to words, titles, etc. It assists people to understand acronyms. It helps move the EMS forward. It reduces the potential for confusion.

When developing your system, you should seek to provide common terminology for such things as

- Position titles
- Incident classification systems
- Chapters of the basic plan
- Appendices to the plan
- Emergency plan implementing procedures
- Emergency facilities

I'm sure you can come up with other examples. Once you establish a common terminology, document it, publish it, track it, and incorporate the documentation into the plan as an appendix. Ensure that it is periodically updated and that everyone is using it.

Efficiency of Implementation

The primary goal of your program should be emergency preparedness. As you begin or continue the process, you should be asking yourself, "What do we need to facilitate an adequate response to an incident?" You must understand and promote the idea that we do not ensure preparedness by merely satisfying government agency requirements. The production of the plan is not an end-all. In the same vein, you can hardly expect to implement a plan understood by few. The planning documents must be user-friendly. In most instances, they will not be. In most instances, personnel responding to an incident will not access their plans. Why?

The most common reason given is that the plan is too cumbersome! This, in many instances, is true. It is also true that when you have to activate your response organization or response system to respond to an incident, you might as well put some compliance issues aside, for you are essentially out of compliance at that point.

So, what's needed? The answer was provided in Chap. 2. It has been my experience that the three-tier approach, with variations for custom fitting, seems to best facilitate the efficiency of implementation. Essentially, the working component, that part used in the response, is the *emergency plan implementing procedure(s)* [*EPIP(s)*]. The plan and appendices become reference material. In some cases, the EPIPs have been consolidated into position booklets or condensed into simple, task-oriented statements, supplemented with checklists and flowcharts and supported by status boards, worksheets, maps, and computer programs. The EPIPs should contain only that information which can be used at the time of the incident. All other information is irrelevant and potentially distracting.

The basis for the EPIPs, however, is the plan and associated appendices. Therefore, it is necessary to ensure compliance through a well-developed plan and supporting materials (appendices, EPIPs) yet have a system flexible enough to allow for efficiency in response.

This is the basic premise upon which the remainder of this book is written. It provides a workable, manageable format for managing and responding to emergencies.

Planning Factors

We have reviewed in Chaps. 1, 2, and 3 how to establish and document the planning premises. Critical to an effective system is a well-thought-out and well-executed hazard analysis. This analysis forms the basis for your all-hazards EMS. Once completed, it should become an appendix to the plan. A schedule for periodic reevaluation should be established. An example of a hazard analysis is also provided at the end of this chapter.

Next, you must select a time horizon. By this, I mean you must decide when your system will be in place and to what degree you are willing to accept the risk that not all components are fully addressed. In essence, you have to have a plan to plan. This plan to plan should be carried forward through the administration of the system.

Once your plan to plan is defined, you need to do the following:

- Review existing and past practices.
- Develop and state assumptions.
- Determine key variables.
- Determine plausible ranges for the variables.
- Build scenarios (most probable case, worst case).
- Develop a strategy for each scenario.
- Check for effectiveness of each strategy.
- Select optimum strategies.
- Develop and implement the strategies.

Your goal should be to provide a mechanism for continuous assessment, evaluation, and development of the system.

Outcomes like this will not occur automatically. You must develop and implement policies and procedures that ensure optimum system responsiveness. Everyone in your organization must become an owner of the system, with a vested interest in its success. Administration of the all-hazards EMS, like any emergency plan or response management system, must become part of the daily routine of doing business and not just a quarterly, semiannual, or annual event.

Your emergency management system must be developed so that information sharing and a high level of involvement from all user groups can be achieved. If you use the administrative aspects of the all-hazards system presented here as a guide for establishing high-level, effective, continuous learning and improvement, then management of change to the system, as new requirements are addressed, will be less painful, less costly, and less time-consuming.

The examples at the end of this chapter are provided for your use. These reflect working samples that have been developed, implemented, and tested over time. They are presented in the following sequence:

- Sample all-hazards emergency management plan, section: administration

- Sample supporting materials: administrative appendices

- Sample implementing procedures: administrative emergency plan implementing procedures

Sample

All-Hazards Emergency Management Plan

Section: Administration

Sample

Purpose

Here you should state the premise for your plan. For example:

> The plan has been specifically designed to serve as a basis for dealing with incidents at the [LOCATION]. The all-hazards *emergency management plan (EMP)* contains specific plan sections, appendices, and emergency plan implementing procedures (EPIPs) addressing significant actions and anticipated response activities. Every effort has been made to integrate the applicable regulatory requirements into this plan. In this regard the EMP is consistent with existing authorities, planning assumptions, systems, and procedures.

Objectives

Here you should state the objectives of the EMP. For example:

- Delineate action plans which will minimize hazards to life and property and will reduce adverse impacts upon the environment from incidents occurring at or near the [LOCATION] boundaries.

- Establish procedures to provide for well-coordinated efforts on the part of the [COMPANY] and regulatory agencies in the management of emergency response.

- Identify emergency organizations, equipment, and other resources which can be employed during such a response.

Incident Information Summary

Initial information during an incident can be critical. Guidelines for gathering essential information about the incident and reporting it should be defined here. This may include, but will not be limited to, the following:

- Date and time
- Name of the facility and person, including emergency title, placing the call
- Name of person receiving the call
- Name and telephone number of on-scene contact
- Location
- Nearby populations

- Incident description
- Time of release (if any)
- Possible health effects
- Number of injured
- Medical emergency information
- Where injured are being taken
- Name of material released, and (if known):

  Manifest, shipping invoice, billing label
  Shipper and manufacturer identification
  Container type
  Railcar or truck four-digit identification numbers
  Placard or label information
  Characteristics of the material (only if readily detectable)
  Present status of material
  Total amount of material that may be released
  Other hazardous materials in area
  Amount of material released so far, duration of release
  Whether significant amounts of material appear to be entering the atmosphere, nearby water, storm drains, or soil
  Direction, height, color, odor of any vapor clouds or plumes
  Weather conditions (wind direction and speed)
  Local terrain conditions
  Personnel at the scene

Planning Factors

A summary of key planning factors should be provided. For example:

Mission

- Prevent loss of life and minimize the risk of bodily injury.
- Prevent damage to the environment.
- Prevent or minimize property damage to [LOCATION] and the surrounding community.
- Provide maximum safety for emergency response personnel at the scene of the emergency.

Physical Location Description

A brief description of the physical location should be provided. Key information includes

- Number of acres
- Key border identifiers (streets, landmarks, etc.)
- Latitude coordinates
- Longitude coordinates (Federal Aviation Administration requires this information in order to order the airspace evacuated.)
- Location street address and mailing address

Other information that may be useful includes the following:

- Land use near the location
- Major products
- Potentially hazardous chemicals located at [LOCATION]

These should be highlighted and a separate appendix provided for detailed information:

- Use of chemicals in process
- Storage location of chemicals
- Releases and release pathways

A brief summary of the types of releases and release pathways should be provided. A separate portion of the hazard analysis should detail the releases and release pathways.

Sample

All-Hazards Emergency Management Plan

Supporting Materials

Administrative Appendices

Sample

[COMPANY]

[LOCATION]

APPENDIX __

Hazard Analysis

[DATE]

General Information

Provide a description of physical location including a discussion on major roadways, acreage, average elevation above sea level, coordinates (latitude _____ and longitude _____). Also note the county and state in which the facility is located. Conclude this paragraph with a brief discussion of cities, towns, and locales within, say, an hour's drive of the location or within an established emergency planning zone.

Also included in this introductory statement should be a brief description of the following, as they apply:

- Offshore transportation-related facilities
- Offshore non-transportation-related facilities
- Water intakes and outfalls, effluent lines, discharge areas
- Major industries bordering the facility
- Major roadways and points of reference
- Major medical facilities
- Law enforcement and fire protection services (include federal agencies if applicable, e.g., the FBI)
- Educational, day care, or other highly sensitive areas and special populations

Assignment of Responsibility for Emergency Planning

Describe briefly what position title is responsible for emergency planning. Do not, however, include names. People change, but position titles generally do not. For example:

> Responsibility for emergency preparedness at [LOCATION] has been assigned to [POSITION, TITLE, DEPARTMENT]. Specific procedures for auditing, maintaining, improving, and exercising emergency preparedness appear in sections _____ and _____ of the all-hazards plan and in _____ series and _____ series EPIPs.
>
> For United States–based operations, the following regulatory guidance should be considered as it applies, in assessing hazards associated with [LOCATION] processes and operations:
>
> - Code of Federal Regulations (CFR) 29, 40, and 49
> - OSHA 29 CFR 1910.36, "Means of Egress" (evacuation)
> - OSHA 29 CFR 1910.38, "Employee Emergency Plans and Fire Prevention Plans"
> - OSHA 29 CFR 1910.119, "Process Safety Management of Highly Hazardous Chemicals"

- OSHA 29 CFR 1910.120, "Hazardous Waste Operations and Emergency Response"
- OSHA 29 CFR 1910.1030, "Occupational Exposure to Bloodborne Pathogens"
- OSHA 29 CFR 1910.156, "Fire Brigades"
- OSHA 29 CFR 1910.165, "Employee Alarm Systems"
- OSHA 29 CFR 1910.1200, "Hazard Communication"
- Comprehensive Environmental Response, Compensation, and Liability Act (CERCLA), section 105
- EPA 40 CFR 112, "Oil Pollution Prevention"
- EPA 40 CFR 261, "Identification and Listing of Hazardous Wastes"
- EPA 40 CFR 300, SARA Title III of the Superfund Amendments, and Reauthorization Act of 1986
- Oil Pollution Act of 1990 (OPA 90)
- Any state regulations applicable to the location
- Any local regulations applicable to the location

Note: This list is not all-inclusive. As new regulatory requirements are promulgated, you should review the *Federal Register* or other sources to determine the status of promulgation and applicability to your operations. Foreign operations should seek applicable guidance from the country in which they operate.

Identification of Potentially Hazardous Materials

You should list the potentially hazardous materials located at your site, using the following breakdown and any applicable regulatory requirements as guidance.

Classification systems

There are three major regulatory bodies concerned with potentially hazardous chemicals and materials in the United States: the *Occupational Safety and Health Administration* (OSHA), the *Environmental Protection Agency* (EPA), and the U.S. Legislature, which drafted SARA Title III. Each of these regulatory bodies uses classification systems, complete with definitions for materials and chemicals. Other recognized sources are the *National Fire Protection Association* (NFPA), *Hazardous Materials Identification System* (HMIS), and the *National Institute for Occupational Safety and Health* (NIOSH). A discussion of some of their provisions appears below.

OSHA.   The Occupational Safety and Health Administration defines a *hazardous chemical* as "a chemical for which there is statistically significant evidence, based on at least one study conducted in accordance with scientific principles, that acute or chronic health effects may occur in exposed employees."

The definition also includes chemicals for which there is scientifically valid evidence that they fit one of the following categories:

- Combustible liquid
- Explosive
- Organic peroxide
- Pyrophoric
- Water-reactive
- Compressed gas
- Flammable
- Oxidizer
- Unstable (reactive)

Under other regulations, hazardous substances include any

- Substance designated as hazardous under section 311 of the federal Clean Water Act
- Substance designated as hazardous under CERCLA, section 102
- Waste listed as hazardous, or substance which has hazardous waste characteristics under RCRA
- Toxic pollutant under section 307(a) of the federal Clean Air Act
- Hazardous air pollutant under section 112 of the federal Clean Air Act
- Imminently hazardous chemical substance, under section 7 of the federal Toxic Substance Control Act, for which the EPA administrator has taken action

SARA Title III.   SARA Title III levies many requirements on entities that are involved with hazardous chemicals. The law further recognizes the need to establish and maintain contingency plans for responding to chemical accidents.

Three classes of chemicals are recognized in SARA Title III:

1. *Hazardous chemicals.*   These chemicals fall within the hazard communication standard's (OSHA 29 CFR 1910.1200) definition of a hazardous chemical. If a hazardous material is not included on one of the EPA lists, it is still regulated as a hazardous waste if it meets one or more of four characteristics, including

- Ignitability
- Reactivity
- Corrosivity
- Extraction procedure toxicity

2. *Extremely hazardous substances.*   The list includes 403 chemicals, now appearing in appendix A of the EPA's Chemical Emergency Preparedness program.

3. *Extremely toxic substances.*   The states of Maryland and New Jersey have developed lists of 311 environmentally hazardous chemicals. Additions are made if a chemical is known or anticipated to cause chronic or acute health effects or adverse environmental effects. These lists serve as reference for the EPA's definition of *extremely toxic substances.*

If your facility uses chemicals which have been classified, under SARA Title III, as extremely hazardous, they should be listed. An example follows:

Extremely Hazardous Substances List

Item	Chemical name	RQ (lb) 1987	DOT guide no.	UN no. (ID no.)

[Insert your list here.]

RQ means *reportable quantity.* This number shown is in pounds. The Department of Transportation (DOT) guide number refers to the appropriate page in DOT P 5800.4, *Emergency Response Guidebook—Guidebook for Initial Response to Hazardous Materials Incidents.*

The UN number (ID number) refers to the four-digit identification number assigned to each chemical listed in the DOT *Emergency Response Guidebook.*

You should also provide a list of materials that may cause concern but are not on the EPA list. These include familiar products, such as gasoline, diesel fuel, and propane.

Information on the specific use of each chemical is generally beyond the scope of this type of hazards analysis. However, you may wish to cite other studies such as hazard operability, process safety management program studies, and supplementary materials as resources here.

You should provide a list of the locations where *material safety data sheets (MSDSs)* are maintained.

If your location experiences an incident in which a release of a potentially hazardous chemical substance occurs, you should identify the chemical and its release state. An example follows:

Item	Chemical	Release state
1	Chlorine	Gas
2	Ammonia	Gas, liquid
3	Hydrogen sulfide	Gas
4	Sulfur dioxide	Gas
5	Sulfuric acid	Gas, liquid

You should also include, as applicable, the release pathways for potentially hazardous materials. An example follows:

Release pathway	Item	Description
Air	Vertical flare	Vent gas
Air	Ground flare	Vent gas
Water	Docks	Barge or ship loading or unloading incident
Ground	Tank farm	Rupture of storage tank
Ground	Pipeline	Pipeline rupture
Ground	Truck	Traffic accident
Ground	Railcar	Derailment

Release History

An overview of the location's release history should be provided. Also you should describe any systems used to retain the data on release history. Proposed new regulations seek a 5-year history of past incidents and releases. You should carefully document the release history to ensure consistency in defining the release and incident parameters.

Hazard Analysis

In this section, you should describe the methodology used to conduct the hazard analysis. Consider the following example.

HAZOP methodology

A HAZOP study is a procedure used to review the design and operation of a process facility. It is used to identify all causes of deviation from normal, safe operation which could lead to any safety hazard or operability problem. The study is a team effort, undertaken to identify potential causes and consequences of a problem and to recommend changes or further study to overcome it. It is normal for the study team to prepare a draft report listing the recommendations made, the circumstances requiring the changes, etc. A final report is produced later, including actions taken and future actions planned.

Hazard and operability studies are undertaken by the application of a formal, systematic, and critical examination of the process and engineering intentions of a process design. Individual items of equipment are reviewed in detail. In this fashion, overall system hazards can be identified before an incident occurs. This examination of the design is structured around a specific set of guide words, which ensures thorough coverage of all possible problems while allowing sufficient flexibility for an imaginative approach.

To summarize, there are four overall aims for any HAZOP study:

- To identify all potential deviations from the way the design is expected to work, their causes, and all the hazards and operability problems associated with these deviations
- To decide whether action is required to control the hazard or the operability problem, and if so, to identify the ways in which the problem can be solved
- To identify cases where a decision cannot be made immediately and to decide what information or action is required
- To ensure that actions decided upon are followed through

Hazard Categories

In this section, you should identify the hazard categories of concern. For example:

External hazards: tornadoes, floods, wildfire, hurricanes or severe storms, earthquakes, nuclear attack, terrorist attack

Hazardous materials incidents: roadway, railway, pipeline, fixed site

Major transportation accidents (Non-HAZMAT):   roadway, railway, airway, waterway

Mechanical failure: corrosion, fatigue, erosion, etc.; curtailment or loss of utilities; curtailment or loss of cooling water; curtailment or loss of natural gas

Human error: operator error, maintenance error

A more detailed discussion of each of these hazards should follow on succeeding pages.

Additional information about your location's operations and the potential areas where involvement in hazardous materials incidents could occur should be summarized as applicable. The following are examples.

- Summary of process units and processes
- Oil, chemical, and bulk storage areas

- Transfer locations
- Control stations
- Aboveground and below-ground piping
- Monitoring systems
- Leak detection systems
- Location of safety protection devices
- Highly toxic materials handled

Other Major Risks

In this portion of the hazard analysis, you should identify and discuss other potential risks, such as

- Spills: oil and/or hazardous materials
- Major transportation incident (identify specific modes)
- Mechanical failure
- Human error

Other Hazards

This section of the hazard analysis should provide a brief summary of other recognized hazards or potential concerns associated with neighboring industrial or other types of facilities.

- Neighboring industries
- Surface waters
- Groundwater
- Public water supplies
- Public and private water wells and springs
- State and/or federal wildlife management areas, wildlife refuges, management areas, and sanctuaries
- Property listed on the national register of historic places and property listed on the national register of historic landmarks
- Lists of potentially hazardous wastes
- Other waste streams

Incident Scenarios

The hazard analysis discussion concludes with a summary of incident scenarios that could have adverse effects on the community. These should be listed in the order of consequence. You will want to prepare most-probable-case and worst-case scenarios. Subsequent to each listing, provide a discussion that includes general information and information on what has been done to prevent the event from occurring.

This appendix should also discuss any historical records management system for incidents, if your company has one.

[COMPANY]

[LOCATION]

APPENDIX __

Community Maps

[DATE]

Another administrative consideration, especially if personnel will be coming to your location from far away, is community maps. You may wish to create an appendix to your all-hazards *emergency management plan (EMP)* which contains community maps.

You can generally secure adequate quality maps from the following:

- Chamber of Commerce
- Department of Transportation
- Commercial outlets
- Aerial photography services
- Topographic mapping services
- National Oceanic and Atmospheric Administration (NOAA)
- Civil Defense/Emergency Management Agency
- Department of Commerce

Community maps also help to establish the potential impact of an incident on the community. *Emergency planning zones (EPZs)* can be established, based on incident scenarios, which can be overlaid on the maps to determine potential off-site protective action recommendations.

Sample

All-Hazards Emergency Management Plan

Administrative

Emergency Plan Implementing Procedures

The following sample emergency plan implementing procedures are provided as examples of practical working documents used on a daily basis to administer the all-hazards system.

Emergency Plan Implementing Procedures

Emergency plan implementing procedures (EPIPs) contain specific detailed instructions and guidance for all aspects of the all-hazards EMP. They assign responsibilities to personnel and include flowcharts and checklists, where appropriate, to improve emergency management and response. The key plan sections introduce concepts which are expanded upon and supported by the appendices. EPIPs, however, are the tools used to implement the plan.

Number your EPIPs so they can be cross-referenced to the section of the all-hazards plan to which they relate. Thus, EPIPs will fall into series, with the 100 series relating to section 1.0 of the EMP, the 200 series to section 2.0, etc. This is important because you will want to ensure an adequate cross-reference between the EMP, appendices, and EPIPs.

EPIP format

Each EPIP should be sufficiently detailed as to guide designated individuals or groups during emergencies or potential emergencies. The EPIPs should be written so that these individuals or groups will know in advance the course of events that identifies an emergency condition and the actions that should be taken immediately.

Since incidents do not follow any generally anticipated patterns, the EPIPs should provide sufficient flexibility to accommodate various situations. The format for EPIPs should include the following provisions:

Detailed instructions to cover step-by-step actions to be taken by designated individuals or groups for the implementation of, and subsequent use of, the EPIP(s).

Supplemental background information to further aid designated individuals or groups in the implementation of the EPIP(s).

The format used for the sample EPIPs contained in this book is as follows:

1.0 *Purpose.* This is a statement indicating the basic purpose of the EPIP. It should include sufficient leeway in the wording to provide flexibility for the user, e.g., a statement such as "This procedure provides guidance and instructions..." A statement such as this allows the user some latitude to adjust decision making to the vagaries of the situation.

2.0 *Applicability.*   This item describes to whom the procedure applies. There should be a one-line paragraph indicating the effective date on which the procedure becomes implementable. A statement such as "This procedure becomes effective when issued" is sufficient. All the EPIPs should be reviewed at least quarterly, so it is likely that any individual EPIP will contain errors. Revision dates and review intervals are not necessarily valid indicators of the accuracy of currency of an EPIP. A careful and detailed assessment should be made annually.

3.0 *Definitions.*   With the overabundance of acronyms, abbreviations, and shortened wordings, it is advisable to define any new or unusual terminology. This section of the procedure also clarifies terms.

4.0 *Instructions.*   Section 4.0 is broken down into subparts. These may include, but are not limited to, responsibilities, general information, initial actions, and subsequent actions.

5.0 *References.*   References to the EMP, other EPIPs, appendices, technical documents, and other sources of information should be listed in this section. It is a very common practice for the instructions in one EPIP to refer users to other procedures for additional instructions concerning some part of the activity. Also, the referenced procedure may contain instructions that experienced persons are expected to know, and so there is no need to repeat it within the procedure. However, it is also known that persons are less likely to obtain information if they must seek it in a document other than the primary one they are using. As a consequence, they are apt to overlook needed information. Surveys suggest that referencing to other procedures is overused.

As a general rule, all the information necessary to accomplish the immediate actions should be provided by one EPIP to ensure, among other objectives, that all necessary information is indeed reviewed periodically in accordance with facility policies.

6.0 *Attachments.*   This section contains information pertinent to the accomplishment of the function or task prescribed in the EPIP. This information may include applicable drawings, telephone lists, data sheets or forms, checklists, flowcharts, and maps. If there are none, the EPIP should so state.

The cover page of each EPIP should contain the following information: company name, facility location, full title of the EPIP, EPIP number, revision number, party responsible for preparing and submitting the EPIP, date of submittal, approving authority, and date of approval/issue.

[YOUR COMPANY]
[LOCATION]

Emergency Management
Plan Manual

Controlled Distribution of the
All-Hazards Emergency
Management Plan

EPIP-_____
Revision 0

[DATE]

SUBMITTED BY: _____ **DATE:** _____

APPROVED BY: _____ **DATE:** _____

1.0 Purpose

An executive summary of the all-hazards plan, appendices, and EPIPs will be distributed to specific representatives of external organizations in accordance with all applicable federal, state, and local regulations. Distribution of this material must be carefully controlled so that all material is up to date. This procedure provides guidance for the distribution and maintenance of controlled copies of the all-hazards EMP.

2.0 Applicability

This procedure applies to [COMPANY] personnel assigned the responsibility of ensuring the availability of the all-hazards EMP.

3.0 Definitions

Controlled copies. Numbered copies of the all-hazards EMP are issued to specific individuals. These individuals have signed for the numbered copy. Such distribution is documented so that future revisions may be transmitted to these individuals in order to keep distributed material current.

4.0 Instructions

4.1 Materials to be distributed

Each external organization or agency requiring information contained in the all-hazards EMP will be sent an executive summary as defined above. Upon request and internal approval, [COMPANY] will provide additional information from the all-hazards EMP.

No external organization or agency will be sent a copy of any other part of the all-hazards plan, appendices, or EPIPs unless it is specifically requested by that external organization or agency and only after the individual who is to receive these materials has signed the nondisclosure agreement on behalf of the external organization or agency (see attachment 3).

The all-hazards EMP will be readily accessible for inspection by employees, their representatives, and regulating agencies. *No individuals from outside the company shall copy any part of this all-haz-*

All-Hazards	Issue Date	Procedure No.
Emergency Plan Manual	_/_/_	EPIP-___

Controlled Distribution of	Rev. Date	Revision No.
Emergency Management Plan	_/_/_	0
		Page __ of __ Pages

ards EMP until they have signed the nondisclosure agreement (see attachment 3).

4.2 Precautions

No changes are permitted to any elements of this all-hazards EMP except by the [POSITION, TITLE OF RESPONSIBLE INDIVIDUAL].

Any modifications to this all-hazards plan may be initiated by following EPIP-_____ , "Revision, Approval, and Control of the All-Hazards Emergency Plan and Plan Implementing Procedures."

All revised pages will be printed by the [POSITION, TITLE OF RESPONSIBLE INDIVIDUAL]. These revisions will be forwarded to the all-hazards plan holders for local distribution.

All copies of original and revised all-hazards plan elements shall be sent to external holders by certified mail with return receipt requested or by registered mail.

4.3 The controlled-copy list

The [POSITION, TITLE OF RESPONSIBLE INDIVIDUAL] shall establish and maintain an official list of external holders of controlled copies of the all-hazards EMP. The controlled-copy list shall include the following information for each entity listed:

Name, address, and phone number of receiving entity

Name and title of person taking possession of the EMP

Date of original transmittal of the all-hazards EMP

4.4 Distribution procedures

The [POSITION, TITLE OF RESPONSIBLE INDIVIDUAL] will

Generate cover letters of transmittal

Make copies of the revised pages as needed

Send copies to all currently listed entities on the controlled-copy list by registered mail

Maintain copies of mail receipts in files for not less than 5 years

When revised all-hazards plan elements are received from [POSITION, TITLE OF RESPONSIBLE INDIVIDUAL], all-hazards plan holders will sign and return the receipt-acknowledgment cover letter to the [POSITION, TITLE OF RESPONSIBLE INDIVIDUAL].

5.0 References

EPIP-_____ , "Revision, Approval, and Control of the All-Hazards Emergency Plan and Plan Implementing Procedures"

6.0 Attachments

1. Sample letter of transmittal and return-acknowledgment request
2. Sample letter of transmittal for all-hazards plan revisions
3. Nondisclosure agreement

All-Hazards	Issue Date	Procedure No.
Emergency Plan Manual	__/__/__	EPIP- ___

Controlled Distribution of	Rev. Date	Revision No.
Emergency Management Plan	__/__/__	0
		Page __ of __ Pages

Attachment 1
Sample Letter of Transmittal for Original Transmittal
Rev. 0
[DATE]

Person's name

Person's title

Organization name

Organization address

Dear _____:

Please find enclosed the all-hazards EMP for [COMPANY][LOCATION].

The enclosed material consists of an Executive Summary of the [COMPANY] all-hazards EMP, appendices, and emergency plan implementing procedures.

The complete all-hazards EMP manual for this [LOCATION] is available at the [LOCATION] during normal operating hours for your inspection or as needed in the event of an emergency.

Please sign and return a copy of this letter to acknowledge receipt of this transmittal. If there are any questions concerning this revision, please do not hesitate to call me at [TELEPHONE NUMBER].

Sincerely,
[POSITION, TITLE OF RESPONSIBLE INDIVIDUALS]

I hereby acknowledge receipt of the materials described above.

Signed _____   Date: ___ / ___ / ___

All-Hazards	Issue Date	Procedure No.
Emergency Plan Manual	_/_/_	EPIP-___

Controlled Distribution of	Rev. Date	Revision No.
Emergency Management Plan	_/_/_	0
		Page __ of __ Pages

Attachment 2
Sample Letter of Transmittal for All-Hazards Plan Revisions
Rev. 0
[DATE]

Person's name

Person's title

Organization name

Organization address

Dear _____:

Please find enclosed the following revised sections of the all-hazards EMP for [COMPANY][LOCATION]:

Section name   Revision no.   Revision date

_____   _____   _____

Please remove and destroy prior versions of these sections from your copy of our all-hazards plan and insert these new pages. If there are any questions concerning this revision, please do not hesitate to call me at [TELEPHONE NUMBER].

Sincerely,
[POSITION, TITLE OF RESPONSIBLE INDIVIDUALS]

All-Hazards	Issue Date	Procedure No.
Emergency Plan Manual	_/_/_	EPIP-___

Controlled Distribution of	Rev. Date	Revision No.
Emergency Management Plan	_/_/_	0
		Page __ of __ Pages

Attachment 3
Nondisclosure Agreement
Rev. 0
[DATE]

In the course of performing mutual aid services in accordance with the Mutual Aid Agreement dated _____ between [AGENCY] and [COMPANY], or in connection with such services, [AGENCY] will receive from [COMPANY] data, information, documents, and other materials belonging to, prepared by and for, or concerning [COMPANY] and its customers, employees, and software and trade secret licensers.

For purposes of this Agreement, all such data, information, documents, and other material, including all summaries, extracts, copies, compilations, analyses, interpretations, presentations, and other materials derived therefrom, shall be called "Proprietary Information" and/or "Work Product." [AGENCY] agrees that until such time as any such material becomes a part of the public domain without breach of this Agreement by any agent or employee of [AGENCY], and in any event for at least five (5) years after the termination of this Agreement, [AGENCY] shall:

1. Treat, and obligate [AGENCY] employees, if any, to treat as secret and confidential, all such Proprietary Information whether or not it be identified by [COMPANY] as confidential

2. Not disclose any such Proprietary Information or make available any reports, recommendations, and/or conclusions which [AGENCY] may make for [COMPANY] to any person, firm, or corporation or use it in any manner whatsoever without first obtaining the written approval of [COMPANY]

3. Reveal the Proprietary Information only to such of [AGENCY] employees who require access to such Information in order to perform the Services hereunder

4. Not to employ the Proprietary Information to [AGENCY] advantage, other than as herein provided

This agreement shall become effective on the date written below and shall continue until terminated in writing by either party. The obligation to protect the confidentiality of Proprietary Information received prior to such termination shall survive the termination of this agreement.

[AGENCY]

BY: _____ **DATE:** _____

TITLE: _____

[COMPANY]

BY: _____ **DATE:** _____

TITLE: _____

Organizational Considerations

Establishing and developing an effective organization that can respond to an incident and manage nonaffected operations as well is essential. This chapter will provide an overview of various organizational considerations. *Organization,* in the context of the all-hazards emergency management system (EMS), is defined as follows:

> *Organization:* The emergency management/response organization (EMRO) forms the basic building block for incident response, mitigation, and management activities. The EMRO structure is based on an application of the basic incident command system components (command, planning, operations, logistics, finance, and administration) to a business and/or industrial type of setting. This includes, but is not limited to, management support personnel and response personnel responsible for direction, control, mitigation, and postincident activities.

Chapter organizer: What this chapter is about

- *Organizational considerations for effective emergency management.* You must define the structure, functions, and span of control for the emergency management/response organization (EMRO). In part this is based on the assets you have on hand. How the EMRO and external support elements interface is also important.

An inherent lack of manpower should not inhibit the development of an effective organizational structure and response strategy. You may be more dependent on external resources and therefore will need to develop effective strategies for meeting not only management/response requirements but also regulatory requirements.

- Organizational considerations for spill situations and how they differ from fixed facility considerations. Due to their very nature, spills and spill management/response will require skills not normally represented at fixed-site facilities. As such, the differences must be addressed and your organizational structure adjusted accordingly.

Organizational Considerations

The effectiveness of the all-hazards *emergency management plan* (EMP) is dependent on the ability of your normal operating organization to become an EMRO capable of effectively responding and managing during an incident. Your emergency organization's basic composition should be based on capabilities present in the normal operating organization. This includes operations in the short term and incidents of long duration requiring extended organizational capabilities.

The examples and recommendations presented here focus on assisting you in developing a responsive organization structure. In my previous book, *It Can't Happen Here: All Hazards Crisis Management Planning,* I gave position descriptions for an organizational structure based on an enhanced incident command system.

The enhanced incident command system evolved from the standard incident command structure. However, an identification of the differences in organizational structure in the typical industrial and/or business setting required that the standard *incident command system* (ICS) be modified. You can access a variety of sources for position-specific references. In this chapter, we will explore the application of the enhanced ICS and will expand our discussion to organizational requirements at different levels and for varying capabilities represented in the normal operating organization. We will not seek to provide you with additional position description functions, duties, and task lists.

It is also essential to our discussion that you look beyond the pure response aspects of organizational structure. You must recognize the management aspects of organizational structure and integrate these into the overall structure you create for your plan. Additionally, you need to think in terms of function versus workforce. You must address the functions to be performed by the organizational structure as well as the workforce needs to fill the blocks on the organizational chart.

With this brief introduction and caution on function versus organizational chart blocks, let's proceed to our discussion of organizational considerations.

As with Chap. 4, I have included examples for your use. As with all examples, some fit; others do not. You must not use this as a fill-in-the-blank exercise. Rather, use the examples to develop your own unique all-hazards system.

Achieving a high quality in decision making comes from understanding the differences between management decision making and response decision making and being able to bring the two into harmony so balance can be maintained.

A question often asked is, Is there a difference between management and response leadership? The answer is yes. It depends on the results that you seek to achieve and how you go about achieving them. Moreover, we describe decision making and pragmatic leadership here; your initial responders can also be leaders. Remember, the first person on the scene in essence is your EMRO, ICS, or whatever you refer to your emergency organization as.

It is therefore essential to establish an operational framework and develop a cadre of knowledgeable and skilled personnel who can identify and take care of the decision making critical to effective response and provide value-added supervision through coordination, facilitation, and support of the efforts of others.

Effective incident operations integrate management and response in ways that increase productivity (effectiveness of the response effort) and improve the quality of decision making.

Planners are not solely responsible for creating and installing effective decision-making systems. All personnel involved in the process of emergency management and response should have the ability to input to the system and have inputs considered. However, once a framework is established, all personnel must embrace it if it is to be effective. Eight elements should be considered:

1. *Shared operational framework.* Develop a comprehensive, integrated system of management to provide a shared operational framework and a common language for managing crisis situations. A key aspect is information feedback.

2. *Role clarity.* Make sure that all personnel assigned to perform functions during an incident understand their roles and the key ways in which they can add value to the process.

3. *Criteria for selection.* Establish criteria for the selection and assignment of personnel to the EMRO. Choose people who can use the all-hazards approach to enhance the process of managing and responding to an incident. Just because a person occupies a managerial position in the normally operating organization does not mean that he or she is qualified to hold a position in the EMRO. Make sure that personnel have the interpersonal skills needed to effectively integrate diverse activities and personalities.

4. *Performance feedback system.* Develop a system to assess performance and provide feedback that focuses on improving performance. Make sure the system is owned by all levels within the organization. That is to say, everyone who has a role in the system must embrace the

structure and make it part of their work practices. Make assessment and feedback activities a process of continuous improvement, part of the way you do business, rather than a reaction to issues.

5. *Levels of management.*   Establish only as many levels of management as are needed to serve the EMRO. Make sure that personnel understand the roles of other people within the organization, with whom they will have external interfaces, and their relationships to them so that all their efforts can be integrated.

6. *Selection of managers and responders.*   Choose managers and responders on the basis of their potential to perform within the context of the all-hazards EMS. Choose people you want to manage, supervise, and work with effectively under pressure situations demanding teamwork.

7. *Development of personnel.*   Make sure that personnel have the basic knowledge and skills to work within the EMS. Continually develop personnel in order to help them improve their effectiveness.

8. *Position succession planning.*   Make sure that there is a steady stream of people capable of assuming EMRO position responsibilities. Develop a cadre of alternates through training, drills, and exercises. And let them perform before an actual incident puts them into a "have to" situation.

There are no pat formulas to be used. While the principles are clear (for instance, ensure that personnel have the interpersonal skills needed for effective management/response integration), each organization has to work out its own formula. For many, unfortunately, creating effective emergency/crisis management systems is not high on the priority list.

Pragmatic Leadership

Like excellence, leadership is a familiar concept but is hard to define, because it is so complex. Leadership is one of the most observed but least understood phenomena on earth.

If we are to speak meaningfully about effective incident management, we must first understand what pragmatic leadership means and what kind of incident management our particular organization needs. It is impossible to discuss the all-hazards approach to emergency/crisis management effectiveness without including pragmatic leadership. One principle is clear: You need to develop leadership skills at every level of the EMRO to provide flexibility and responsiveness to ever-changing situations.

In his book *Adding Value* (San Francisco: Jossey-Bass, 1993, 236 pp.), Gerard Egan presents a summation of leadership traits. I feel it is of benefit.

The essence of leadership: Performance beyond the ordinary

Leadership refers to those who deliver results beyond the ordinary, either in a single instance, or in some ongoing way. Leadership is in direct contrast to mediocrity.

On the other hand, "results beyond the ordinary" is not the same as "extraordinary" results. If it were, then leadership would be beyond the reach of almost everyone; it would refer only to the heroes and heroines among us. For now, suffice it to say that leadership needs to be rescued from those who would make it mean too much or too little. Everyone in the organization needs to know what it means. And whatever it means in the context of a specific company, personnel at all levels must be capable of achieving it.

Emergency Management/Response Organization

It has been said that the organization is a key driving force. Time management—the ability to organize, prioritize and manage tasks efficiently—offers a basis for the development of your EMRO strategy.

A basic truth of emergency response is that *whoever first discovers or identifies that an incident has occurred or exists is your EMRO—until such time as various functions can be properly turned over to others with the appropriate authority, skills, knowledge, and training to assume those functions.*

By having a well-conceived organizational structure, one that is publicized and understood by all, your ability to transition smoothly into emergency operational mode is greatly enhanced. This is especially critical where human resources are at a premium.

In the evaluation items in Chap. 3 under the heading "Emergency Management/Response Organization," to how many questions can you give a positive answer?

Your EMRO should reflect your normally operating organization's capabilities. In the immortal words of Clint Eastwood's character Dirty Harry, "A man's got to know his limitations." I would add that this applies also to women who work in this area.

In his book *Adding Value,* Egan presents an excellent discussion of how to manage more effectively. I have modified some of these points to apply them to the context of EMRO structure and functions. I recommend his book as a good basis for assessing your capabilities and for focusing your training program development and implementation process.

The potential for improving emergency management systems and the effectiveness of individuals responsible for incident management and response can be realized by applying some of these points. The following set of guidelines can be applied in the development of your own EMRO:

- Choose personnel to fill key positions who have the capability to become self-starting, self-directing, and autonomous.
- Make sure that all personnel assigned to the EMRO really know what their jobs entail.
- Choose an EMS that effectively enhances your organization's ability to perform during an incident.
- Make it as easy as possible for people to communicate and access information.
- Establish management/response goals, find the resources needed, and then train your organization to meet those goals.
- Make emergency management/response more effective by supplementing the plan with tools such as emergency plan implementing procedures, planning meetings, and communications that add value to incident mitigation efforts.
- Provide ongoing guidance and feedback on performance.
- Establish an organizational culture of collaboration, not confrontation.
- Develop a common terminology that allows everyone involved understand the issues at hand and facilitates working with others.
- Make senior managers part of the process. Give them a role in emergency management/response activities.
- Make sure your managers know how to manage.
- Set strategy; keep it evergreen (responsive to changes in operations, hazards, regulations).
- Stay abreast of changes in regulatory requirements.
- Make sure the organization is structured to enhance access to information needed to make decisions.

Egan continues his discussion with an overview of the value of shared models of management. This summarizes his basic discussion and its application to the development of an effective and responsive organizational structure. I have used brackets to indicate where I have replaced his text with emergency planning text:

The role of shared models of [emergency] management

The trick, of course, is to know what to do to add value [to the response effort], which is the basic premise of this book:

1. [Emergency] Managers would manage more effectively and add greater value to the [response effort] if, like other professionals, they trained in and worked from comprehensive, integrated models of effective [emergency] management.
2. The [emergency management system] model should be derived from the needs of the [organization] and be shared by all [personnel with a role in response and mitigation efforts—this includes external entities].
3. The [emergency management system] model should serve as the basis for [personnel] selection, training, and development.

Figures 5.1 through 5.5 depict typical organizational structures developed by using the enhanced ICS and the standard ICS structure.

With this basic framework in mind, I have prepared the following examples to provide you with practical applications for developing your own organization discussion section and supporting materials.

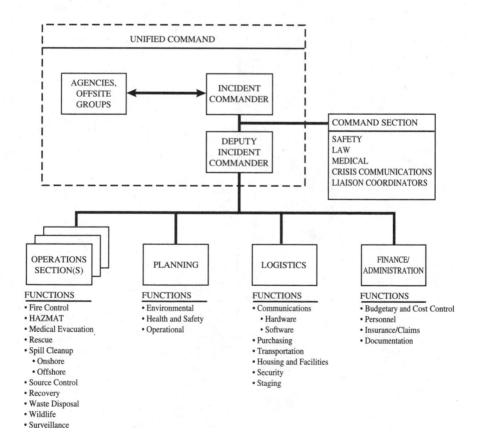

Figure 5.1

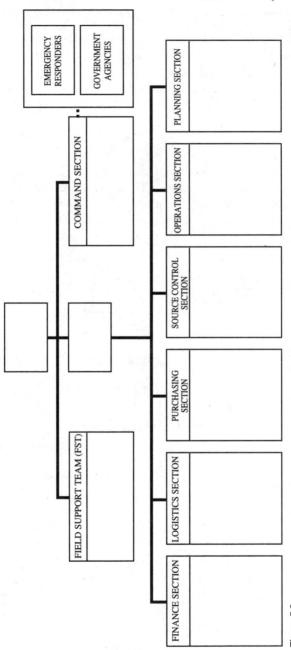

Figure 5.2

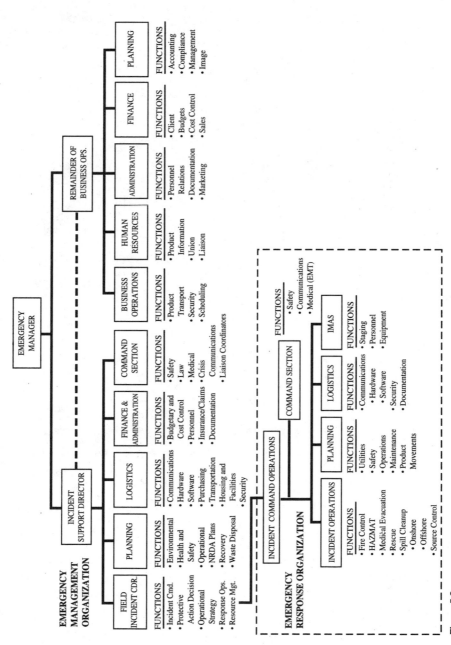

Figure 5.3

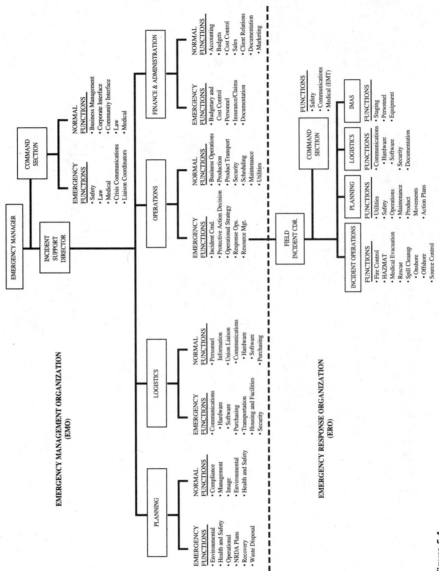

EMERGENCY MANAGEMENT ORGANIZATION (EMO)

EMERGENCY RESPONSE ORGANIZATION (ERO)

Figure 5.4

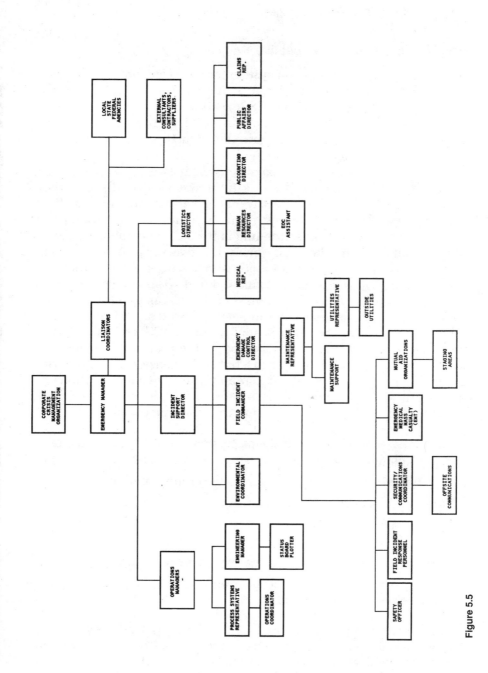

Figure 5.5

Incident Command: A Perspective

Adopting an incident command system for your company is a decision that should be carefully considered. While there is a wealth of literature available today describing ICS structure and employment, business needs to carefully choose how it will structure incident command. Even more important is how this structure and its functions are communicated to external audiences.

It has become clear in my experience that two people using the same ICS terminology can be talking about two totally different applications. Each will be correct in his or her meaning and application. However, each will be 180° from the other as they attempt to apply their versions or understanding of incident command. To identify the differences and hopefully bring the two applications to some common ground, I will refer to tactical and strategic applications of ICS concepts. Tactical incident command and strategic incident command both embrace the central tenets of the ICS as prescribed by the National Inter-agency Incident Management System (NIIMS).

For our purposes, the tactical application of ICS terminology and functions is defined, based, and focused on the proven fireground tactics applied by most, if not all, fire-fighting agencies and industrial fire brigades. Tactical incident command focuses on operations of short duration. I will provide more detail on this later. Tactical incident command can be subdivided into the following components:

Command consists of the incident commander and staff. This may include planning, operations, logistics, and finance.

Sectors are sections, branches, divisions, groups, and units.

Staging consists of uncommitted resources and support.

Safety consists of a safety officer responsible for incident scene safety operations.

Medical services consists of emergency medical services.

Suppression is the response portion of the system, focused on response and mitigation operations.

The strategic application of ICS terminology and functions is defined, based, and focused not on fire tactics, but on the application of ICS methodology involving a broader spectrum of resources, i.e., a combination of management and response functions applied to longer-term operations (as opposed to the short-duration situations where tactical incident command is focused). Strategic incident command can be subdivided into the following components:

Command is generally a unified command structure consisting of management, external agency representatives, and support personnel.

Planning consists of personnel focused on longer-term issues, such as material resource damage assessment, waste management, and response strategy development and resource management.

Operations consist of field operations encompassing the tactical incident command application and the necessity to focus on a greater span of control concerns.

Logistics is comprised of specialists in purchasing, administration, communications, documentation, transportation, security and human resource services.

Finance consists of specialists in accounting, claims administration, and financial management services.

The Decision—Tactical, Strategic, or Combined

The decision to choose a tactical, strategic or combined ICS approach really is not a difficult one. This is due in part to the various environmental, safety, and health regulatory compliance requirements promulgated by federal, state, and local authorities. You may also find that by conducting a comprehensive hazard analysis, your decision on an incident command system has been made. In fact, once you determine the spectrum of events, you may be faced with the decision to opt for a combination of strategic and/or tactical incident command.

I have discussed this application in previous papers and have applied it with various clients. Termed the *enhanced incident command system (EICS)*, it combines management and response functions into an organized structure that embraces ICS tenets. It is important to understand the application, since the industrial setting and the government or community setting differ dramatically from the setting found in fire and hazardous materials response organizations. Also note that the combined system allows for the same flexibility as the NIIMS-based system.

Due to the nature of oil spills and large spills in general, the choice of tactical or strategic incident command is critical. A decision must be made early on in the incident and should be based on a simple assessment. If the spill occurs on land, it should be safe to think in terms of square feet or square yards of potential exposure. On the other hand, if the spill occurs on water, immediately start thinking in square miles! This should provoke immediate consideration of the span of control issues. Because of the nature of a large spill on water, a far greater amount of resources will be involved in the response, at potentially greater distances than would normally be the case for a fire, explosion, or related type of incident.

Sample

All-Hazards Emergency Management Plan

SECTION __: ORGANIZATION

Sample

Normal Organization

A brief introductory statement about the normally operating organization and how it will transition to emergency operations should be developed. You may wish to highlight any unique aspects of your normally operating organization, such as management workers, shift workers, security workers, utilities workers, and union representation.

Emergency Management/Response Organization

A brief description of how the EMRO is structured should be developed and presented here. You will want to describe

- Composition, including such features as management levels
- Key personnel specialties

Also describe where the core group of personnel for the EMRO is drawn from. Briefly describe key positions and highlight their functions. You can go into greater detail in supplementary material (appendices and EPIPs).

You may wish to identify any special situations peculiar to your operations and/or location. For instance, many facilities along the Gulf of Mexico are vulnerable to the threat of hurricanes. If your facility maintains a separate organization for hurricane response, you should highlight it here. This applies to spill response, winter weather response, etc.

Corporate Support

Corporate support should be described in a separate paragraph or paragraphs. Refer to any specific corporate crisis management plan that has been developed to set a basic structure and direction for response initiatives in the event an incident occurs that could develop into a crisis for your company.

Off-Site Response Organizations

State organizations

A brief description of the lead state agency should be provided. A discussion of responsibilities should be included.

Local and interjurisdictional disaster agencies and services. A brief description of the local agencies should be included here. Indicate how the agencies interface with your organization in an emergency.

Federal agencies

The federal government's role in major pollution incidents, such as those which could result from hazardous materials spills, is described in the National Oil and Hazardous Substances Contingency Plan. This plan is jointly administered by the Environmental Protection Agency and the U.S. Coast Guard (a branch of the Department of Transportation).

News media

A brief statement identifying and acknowledging the news media should be prepared. Additionally, you will want to designate a spokesperson to deal with the media.

Private response organizations

Here you should describe any mutual aid systems and their composition.

[COMPANY]
[LOCATION]

Appendix __

Emergency Management/Response Organization

Position Descriptions

Instead of devoting page upon page of information to the EMRO position descriptions in your basic plan, a convenient method is to develop an appendix with this information as a supplement to the plan. There are several advantages to having this information in an appendix:

- Ease of maintenance. Because this information is subject to frequent change, it is easier to maintain in an appendix to the plan.
- The appendix is a central repository for information on skills required (especially useful when you have to supplement the organization from external sources).
- The plan is not padded with material primarily of a supportive nature.

The following breakdown has been helpful in preparing the detailed position descriptions contained in the appendix. I have provided a single example for the sake of brevity.

Emergency Management/Response Organization
[POSITION TITLE]

Position holders

List the primary and designated alternates by job title.

Emergency facility location

Identify where the position holders are located in an emergency.

Notification

Identify the primary means and any alternate means for notification of the position holder.

EMRO position you report to

List the primary position the position holders report to.

EMRO positions reporting to you

Describe who reports to this position.

Primary EPIPs you will use

List those EPIPs that the position holders may use in an incident.

Other sources of information needed

List all sources of information the position holders may use.

Major functions, duties, and tasks

Describe the major functions, duties, and tasks position holders are to perform during an emergency. For example, the accounting director will:

- Advise the emergency manager and/or recovery manager and other personnel regarding the status of on-scene accounting activities.
- Coordinate accounting activities through [LOCATION] and corporate accounting departments.

- Request guidance and information regarding any changes in [COMPANY] policy and procedures that may impact accounting activities.
- Coordinate the requisition and ordering of accounting-related supplies through the logistics director.
- Coordinate with the [COMPANY] insurance claims representative as necessary.
- Coordinate with the [COMPANY] law representative as necessary.

This is *not* an all-inclusive list of duties.

Sample

Emergency Plan Implementing Procedure

Duties of the Emergency Manager
EPIP -_____
Revision __

Sample

SUBMITTED BY: _____ DATE: _____

APPROVED BY: _____ DATE: _____

1.0 Purpose

The purpose of this procedure is to provide guidance and identify the required actions, responsibilities, authorities, and interfaces of the emergency manager relative to the overall direction and control of emergency management and response efforts at the [LOCATION].

2.0 Applicability

2.1 This procedure applies to the emergency manager in the event that an emergency condition at the [LOCATION] requires the activation of the [LOCATION] EMRO.

2.2 This procedure becomes effective when issued.

3.0 Definitions

3.1 Emergency classification

A classification system of emergency severity is based on operational and meteorological conditions at or near the site. The emergency classifications in order of increasing severity are as follows:

3.1.1 Level 0: Internally reportable event. A minor incident or problem such as a small localized fire, minor material release, unit upset, or other internal event has occurred which can be handled by in-plant personnel using standard operating procedures. It is not visible off site, requires no emergency response team, and requires no report to local, state, or federal regulatory agencies.

3.1.2 Level 1: Unusual event. A minor emergency or problem such as a fire, material release, unusual noise, unusual odor, abnormal and/or extended flaring activity, or other internal event has occurred which may be visible or detectable off site, but presents no off-site threat and requires no assistance or protective actions by off-site persons. *The situation is under control.*

3.1.3 Level 2: Alert. An emergency such as a fire, explosion, or material release or other event has occurred which has the potential to escalate to a more serious emergency and/or affects plant operations. *The emergency is not under control but poses no threat to off-site areas.*

3.1.4 Level 3: Site area emergency. A serious emergency such as a fire, explosion, material release, or other event has occurred or is imminent and poses a threat to residents or industries in the immediate vicinity of the affected industry and/or seriously affects plant operations. *The emergency is not under control, and protective actions by off-site persons may be necessary.*

3.1.5 Level 4: General emergency. A severe emergency such as a fire, explosion, material release, or other event has occurred or is imminent and seriously affects off-site areas well beyond site boundaries and/or plant operations. *The emergency is not under control, and protective actions by off-site persons for residents and neighboring industries are necessary.*

4.0 Instructions

4.1 Precautions

4.1.1 The emergency manager will not delegate the decision-making authority for declaring an emergency classification and for implementing the all-hazards EMP.

4.1.2 The emergency manager will not delegate the decision-making authority for communicating with off-site agencies.

4.1.3 The emergency manager may designate a communicator to handle the notification to the various agencies in accordance with EPIP-_____ , "Emergency Notification."

4.1.4 The emergency manager will not delegate approval authority for public information and news media releases.

4.1.5 The individuals designated to assume this position are (in descending order of succession)

- [POSITION, TITLE OF RESPONSIBLE INDIVIDUAL]
- [POSITION, TITLE OF RESPONSIBLE INDIVIDUAL]
- [POSITION, TITLE OF RESPONSIBLE INDIVIDUAL]
- [POSITION, TITLE OF RESPONSIBLE INDIVIDUAL]

- [POSITION, TITLE OF RESPONSIBLE INDIVIDUAL]
- [POSITION, TITLE OF RESPONSIBLE INDIVIDUAL]

4.2 Initial actions

- Assume the position of emergency manager and/or conduct a formal transfer of authority from any on-shift emergency manager (OEM), and log the time on an activities record sheet (log form).
- Review the initial assessment of the emergency condition. Determine and declare the appropriate emergency classification, and initiate appropriate sections of the all-hazards EMP.
- Initiate EPIP-_____ , "Emergency Notification," for the [LOCATION] emergency management organization (EMO).
- Ensure that the [LOCATION] emergency organization personnel have been notified, that all personnel have reported to their assigned locations, and that the emergency management organization is properly staffed.
- Establish communications with key on-site and off-site emergency personnel.
- Assemble the management team (EMO) and conduct initial and update briefings periodically and when dictated by circumstance.
- Review and approve all public information and news media releases.
- Authorize the procurement of equipment, materials, and other resources, as necessary.
- Ensure (24-hour) emergency operations capability by scheduling relief for EMO personnel as necessary.
- Designate [COMPANY] personnel to interface with federal, state, and local officials.
- Approve the protective action recommendations that are made to off-site officials.
- Coordinate all on-site and off-site emergency response activities.
- Inform the [BUSINESS UNIT] and/or corporate crisis management organization of the need for resources beyond local capabilities.

- Provide situation updates and ensure that the public affairs director provides updates to internal and external groups.

- Evaluate, coordinate, and control all [COMPANY] response activities until the event is closed out or the [LOCATION/COMPANY] recovery organization is formed.

- Maintain a log. Remember, documentation is important.

4.3 Subsequent actions

4.3.1   In the event of an incident requiring extended operations, complete the following:

- Brief the incoming emergency manager on the current status of the incident and response activities.
- Brief the necessary off-site organizations of the turnover.
- Document the turnover as appropriate.

4.3.2   When the event is to be terminated and a recovery effort initiated, obtain guidance from EPIP-_____ , "Postincident Sampling," and EPIP-_____ , "Reentry and Recovery Operations."

4.3.3   Authorize all reentries into evacuated on-site areas when conditions warrant doing so safely.

4.3.4   Continue briefing EMO personnel on a regular basis until the emergency incident has been stabilized and mitigation has begun.

4.3.5   Ensure that outside support and regulatory agencies are updated promptly as the emergency situation changes. This includes [COMPANY] and non-[COMPANY] groups.

4.3.6   Activate the recovery organization, as described in EPIP-_____ , if needed to return to normal operating conditions, and close out the event when appropriate to do so. (This action should be logged.)

4.3.7   Route completed emergency manager's checklists and activities record sheets to the [POSITION, TITLE OF RESPONSIBLE INDIVIDUAL] for review and subsequent filing in a documentation storage location.

All-Hazards Emergency Plan Manual	Issue Date __/__/__	Procedure No. EPIP- ___
Duties of the Emergency Manager	Rev. Date __/__/__	Revision No. 0

Page __ of __ Pages

5.0 References

5.1 All-Hazards EMP, section _____ , organization

5.2 EPIP-_____ , "Duties of the EMRO during Emergencies"

5.3 EPIP-_____ , "Corporate Support"

5.4 EPIP-_____ , "Emergency Notification"

5.5 EPIP-_____ , "Assessment of Emergency Conditions and Emergency Classification"

5.6 EPIP-_____ , "Protective Action Recommendation Guides"

5.7 EPIP-_____ , "Release of Emergency-Related Information to the Public"

5.8 EPIP-_____ , "Postincident Sampling"

5.9 EPIP-_____ , "Reentry and Recovery Operations"

6.0 Attachments

6.1 Attachment 1, Form EPIP-_____ -1, "Activities Record Sheet"

6.2 Attachment 2, Emergency Manager's checklist

CONFIDENTIAL - WORK PRODUCT

ACTIVITIES RECORD SHEET   DATE:

EMERGENCY TITLE: _____	NAME: _____ PAGE ___ of ___ PAGES

TIME:	SUMMARY OF ACTIVITIES

C
O
N
F
I
D
E
N
T
I
A
L

W
O
R
K

P
R
O
D
U
C
T

ACTIVITIES RECORD SHEET

FORM EPIP-   -1   PAGE   of   PAGES

NAME: DATE

 TIME: SUMMARY OF ACTIVITIES:

SIGNATURE:

EPIP-_____   ATTACHMENT 2

EMERGENCY MANAGER'S CHECKLIST

INITIAL ACTIVITIES   **EMERGENCY MANAGER**

Page 1 of 2 Pages   TIME/INITIAL

1. Assess and Classify
   the Emergency per
   EPIP-___   _____

2. Conduct Notifications
   internal/external   _____

3. Approve press re-
   leases (EPIP-___)   _____

4. Situation Updates
   (EPIP-___)

   A: Internal   _____

   B: EMO(Bi-hourly)   _____

   C: Security   _____

   D: [COMPANY]   _____

   E. NRC (National
      Response Ctr.)
      (4 hours)   _____

5. Initiate Environmental
   Response(EPIP-___)   _____

6. Initiate Evacuation
   Assembly, Accountability
   (EPIP ___)   _____

7. Recommend Protective
   Actions(EPIP-___)   _____

8. Activate Emergency
   Facilities
   (EPIP ___)   _____

EPIP-_____ ATTACHMENT 2

EMERGENCY MANAGER'S CHECKLIST

INITIAL ACTIVITIES   **EMERGENCY MANAGER**

Page 2 of 2 Pages   TIME/INITIAL

9. Responsibility/Authority
   Transferred To:

   A. Emergency Manager   _____

   B. Recovery Manager   _____

10. Initiate Post-Inc.
    Sampling(EPIP-___)   _____

11. Initiate Reentry
    /Recovery Operations (EPIP-___)   _____

12. Close Out Emergency   _____

NOTE: When completed, this checklist will be placed in the
Emergency Response and Recovery Activities Record binder.

                    /s/ _____
                         EMERGENCY MANAGER / DATE

6

Concept-of-Operations Considerations

The further away from the incident, the greater the need for concise, timely, accurate information to aid the decision-making process.
GEARY W. SIKICH, 1994

Once you have developed and implemented your emergency management/response organization (EMRO), you can begin to better define the organization's concept of operations. This chapter will provide an overview of EMRO operational considerations. The term *concept of operations,* in the context of the all-hazards EMS, can be defined as follows:

> The *concept of operations* includes the spectrum of steps necessary to activate the EMRO and successfully execute incident response, mitigation management, and termination operations. This includes, but is not limited to, incident classification, operations planning, direction, control, response, mitigation, termination, and postincident activities. Our definition must, therefore, look beyond purely incident response and mitigation considerations and expand to consider the broader issues of business impacts, resource management, project management, and pragmatic leadership.

Chapter organizer: What this chapter is about

■ *Operational considerations and how they vary with the level of the organization.* Defining and delineating the operations considerations and responsibilities for various levels of management will facilitate effective operations execution. Within this context, you must address the decision-making functions, support activities, and span of control for all elements with a role in response. You must define how the EMRO will execute its functions, duties, and tasks. Again, the interface among various components is important.

- *Operations considerations for spill situations and how they differ from fixed facility considerations.* The duration of the majority of industrial incidents is short. A fire, explosion, or similar incident generally has an immediate short-term impact. Spills, on the other hand, are generally longer-term situations, spanning hours, days, weeks versus minutes or hours. Therefore, special considerations exist for spill operations.

Operational Considerations

Eight issues predominate in the area of operations:

- Execution of the emergency management plan
- Decision making: assessing the incident
- Timely mitigation of the incident
- Organizational interfaces (discussed in Chap. 5)
- Pragmatic leadership (discussed in Chap. 5)
- Effective use of resources
- Management response
- Response management

Typically, the concept-of-operations discussion is narrowly focused. It generally revolves on a discussion of how to implement an effective response and achieve timely mitigation of the incident. While these are two essential operations issues, they are not reflective of the typical industrial situation, where one must look at and analyze long-term, medium-term, and short-term business impacts as well.

Execution of the Emergency Management Plan

If it is written, you had better be able to execute it. In other words, do not put it on paper unless you intend to fulfill the obligation to perform.

Timely execution of the emergency management plan (EMP) under incident conditions is essential. Personnel must know their assignments and be capable of executing them. It is therefore essential that the concept-of-operations portion of the all-hazards EMP clearly define how your organization intends to operate during an emergency.

These are some of the considerations:

- *Governing principles:* incident command philosophy, components of the incident command system (ICS), incident command operations.

- *Assessment of incident conditions:* Establish the level of severity of an incident, determining the impact by assessing seven key factors: safety concerns, environmental impacts, business operational status, geographic area impacts, commodity, meteorological conditions, and response capabilities and actions and appropriate execution.

- *Integrating operations:* Create a unified command focused on mutually acceptable objectives and effective management of all available resources.

- *Consistent decision making:* Implement pragmatic leadership to manage the process and supervise the organization at all levels. Resolve conflicts, maintain an overall perspective of the primary goals, establish a cohesive work environment, work toward a common goal, and do not mistake activity for productivity.

Decision Making: Assessing the Incident

We closed our highlights on execution of the all-hazards EMP with an item on consistent decision making. Effective and timely decision making is essential to achieve high-quality performance in the implementation of incident-related operations.

Incident Assessment: The Key Factor

Initial assessment of an incident is critical. Proper assessment of the potential magnitude of an incident provides a basis for implementation of the *enhanced incident command system* (EICS). It is, therefore, imperative to train personnel, who are initial responders, to properly assess the incident. This means that a broader preview of potential impacts is needed. One can no longer opt for a narrowly focused assessment based upon an analysis of limited factors.

Seven issues and factors have come to the forefront as essential to determining the full impact of an incident. To effectively implement a coordinated response, you must consider these factors:

Safety—injury, fatality, and protective action considerations

Environment—establishment and assessment of potential impacts to the environment (air, land, water)

Operations—considerations such as facility status, continuity of operations, and reentry and recovery issues

Commodity—the identification of the material involved, quantity, toxicity, and other characteristics

Meteorology—assessment of short-term and long-term conditions

Response capability—assessment of management/response capabilities, including human resources and equipment resources (also evaluation of response strategies)

Geographic location—the location or proximity to community areas or other industries

Personnel need to embrace this broader assessment perspective in order to implement an effective response and manage the impact of an incident.

Management/Response: Communicating Effectiveness

We have employed the ICS in the traditional fire and hazardous materials manner, i.e., a tactical approach based on fire ground command and control techniques. While extremely effective for the vast majority of incidents occurring in a facility, this approach is limited when employed as the primary response system for an oil spill.

These types of incidents require the use of a strategic ICS. This system, referred to as the enhanced incident command system, is structured along the recognized ICS structure as previously discussed.

The EICS combines the tactical and strategic approaches into an effective, highly flexible, and responsive structure required to deal with a long-term event, such as an oil spill.

The organizational structure needed to employ the EICS consists of management and response personnel, combined to effectively address management/response functions. The EMRO is critical to the successful mitigation of any large-scale, long-term, high-impact incident. This includes not only oil spills but also a variety of incidents and situations in which a purely tactical ICS approach is not practical, applicable, or adequate to handle the situation at hand. Figure 6.1 depicts the reactive and proactive phases typically encountered during an incident.

Effective Use of Resources

From an operations perspective, effective use of resources is probably the most talked about, but least effectively implemented operations

PRE-INCIDENT	REACTIVE	PRO-ACTIVE		RECOVERY
PREPARATION	INITIAL RESPONSE	SUSTAINED RESPONSE	POST-INCIDENT	RECOVERY
Planning	Identify	Sustain & Augment	Transition to Recovery Organization	Recovery Organization
Hazard/Vulnerability Analyses	Assess	Mitigate	Project Management Mode	Incident Investigation
Regulatory Compliance	Defensive Action	Offensive Action	Resource Management	Demobilization
Training. Drills & Exercises	Notification	Communication	Communications	Claims
Resource Identification/ Resource Agreements	First Response	Resource Management	Documentation	Documentation Discovery
		Forward Planning		Regulatory Compliance
		Demobilization Planning		Hazard/Vulnerability Analyses
		Incident Investigation Planning		Revision of Emergency Management Plan

Figure 6.1   All hazards emergency management system phases.

135

concept. First you have to identify, define, categorize, and ensure your available resources.

Identification is a relatively simple procedure, as are defining and categorizing the capabilities of the resource. Ensuring the availability of the resource and the willingness of the resource to participate is another matter altogether.

You will recall from our earlier discussion in Chap. 4 that I spoke of developing letters of understanding, letters of agreement, mutual aid pacts, etc. This is when these efforts begin to pay off. By having these arguments in place, you can invoke participation and be assured of the response by the identified resource.

Effectively using the resources once they appear on scene is another issue. It is critical that you make use of all available resources to their maximum potential. Just look at the issue of the *natural resource damage assessment* (*NRDA*). To effectively be addressed, every resource in your EMRO must play a contributing role. In developing your concept of operations, you must identify and plan for issues such as NRDA to be addressed, early on. If you do not, you will end up constantly reacting to the situation instead of controlling and managing the incident.

Management Response and Response Management

I have grouped these last two points for a reason. They are inextricably interlinked. It is like the chicken or the egg—which came first?

As I view these two areas, it is a two-way vertical and horizontal process. You cannot do one without the other for long. And if you do one effectively and one less effectively, both will suffer in the end.

Management response from an operations standpoint deals with not only incident-related issues but also non-incident-related issues that keep the enterprise in balance. Effective communications, superior information management, upward management, and downward management make up the components of effective management response.

Response management, on the other hand, deals with effectively implementing the concept of operations as it applies to the use of resources (human and otherwise) toward mitigation of the incident.

Summary

I have presented a brief discussion on concept-of-operations considerations. The following examples highlight potential practical applications.

Sample

**[COMPANY]
[LOCATION]**

**All-Hazards Emergency
Management Plan**

**SECTION __: CONCEPT
OF OPERATIONS**

Sample

Governing Principles

You should provide a summary of how your organization will perform direction and control during an incident. Included should be a discussion of the ICS that has been developed and implemented, with reference to specific EMRO positions and various support organizations. Take the following example.

Incident Command Philosophy

The generalized incident command system is a proven system for managing all emergency incidents. An ICS consists of personnel, facilities, equipment, communications, and procedures operating within a common organizational structure to gain control of an incident. Major sections of a typical ICS are as follows:

- Command
- Planning
- Operations
- Logistics
- Finance

An ICS provides a flexible structure for response to *all* incidents. Transition from incident scene to expanded operations requires a minimum of adjustment.

Management of all major functions is initially the responsibility of [POSITION, TITLE OF RESPONSIBLE PERSON]. As the need for expanded operations is identified, activities management is assigned to additional personnel. This results in efficient operation and provides a prudent level of control.

The organization of an ICS evolves from the time of initial response until the requirement for incident management and response operations no longer exists. The organization changes as the incident progresses, depending on the requirements of the situation. The basic organizational structure is applicable to small incidents, major incidents, and incidents not directly involving process-related hazards, such as natural disasters, product tampering, spills, or business disruption.

Sections and divisions within the ICS will be activated only when required by the incident.

Components of the ICS

The ICS has a number of components. These components provide the basis for effective response to emergencies:

Common position titles.   A standard set of position titles and sections has been established for the EMRO. The ICS provides the core element for this application.

Resource titles and specifications.   Common names and specifications have been established for all resources used within the ICS.

Facilities.   Common identifiers are used for those facilities in and around the incident area which will be used during the course of the incident. These facilities include such things as the command post, emergency operations center (EOC), and staging areas.

Flexible organizational structure.   The ICS structure builds from the top down, with responsibility for performance placed initially with the command section. As the need exists, separate sections can be activated (planning, logistics, etc.). The organization established for any given incident will be based upon the response needs. *If one individual can simultaneously manage all the sections, no further positions are required.*

Incident Command at the [LOCATION]

The ICS adopted by the [LOCATION] is designed to complement normal shift operations. The ICS can be implemented in a variety of emergencies, such as fires, floods, tornadoes, and hazardous materials or other process-related emergency incidents. The ICS is a long-term, all-hazards concept for response to emergencies that could affect the operations of the [LOCATION] and/or have potential life-threatening effects on employees, contractors, or the general population.

Generally, the ICS is implemented in phases according to the severity of the emergency.

The normal operating shift at the [LOCATION] is present from [TIME, NORMAL WORK WEEK]. During each shift a full complement of the [LOCATION'S] shift employees are present. This group provides support for the EMRO, following established safety guidelines.

In the event of an emergency at the [LOCATION], a *mobile command center (MCC)* will be established [near the incident scene or where you will want it located]. The MCC generally serves as the base of operations of the *field incident commander* (*FIC*) during the emergency. As warranted by the emergency condition and emergency classification, other emergency response facilities will be activated.

The FIC will be the designated lead [COMPANY] representative *at the incident scene.*

Once potential emergency conditions have been identified, the *emergency manager* (*EM*) notifies the FIC as appropriate. The FIC and EM implement EPIP-_____, "Assessment of Emergency Conditions, Emergency Classification and Protective Action Recommendation Guides," classifying the emergency condition into one of five emergency designations. [These are discussed in a later example and have been presented in my earlier book.]

Upon classification of the emergency, the EM, with advice from the FIC, is responsible for further activation and notification of the *emergency response organization* (ERO). The extent of activation will vary with the severity and classification of the emergency. The FIC will ensure that the appropriate emergency classification is made and that primary responders are notified [insert the means you will use]. The FIC will also ensure that outside agencies are notified of the emergency classification, as appropriate.

Emergency Response Organization and Operation

The ERO forms the core of the operational response, as depicted in the following functional task chart (Fig. 6.2).

You should provide a brief description of the section responsibilities and personnel assignments for each ERO component of the EMRO. Here is an example:

ERO command section (FIC)

The command section is responsible for overall management of the incident at the incident scene. The command section also includes certain staff functions. The transition from the initial response of the ERO to the EMRO will be evolutionary, and positions will be filled as the corresponding tasks dictate.

In most instances, the FIC will be the [POSITION, TITLE OF PRIMARY POSITION HOLDER]. In the event of [POSITION, TITLE OF PRIMARY POSITION HOLDER'S] absence, the command section may be assumed by one of the [LIST ALTERNATE POSITION HOLDERS] or during off-shift hours by the [POSITION TITLE].

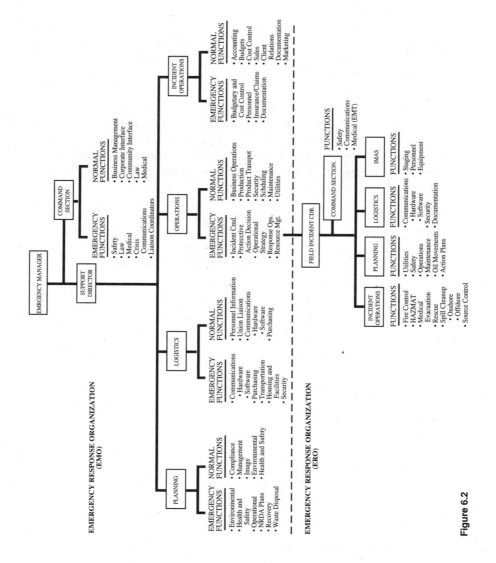

EMERGENCY RESPONSE ORGANIZATION (EMO)

EMERGENCY MANAGER

COMMAND SECTION

NORMAL FUNCTIONS
• Business Management
• Corporate Interface
• Community Interface
• Law
• Medical

EMERGENCY FUNCTIONS
• Safety
• Law
• Medical
• Crisis Communications
• Liaison Coordinators

SUPPORT DIRECTOR

PLANNING

NORMAL FUNCTIONS
• Compliance
• Management
• Image
• Environmental
• Health and Safety

EMERGENCY FUNCTIONS
• Environmental
• Health and Safety
• Operational
• NRDA Plans
• Recovery
• Waste Disposal

LOGISTICS

NORMAL FUNCTIONS
• Personnel Information
• Union Liaison
• Communications
• Hardware
• Software
• Purchasing

EMERGENCY FUNCTIONS
• Communications
• Hardware
• Software
• Purchasing
• Transportation
• Housing and Facilities
• Security

OPERATIONS

NORMAL FUNCTIONS
• Business Operations
• Production
• Product Transpot
• Security
• Scheduling
• Maintenance
• Utilities

EMERGENCY FUNCTIONS
• Incident Cmd.
• Protective Action Decision
• Operational Strategy
• Response Ops.
• Resource Mgt.

INCIDENT OPERATIONS

NORMAL FUNCTIONS
• Accounting
• Budgets
• Cost Control
• Sales
• Client Relations
• Documentation
• Marketing

EMERGENCY FUNCTIONS
• Budgetary and Cost Control
• Personnel
• Insurance/Claims
• Documentation

EMERGENCY RESPONSE ORGANIZATION (ERO)

FIELD INCIDENT CDR.

COMMAND SECTION.

FUNCTIONS
• Safety
• Communications
• Medical (EMT)

INCIDENT OPERATIONS

FUNCTIONS
• Fire Control
• HAZMAT
• Medical
• Evacuation
• Rescue
• Spill Cleanup
  • Onshore
  • Offshore
• Source Control

PLANNING

FUNCTIONS
• Utilities
• Safety
• Operations
• Maintenance
• Oil Movements
• Action Plans

LOGISTICS

FUNCTIONS
• Communications
• Hardware
• Software
• Security
• Documentation

IMAS

FUNCTIONS
• Staging
• Personnel
• Equipment

Figure 6.2

141

When other agencies with jurisdiction are involved, due to the nature of the incident or the kinds of resources required, the FIC will ensure that those organizations are involved in developing incident objectives and strategy and are kept informed of the action plan and its implementation.

The command section should determine when to divide the organizational responsibilities for the incident by creating sectors and, when needed, assign a [POSITION, TITLE] to take over the tactical implementation of the plan created by the command section. In the following situations, the command section may divide the incident's organization:

- When the command section can forecast a situation which will eventually involve a number of responders beyond their capability to directly control. A good rule of thumb is whenever there are more than five functions reporting to the responders.

- When the command section can no longer effectively observe the activities of all responders because of physical barriers, such as walls inside a building or other obstructions to vision.

- When close coordination of personnel is required, such as during hazardous materials response.

Summary of the FIC's duties

- Assessing incident situations
- Setting up the mobile command center
- Managing incident operations
- Authorizing implementation of the incident action plan
- Activating incident command sections as necessary
- Giving status reports to the incident support director
- Calling for additional support as needed
- Obtaining initial information on personnel and process status
- Coordinating maintenance and utilities assistance
- Coordinating external resources
- Supporting activities of the responders
- Coordinating movement of equipment and/or supplies to emergency

Emergency Management Organization and Operation

The *emergency management organization* (EMO) supports the emergency response organization ICS with, but is not limited to, management, administrative, and operations expertise as needed. The EMO incorporates the following ICS principles as they have been applied to the industrial setting. These sections are

- Command
- Planning
- Logistics
- Finance
- Operations

Section responsibilities and personnel assignments for each area appear in the following paragraphs (also refer to the function chapter presented earlier).

EMO command section

The EMO command section is responsible for overall management of the incident. The EMO command section provides support to the ERO by forming a core management group to facilitate field response operations. This management group consists of the emergency manager, incident support director, assistant emergency manager, and staff.

They perform liaison, public, and government relations and interface functions with [COMPANY] and [NONCOMPANY] organizations. Specific functions are outlined in Section _____, EPIPs, and Appendix _____, discussing EMRO position and function descriptions.

EMO planning section

The EMO planning section is responsible for safety, health, environment, strategic planning, natural resource damage assessment, and documentation support to the EMRO. [Specific functions should be developed and presented in an appendix and emergency plan implementing procedures.]

EMO logistics section

The EMO logistics section is responsible for logistics, purchasing, emergency damage control, engineering and inspection, contract support, and claims support to the EMRO. [Specific functions should be developed and presented in an appendix and emergency plan implementing procedures.]

EMO finance section

The EMO finance section is responsible for human resources, medical support, media, employee information, and humanitarian assistance support to the EMRO. [Specific functions should be developed and presented in an appendix and emergency plan implementing procedures.]

EMO operations section

The EMO operations section is responsible for affected unit operations, balance of business operations, communications, security, and administrative and operational documentation support to the EMRO. [Specific functions should be developed and presented in an appendix and emergency plan implementing procedures.]

Emergency Classifications

[Insert a discussion of the emergency classification system that your organization has developed. If you do not have one, see the examples presented in Chap. 8 or in my previous book.]

Local and State Government Responses

[Insert a brief discussion on how your plan integrates with those of local and state government agencies.]

Federal Government Response

[Insert a brief discussion on how you will contact the National Response Center (NRC) and how your plan will be integrated with the National Contingency Plan (NCP).]

Sample

Emergency Plan Implementing Procedure

Fire or Explosion
EPIP-_____

REVISION __:
[DATE]

Sample

SUBMITTED BY: _____ **DATE:** _____

APPROVED BY: _____ **DATE:** _____

1.0 Purpose

The purpose of this procedure is to provide guidance and to initiate actions necessary for evaluation, isolation, and mitigation in the event of a fire, explosion or release (with the potential of ignition).

2.0 Applicability

This procedure is applicable to all personnel at the [LOCATION].

3.0 Definitions

3.1 *Release*—any spilling, leaking, pumping, pouring, emitting, emptying, discharging, injecting, escaping, leaching, dumping, or disposing into the environment.

3.2 *Incipient-stage fire*—in the first stage of existence, just beginning to exist or to come to notice.

3.3 *Explosion*—detonation of any form due to friction, impact (blows), shock, and/or heat. Detonation generally results in a very rapid release of energy that usually creates very high pressures.

4.0 Instructions

4.1 *Precautions*

4.1.1 In the event of a release (with the potential of ignition), fire, or explosion which creates an immediate operational or personnel hazard, the person discovering the condition will promptly notify the [POSITION/TITLE] [insert how notification will be made]. *Make sure you tell someone to get help before you attempt to extinguish a fire!*

4.1.2 [If an internal alarm system is available, describe how it will be activated.]

4.1.3 Personal protective clothing and respiratory requirements will be determined, based upon the type and magnitude of the situation, prior to deploying personnel for response activities.

4.1.4 The field incident commander (FIC) or emergency manager may receive advice on protective actions from the incident support director, safety coordinator, or environmental health and safety department.

4.2 *Initial actions* include but are not limited to:

On-scene observer

- [Describe notification activity.]
- Take appropriate action to mitigate the incident, if this can be done safely.

Affected area supervisor

- Assess the situation. If necessary, call _____ to request assistance.
- Sound emergency alarm (if this is appropriate).
- Initiate appropriate actions as indicated by the situation and standard operating instructions.
- Assist field incident commander (FIC) in incident classification per EPIP-_____ .
- Coordinate any activities which might impact response efforts with the field incident commander.

Field incident commander

- Activate mobile command center.
- With input from the affected area, classify the incident.
- Announce incident classification.
- Ensure that emergency response organization (ERO) and emergency management organization (EMO) have been activated, if required.
- Coordinate activities with arriving response personnel.
- Keep log.

Operations (unaffected areas)

- Prepare to shut down operations, as necessary.
- Account for all unit operations personnel.

Incident support director

- Ensure EMRO activation is adequate.
- Review incident for *reportable quantity* (RQ) issues, as appropriate.

- Call appropriate agencies.
- Monitor incident.
- Support FIC as needed.
- Keep log.
- Prepare follow-up report (postincident investigation).

Operations managers

- Coordinate and communicate with EMRO.
- Support shift supervisors as needed.
- Coordinate operations.
- Keep log.

Security
[Insert steps for the security section to perform.]

4.3   *Subsequent actions*

4.3.1 The incident support director will prepare a written report to the appropriate regulatory agencies in accordance with reporting guidelines.

5.0   References

5.1 All-Hazards Emergency Management Plan, concept of operations

5.2 EPIP-_____, "Emergency External Notification"

5.3 EPIP-_____, "Assessment of Emergency Conditions, Emergency Classification, and Protective Action Recommendation Guides"

5.4 EPIP-_____, "Evacuation, Sheltering, and Accountability"

6.0   Attachments

6.1 Figure 6.3, the fire or explosion response flowchart

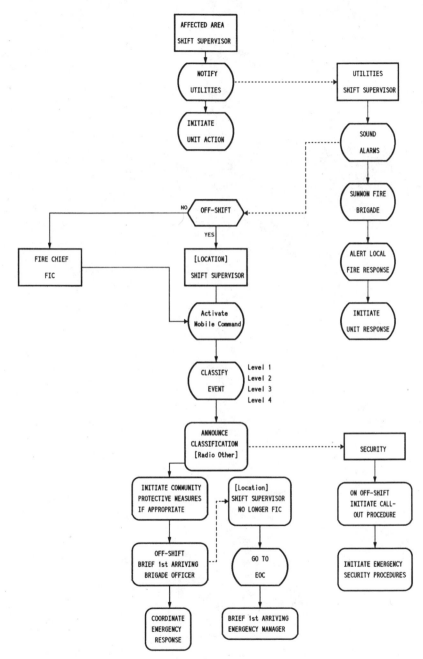

Figure 6.3 Fire or explosion response flowchart.

Communications Considerations

Communications is a word with so many possibilities. In our context, we define it as any and all means used to send, receive, and act upon information. I recommend that when you are developing this portion of your all-hazards emergency management system (EMS) that you seek to clearly define the scope of your current communications capabilities.

The best way to get started is to define what currently exists in the following areas:

- Hardware
- Software
- Temporary support systems
- Communication infrastructure
- Vertical communication requirements
- Horizontal communication requirements

Chapter organizer: What this chapter is about

What are the communications considerations for the emergency management system? Notification, assessment, and seamless communication linkages are crucial to the effectiveness and usefulness of the EMS. Within this context, you must address the communication contact procedures, capabilities, and expected response by all parts of the emergency management/response. You must identify the internal and external communications capabilities. Primary systems and backup systems need to be established. You should also determine the compatibility of communications systems.

The examples and recommendations presented here are focused on assisting you in developing a responsive communication structure. In my previous book, *It Can't Happen Here: All Hazards Crisis Management Planning,* I discussed basic communications considerations. In this chapter, we will see how these basic considerations are developed and implemented.

Critically important to everything we do in putting all the pieces together for our crisis management program is the element called *teamwork.*

Information Management

The need to establish and maintain two-way (vertical and horizontal) communications is clear. The establishment of a defined information management system structure that will ensure adequate communications will be available when needed is important.

The emergency management/response organization (EMRO) and associated entities must be kept well informed. Information is an asset. Information can be expensive. It must be shared and managed effectively. Information management is also critical during a crisis. The need for active systems to provide information on materials and personnel, and capabilities information on materials, personnel, capabilities and processes is paramount. It is extremely important to have a communication system (and adequate backup systems) in place that facilitates two-way exchange of information. In this way, you can effectively identify, catalog, and set priorities and track issues and commitments relating to crisis management and response activities.

Communications Management

Ensuring the adequacy of the communications system cannot be overlooked. One thing you can be assured of, however, is that during an incident there will never be enough telephone, fax, radio, computer, or hardware systems available to adequately address your communications needs.

It is not the intention of this book to provide a checklist for your communication system's design. Rather, I want to offer some guidelines for managing your communications and maximizing your current equipment assets.

We'll start at the incident scene. One thing will be apparent. Generally, at or near the incident scene communications will be almost nonexistent—at least initially. It is, therefore, extremely important to maximize your communications assets.

Your first responder or initial person on the scene may or may not have access to a telephone or radio. Your plan must address this issue. One way is to provide a standard set of instructions for initial response, regardless of who (it might be an administrative person) discovers the incident. In most instances, the initial responder will have some means of communication, generally a radio.

After the initial contact from the incident scene to support personnel is made, the channel should be kept clear for strictly emergency-related communications. You may wish to consider establishing a separate emergency channel if this is a viable option. If you have a response organization, such as a fire brigade or hazardous materials team, they will require some formal communications protocols.

One of the key communications requirements—and an essential element to the success of managing the crisis—is to keep management informed. Keep them informed of what is going on and ask them to support the response effort. This does not mean that they are to take over the response effort. It means that they have a role to play and need to accomplish their tasks in order for the response and mitigation effort to be successful.

Management is never put to the test more strongly than in a crisis situation. The objectives are immediate, and so are the results. What you and those around you do and do not do will have long-lasting implications. One of the most important tasks in support of the initial response effort that management can do is to notify internal and external groups. This includes but is not limited to

- The next higher level of management
- Any internal notification center
- Emergency management/response organization
- Regulatory agencies (federal, state, local)
- External response organizations (fire, police, medical, contractors)

The following examples provide guidance for the development of your communications section and communications protocol in the all-hazards EMS.

Sample

All-Hazards Emergency Management Plan

SECTION __:
COMMUNICATIONS

Sample

Communications Systems at [LOCATION]

There should be a brief introductory statement regarding your company's communication system. A summary of considerations follows:

- Computer communications system
- Fire/security system
- Telephone systems
- On-site alarm systems
    Fire alarm system
    Unit emergency horn signals
    Operations building fire alarm system

Emergency Response Notification

Include a brief discussion on how initial and follow-up notifications will be accomplished. Some considerations:

- Internal notification
- Internal notification outside [location]
- External notifications
    Community
    Regulatory agencies
    Contractors
    Mutual aid
- Internal reporting procedures
    Reporting injuries
    Ambulance calls
- Environmental incident reporting
- Radiation incident reporting
- Transportation incident emergency communications
- Customer facility emergency communications
- Emergency information

Some considerations for information to be communicated include

1. Status of the incident
2. Location

3. Agencies notified

4. Facts of incident (date, time)

5. Incident classification

6. Type of release

7. Release to the environment

8. Potentially hazardous material involved

9. Health risk and medical advice (as required under SARA Title III)*

10. Recommended protective actions (as required under SARA Title III)*

11. Affected area of the facility

12. Estimated quantity involved

13. Wind direction and weather data

A format for follow-up reports should be provided. This may include

- Intracompany notification process
- External agency notification
- Other notification

---

*Note: Health risks, medical advice, and protective action recommendations shall be in accordance with the most currently available copy of the Department of Transportation (DOT) *Emergency Response Guidebook* (DOT-P 5800.5) or the appropriate material safety data sheet (MSDS).

[COMPANY]
[LOCATION]

APPENDIX __

Emergency Management Agencies (Federal, State, Local), Police Departments, Fire Departments

[DATE]

You should consider listing contacts for the following at a minimum:

- Local emergency agencies
    Public safety
    Fire
    Police
    Emergency services
- Federal and state emergency agencies
    National Response Center
    U.S. Coast Guard
    Department of Transportation
    State emergency response commission
- Contractors, consultants, laboratories, etc.

[COMPANY]
[LOCATION]

APPENDIX __

Emergency Radio Channels

[DATE]

Considerations here should include:

- Radio channels
    Frequency assignments
- Cellular telephone
    Number assignments
- Computer network
    User codes
- Facsimile
    Number assignments

[COMPANY]
[LOCATION]

APPENDIX __

FORMS

[DATE]

Considerations include the following:

A Table of Contents listing the forms included in the Appendix

Forms:

- Activities Record Sheet
- Emergency Response Team Assignment Sheet
- Injured Personnel Medical Data Record Sheet
- Spill Incident Report Form
- Recovery Manager's Checklist
- Evaluator's Checklist
- Evaluator's or Controller's Log Sheet
- Temporary Leak Repair Authorization
- Field Report Information
- Emergency Reporting
- Letter of Transmittal for Original Transmittal of Plan
- Letter of Transmittal for Plan Revisions
- Nondisclosure Agreement

Sample

EMERGENCY PLAN
IMPLEMENTING PROCEDURE

EMERGENCY NOTIFICATION
EPIP - __
REVISION __
[DATE]

SUBMITTED BY: _____ DATE: _____

APPROVED BY: _____ DATE: _____

Sample

1.0 Purpose

This procedure provides guidance and instructions for notifying company, corporate, federal, state, and local authorities in the event of a declared emergency.

2.0 Applicability

This procedure applies to designated emergency management/ response organization (EMRO) personnel with emergency notification responsibilities.

3.0 Definitions

There are none.

4.0 Instructions

4.1 Precautions

4.1.1 For external emergency notifications, the initial message will be transmitted by voice communications. Follow-up messages should be sent by telecopier (facsimile) for legal records; however, voice communications are acceptable if it is impractical to use fax for any reason.

4.1.2 An emergency message form is located as attachment 4 to this EPIP, Telephone Incident Report. When voice communications are used to transmit emergency message form information, cover each paragraph, in sequential order, with specific, concise diction.

4.1.3 Each message form transmitted verbally should be completed in its entirety, using current information or the phrase *not applicable.*

4.1.4 In drill and exercise situations, initial communications related to an event should be *preceded and followed* by *"This is a drill."*

4.1.5 All bracketed information on a message form is considered proprietary data and is not to be released.

4.2 Initial actions

4.2.1 *Notification and reporting.* Insert a description on how you will conduct a notification and reporting activities. Considerations should include

National Response Center (NRC)

State

County

Other regulatory agencies

See attachments to this section for phone numbers and associated report forms. Required notifications also include

- Oil spills to the land
- SARA reportable release
- CERCLA reportable release

4.3 Subsequent actions

4.3.1 *Record-keeping requirements.* All personnel with assigned communication responsibility, once in position, will maintain a communication log, using form EPIP-_____-__, Activities Record Sheet. Upon termination of the emergency, ensure that all communication records are filed in accordance with standard operating procedures.

5.0 References

5.1 All-hazards emergency management plan, communications section

5.2 EPIP-_____, Duties of the Emergency Management/Response Organization during Emergencies

5.3 EPIP-_____, Emergency Communications

5.4 EPIP-_____, Assessment of Emergency Conditions, Emergency Classification and Protective Action Recommendation Guides

5.5 EPIP-_____, Managing Public Information

6.0 Attachments

6.1 Attachment 1, Notification Instructions

6.2 Attachment 2, Telephone Numbers

6.3 Attachment 3, Incident Report Forms

Attachment 1: Notification Instructions

Page ____ of ____

Emergency message format

When off-site emergency organizations are notified the following format will be used:

1. Assess and classify the incident (EPIP-_____).

2. Determine if an off-site *protective action recommendation (PAR)* is required. If PAR is necessary, notify appropriate authorities.

3. Ensure appropriate activation of the EMRO.

4. Maintain a log of all incoming and outgoing communications, using form EPIP-_____-__.

5. Record the times when notification calls are placed.

Upon contact with off-site entities:

6. Give your name and title.

7. Briefly inform them of the situation.

8. Where appropriate, note which individual was contacted.

9. During the notification process, depending on the time of day, make no more than two attempts at contacting the external organization.

Attachment 2: Telephone Numbers

Page ____ of ____

	Phone
National Response Center	1-800-424-8802
Environmental Protection Agency (EPA) List the appropriate region.	
EPA Emergency Spill Phone	1-215-597-9898
National Chemical Transportation	1-800-424-9300
Emergency Center (CHEMTREC), Washington, D.C.	
Poison Control Center	
State Emergency Response Team (as appropriate)	
Add other pertinent numbers as you get them.	

Attachment 3: Telephone Incident Report

Page ____ of ____

1. Caller: _____ Phone number: _____

2. Call received by: _____ Date: _____ Time: _____

3. Date of incident: _____ Time of incident: _____

4. Location of incident: _____
_____

5. General description of incident: _____
_____

6. Identify all hazardous materials (including products and feedstocks) involved:
_____
_____
_____
_____

7. If spill or leak, estimate gallons spilled: _____
Estimate gallons recovered: _____
Net gallons lost: _____

8. Names of injured (employees and others): _____
_____
_____

9. Names of fatalities (employees and others): _____
_____
_____

10. Estimate value of loss to company property. $_____

11. Estimate value of loss to property of others. $_____

12. Action taken to mitigate incident: _____

13. Circle those who have already been notified by reporting party.

      Location   Claims   Manager of
      manager   administrator   human resources

   Public affairs representative   Medical representative

14. This report has been relayed to:

	Date	Time
Location manager	_____	_____
Manager of human resources	_____	_____
Claims representative	_____	_____
Public affairs representative	_____	_____
Medical representative	_____	_____
Other_____	_____	_____
_____	_____	_____

15. Remind caller to follow up in writing as appropriate.

Report Information

This form provides an outline of the type of information you may be asked for when a call is made to report an incident.

General information

Name:

Position:

Contact phone number(s):

Location of incident?

How did you learn of the incident?

Time incident occurred?

What other notifications have been made?

Any immediate support needs?

When will an update be available?

Type of incident(s) reported
(Check all that apply.)

Release of chemical or hazardous substance to air

Release or spill of petroleum product, chemical, or hazardous substance to land or subsurface

Release or spill of petroleum product, chemical, or hazardous substance to surface water

Incident is reportable to regulatory or other government agencies

Injuries and/or deaths to company personnel, contractors, or the public

Disruption of facility operations

Explosion and/or fire

Serious threats to security

Potential product recall

1. Release of chemical or hazardous substance to air

   - Type and name of chemical or substance and amount released
   - Toxicity or expected environmental impact
   - Projected volume and duration or release and type of container
   - Plume characteristics, visibility, wind direction, speed
   - Background information on population and commercial activity in the surrounding area
   - Facility, property, equipment, personnel, public affected
   - Impacts on surrounding community
   - Nature of company response
   - Authorities notified or response to the incident by other organizations
   - What noncompany organizations are on-scene
   - Community response and reaction
   - Media response, reaction, scope of exposure

2. Release or spill of petroleum product, chemical or hazardous substance to land or subsurface

   - Type and name of product or substance and amount released
   - Toxicity or expected environmental impact
   - Projected volume, duration of release, source of leak
   - Area affected—square feet, type of soil, acres down gradient that might be impacted by subsurface migration
   - Background information on population and commercial activity in the surrounding area
   - Facility, property, equipment, personnel, public affected

- Impacts on surrounding community
- Nature of company response
- Authorities notified and response to the incident by other organizations
- The noncompany organizations that are on the scene
- Community response, reaction
- Media response, reaction, scope of exposure

3. Release or spill of petroleum product, chemical, or hazardous substance to surface water

- Type and name of chemical or substance and amount released
- Toxicity or expected environmental impact
- Projected duration of release, source of leak
- Affected water body, direction of flow, actions taken
- Facility, property, equipment, personnel, public affected
- Impacts on surrounding community
- Authorities notified, response to the incident by other organizations
- What noncompany organizations are on the scene
- Community response, reaction
- Media response, reaction, scope of exposure

4. Incident is reportable to regulatory and other government agencies

- Type and duration of release, name of material, toxicity, volume or amount released
- Source of leak, impacts—human and environment
- Area affected, air, water, land
- Facility, property, equipment, personnel, public affected
- Impacts on surrounding community
- Authorities notified, response to the incident by other organizations
- What noncompany organizations are on scene
- Community response, reaction
- Media response, reaction, scope of exposure

5. Injuries and/or deaths to company personnel, contractors, or the public

   - Type of incident, number and nature of injuries, deaths
   - Projected duration of incident, damage
   - Impacts on surrounding community
   - Authorities notified, response to the incident by other organizations
   - What noncompany organizations are on scene
   - Victims' families notified?
   - Community response, reaction
   - Media response, reaction, scope of exposure

6. Disruption of facility operations

   - Type of incident
   - Projected duration of disruption, shutdown
   - Facility, property, equipment, personnel, public affected
   - Impacts on surrounding community
   - Other company operations affected
   - Market impact, estimated lost revenue
   - Community response, reaction
   - Media response, reaction, scope of exposure

7. Explosion and/or fire

   - Type of incident
   - Projected duration of incident, damage
   - Facility, property, equipment, personnel, public affected
   - Impacts on surrounding community
   - Secondary effects—release, spill, disruption
   - Authorities notified, response to the incident by other organizations
   - What noncompany organizations are still on scene
   - Community response, reaction
   - Media response, reaction, scope of exposure

8. Serious threats to security

   - Type of incident, nature of threat
   - Projected duration of incident, disruption, damage
   - Information on known or suspected source of threat or act of violence
   - Facility, property, equipment, personnel, public affected
   - Impacts on surrounding community
   - Authorities notified, response to the incident by other organizations
   - What noncompany organizations are still on scene
   - Community response, reaction
   - Media response, reaction, scope of exposure

9. Potential product recall

   - Source of information on contamination
   - Is contamination known or suspected? Deliberate or accidental?
   - Type and source of contamination
   - Information on potential market area affected: population, threat of injuries, deaths
   - Media response, reaction
   - Market impacts, estimated lost revenue
   - Recommended short-term action

10. Other (example: drills)

    - Type of incident
    - Projected duration
    - Information on known or suspected source
    - Facility, property, personnel, public affected
    - Impact on community, community response
    - Authorities notified
    - Other organizations involved
    - Media involvement

Form 1: Emergency Reporting

The NRC Watchstanders will need concise and accurate information. Be prepared to report as much of the following information as possible:

1. Your name: _____
   Address: _____
   Phone no: _____

2. Party or individual responsible for the incident
   Name: _____
   Mailing address: _____
   Phone no.: _____

3. The incident occurred or was discovered
   Date: _____
   Time: _____

4. Specific location of incident: _____
   _____

5. Name of material spilled, released:_____

6. Source of spilled material: _____

7. Cause of release:_____

8. Total quantity discharged: _____

9. Material release to air, ground, water,
   or subsurface: _____

10. Amount spilled to water: _____

11. Weather conditions: _____

12. Vessel name, railcar no.: _____

13. Name of carrier: _____

14. Number and type of injuries, fatalities:_____
    _____

15. Have evacuations occurred? _____

16. Estimated dollar value of property damage: _____

17. Description of cleanup actions taken
    and future plans: _____

18. Other agencies you have notified or
    plan to immediately notify: _____

8

Incident Classification Considerations

Developing an effective response strategy depends on identifying and classifying an incident according to its severity. We highlighted assessment issues in Chaps. 5 and 6 as they related to organizational structure and concept of operations. This chapter provides an overview of incident assessment and classification considerations. Here is the definition:

> *Incident assessment and classification* include all activities prior to and during an incident taken to determine the degree of severity of the incident and the hazard associated with the incident and to assess its potential impact on business operations.

Ensuring that all personnel know and understand the rationale for the emergency classification system is important. However, it is perhaps more important, even vital, that all personnel know and understand what constitutes an emergency and/or an incident. This is important because in today's regulatory milieu, reporting incidents, near misses, and other types of reportable information means the difference between being fined and operating within regulatory constraints and ensuring the safety of both employees and the public. A dynamic incident classification system facilitates this process.

Chapter organizer: What this chapter is about

- What are the considerations for an incident assessment and classification system? There are seven considerations basic to incident classification: (1) safety, including injuries, fatalities, and protective actions; (2) environmental impacts, including near-term and long-term; (3) facility status, including the entity involved in the incident; (4) geographic area, location, including more site and off-site areas; (5) commodity, including quantity, volume, and toxicity; (6) meteorological conditions, including near-term and long-term weather forecasts; (7) response capability and actions, including immediate, near-term, and long-term actions and capabilities.

■ How can we apply incident assessment and classification consider-ations to spill situations and how do they differ from fixed facility considerations? Application of the criteria for incident classification to spill situations must depend heavily on the geographic location, time to discovery, response capability, and accessibility of the loca-tion to the response. Additionally, because spills can, by their nature, threaten to cover wide areas, it is essential to be capable of moving from reactive response toward proactive project manage-ment of the spill and cleanup operations.

Incident Assessment and Classification

The purpose of establishing an incident assessment and classification system is to provide

■ Effective coordination of activities among the organizations having a management/response role

■ Early warning and clear instructions to all concerned if an incident occurs

■ Continued assessment of actual and potential consequences of the incident

■ Continuity of business operations during and immediately after the incident

This chapter describes the incident assessment, classification sys-tem assessment, and protective action decision-making process.

The incident assessment and classification system is important because it provides a framework for

Notification

Determining the severity of the incident

Determining the appropriate response

Determining protective action recommendations

Assessing damage

Ensuring the safety of employees and the public

The above list is not meant to be exhaustive; however, it illustrates the need for a system to classify incidents according to severity. A typical assessment classification system is based on seven criteria:

- Safety considerations
- Environmental impacts
- Operational considerations
- Geographic area impacted
- Commodity, quantity, toxicity
- Meteorological conditions
- Response capability, actions

Examples of definitions for classification from my previous book are seen in Figs. 8.1 through 8.5.

Common Characteristics of a Crisis

As indicated in Fig. 8.6, when an incident occurs, there is a surprise; followed by panic, chaos, and confusion. A rapid flow of events occurs. There is missing information. Initial response begins. Resource concentration starts. There is internal conflict—who's in charge?

EMERGENCY CLASSIFICATION CRITERIA
INTERNALLY REPORTABLE EVENT

Criteria: An incident has occurred; however, the incident does not require any notification of off-site or regulatory agencies.

Value: This classification allows for the tracking of incidents at relatively low levels of severity and can serve to spot trends or areas in need of attention.

Figure 8.1

UNUSUAL EVENT

Criteria: An incident has occurred which is reportable to a regulatory or off-site agency. The incident may be noticeable from the facility perimeter; however, no outside assistance is required, and no evacuation outside the incident scene has occurred.

Value: This classification allows for immediate reporting of an incident to the appropriate regulatory agencies. It also facilitates the ability of the organization to augment its response at relatively low levels of security.

Figure 8.2

ALERT

Criteria: An incident has occurred, with the potential to affect nearby off-site locations. Some outside assistance, such as mutual aid organization response, may be required. Any off-site assistance will generally be limited to a single jurisdiction and agency. The alert does not require off-site protective actions; however, on-site protective actions such as evacuation or sheltering may be implemented.

Value: This classification allows for early assessment of the potential impact of the incident on off-site locations. Protective action recommendations are developed early to allow for their implementation by the appropriate off-site agencies.

Figure 8.3

SITE AREA EMERGENCY

Criteria: An incident has occurred; and the entire facility, with the exception of critical employees, has been sheltered on site or evacuated. Off-site areas surrounding the facility may consider implementing protective actions. There is potential threat to life, health, or property.

Value: This classification allows for early coordination of protective actions with the site and off-site locations. The geographic scope is expanded. Coordination and communications with off-site agencies are enhanced.

Figure 8.4

GENERAL EMERGENCY

Criteria: An incident has occurred with off-site consequences. The affected community is implementing protective actions. Serious hazards or severe threat to life, health, and property exist. There is a large geographic impact.

Value: This classification allows for immediate implementation of protective actions by off-site locations. Extensive resource management and allocation can be accomplished under a unified command structure.

Figure 8.5

Employers are forgotten. Initial response escalates into full-scale response. Government agencies become involved. A siege mentality begins to develop. Cries of social ramifications are heard. Intense media scrutiny of your operations results.

Sound familiar? Perhaps, all too familiar. One goal of your all-hazards emergency management system should be to make preparedness a way of doing business, not just something done for an annual exercise. One of the keys to internalizing the system is a universal understanding of what constitutes an event, how to classify the severity of the event, and how to initiate the response. Another key is to be able

Figure 8.6

to communicate the information to an external, nonsystem audience. This involves outreach. You must ensure that your classification system is known and understood by external support agencies in order for them to act appropriately. Imagine the following conversation:

> FACILITY: This is Joe Brown at XYZ Company. We have an emergency.
>
> LOCAL RESPONSE AGENCY: How bad is it?
>
> FACILITY: Real Bad!
>
> LOCAL RESPONSE AGENCY: Can you tell me what is going on?
>
> FACILITY: We need you to get here and help out—*now!*

Click, phone line goes dead.

What kind of response is Joe Brown going to get? He will probably get everything available and then some. And, in doing so, he may endanger more people than was necessary and tie up valuable resources that could be better used elsewhere.

Let's consider the previous conversation in light having a well-defined emergency classification system, one that is understood by internal and external groups.

> FACILITY: This is Joe Brown, Emergency Coordinator, XYZ Company. I'm calling to report a level 3 emergency at our facility. Our call-back number is XXX-XXXX.

LOCAL RESPONSE AGENCY: Mr. Brown, we confirm a level 3 emergency at XYZ Company. Please verify your call-back number XXX-XXXX.

FACILITY: I verify XXX-XXXX. Resources requested per code X.

LOCAL RESPONSE AGENCY: I verify code X response requested. We will arrive at your scene in approximately X minutes.

Obviously, this is a much shorter and more focused conversation. Yes, you can pick apart the conversation in terms of verification, codes, etc. However, you must agree that it is much more effective because the response agency now knows the severity and type of resources needed for effective response.

IPAC

Incident classification and response do not have to be complicated. Logical Management Systems, Corp., has developed a readily usable format that can be custom-fit to any workplace to provide quicker, more efficient, and more effective response to incidents. IPAC is an acronym where

I = Identify

P = Protect

A = Alert

C = Communicate

OSHA 1910.120, *Hazardous Waste Operations and Emergency Response,* requires that companies establish emergency response operations capabilities for releases of, or substantial threats of release of, hazardous substances without regard to the location of the hazard. A site-specific *incident command system* (ICS) consisting of trained personnel must be established. Two of the designated categories of personnel are

- First responder awareness level
- First responder operations level

IPAC is designed as a practical aid to help the first responder awareness level and first responder operations level personnel accomplish emergency response tasks as defined in OSHA 1910.120. A complete IPAC workbook example can be found in Chapter 12.

Figure 8.7, an incident response worksheet, is an example of a simple form that follows the IPAC philosophy. Beyond the individual actions, the following examples of actions by event classification are provided to facilitate your understanding of how an effective classification system can enhance your response and response management capabilities. Figure 8.8 provides a sample of a type of emergency classification system based on the seven key assessment areas.

INCIDENT RESPONSE WORKSHEET

INFORMATION	ACTION	FEEDBACK
IDENTIFY:		
* INCIDENT INFORMATION		

FACILITY STATUS
    GEOGRAPHIC AREA/LOCATION
    COMMODITY, QUANTITY (RQ),
    VOLUME & TOXICITY		

* INCIDENT ASSESSMENT		

SAFETY
    INJURY/FATALITY
    WHAT IS AT RISK
    ENVIRONMENTAL IMPACTS		

* SPECIAL CONCERNS		

METEOROLOGICAL CONDITIONS/
    CONSIDERATIONS
    POPULATIONS-AT-RISK		

* DECISIONS		
RESPONSE CAPABILITY/ACTIONS		
PROTECT:		
* PRECAUTIONS		
APPROPRIATE PERSONAL PROTECTIVE EQUIPMENT AVAILABLE		
* PROTECTIVE ACTION DECISION-MAKING		

ISOLATE AREA
    CONTROL SOURCE
    EVACUATION
    SHELTER
    OFFSITE PROTECTIVE ACTIONS		

ALERT:		
* DEFENSIVE RESPONSE ACTIONS		

SOUND ALARMS
    PROVIDE INSTRUCTIONS
    MOVE PEOPLE AWAY FROM SCENE
    ESTABLISH PERIMETER
    CONTROL ACCESS ROUTES		

* OFFENSIVE RESPONSE ACTIONS		

ERO ACTIVATED
    EMO ACTIVATED
    GO TEAM/CORPORATE SUPPORT
    OTHER SUPPORT		

COMMUNICATE:		
* INITIAL NOTIFICATIONS		

PERSONNEL IN IMMINENT DANGER
    REQUIRED INTERNAL NOTIFICATIONS
    REQUIRED EXTERNAL NOTIFICATIONS		

* FOLLOW-UP ACTIONS		

ADDITIONAL ASSISTANCE NEEDED
    SITUATION UPDATE
    ASSESS FACILITY/PERSONNEL
    STATUS
    ACTION/OPEN ITEMS
    CRITIQUE OF ACTIONS
    NEXT MEETING SCHEDULED (TIME)		

IPACRE1.FCD

Figure 8.7 Incident response worksheet.

	Safety Injury/Fatality Protective Action	Environmental Impacts	Facility Status	Geographic Area/Location	Commodity Quantity (RQ) Volume & Toxicity	Meteorological Conditions/ Considerations	Response Capability/ Actions
LEVEL 1 (Unusual Event)	Minor first aid treatment. Presents no threat. No PAR	Non-environmental sensitive area	Minor disruption to system. Facility Shutdown Facility systems operational	May be visible from facility boundaries	Minor material release. Not Reportable	Not a factor	Minimum ERO activation, notifications
LEVEL 2 (Alert)	Local area near scene evacuation. Injuries require EMS/Hospital care	Release on water. Potential impact environmentally sensitive area	Affects facility /location operations	In or near populated area. Media involved	Reportable Release	Potential to influence release and/or plume coverage. Potential to impact response time	ERO fully activated. EMO partially activated
LEVEL 3 (Site Area Emergency)	Injury/Fatality (single/multiple) Company personnel PAR for Emergency Workers	Environmentally sensitive area impacted Major impact to environmentally sensitive areas.	Significant impact on operations	Impacts large geographic area. Population impact Media involved	Release Reportable, with voluntary callout of National Spill Response Contractor	Impacts response activities. Impacts release zone	EMRO activated. External support activated.
LEVEL 4 (General Emergency)	Injury/Fatality (single/multiple) Non-company and/ or General Public PAR for General Public	Natural resources habitat impact	Major impact on operations. Long-term cleanup required	Interdicts major population group infrastructure (roadway, rail, waterway, etc.) impacted	Worst Case Scenario Event/ Discharge	Significant impact on response activity of operations Significant impact on plume zone coverage	Agencies respond/ takeover command of operations

Note: All seven columns do not have to be satisfied for a particular classification to be invoked.
Outside assistance may be required at any classification level.
PAR = Protective Action Recommendation

Figure 8.8 Emergency classification system.

Sample

All-Hazards Emergency Management Plan

SECTION __:
EMERGENCY CLASSIFICATION

Sample

Emergency Classification System

The purpose of this section is to define the system adopted for classifying emergency conditions. (The emergency classification system should be developed using common terminology found in the emergency plans of the local operating area as defined by regulation or by off-site groups. This minimizes confusion during emergencies and improves coordination of response efforts.)

The emergency classification system provides a dynamic framework for

- Assessing severity of an incident
- Determining appropriate response
- Formulating protective action recommendations
- Notification and communication
- Ensuring the safety of employees and the public
- Assessing damage

The above list is not all-inclusive, however it illustrates the flexibility for establishing criteria to classify emergency conditions. The following considerations guide the development of the classification system:

Ease of use and understanding	Toxicity
Time and space considerations	Exposure concentrations
Margin-of-safety estimates	Types of releases expected
Operational conditions	Meteorological conditions

Emergency Classifications

Here you insert the definitions of each classification level, similar to the examples provided in Figs. 8.1 through 8.5. You will also want to describe the actions to be taken upon declaration of an emergency classification.

Emergency Planning Zones

Based on your hazard analysis, you should develop *emergency planning zones (EPZs)*. The emergency planning zones should be selected based upon knowledge of the potential consequences, timing, and release characteristics of a spectrum of incidents, regardless of their extremely low probability of occurrence.

EPZs are defined as the areas for which planning is needed to ensure that prompt and effective actions can be taken to protect the public in an emergency. The size of the EPZ represents a judgment based upon detailed planning performed to ensure an adequate response.

Dependent upon the severity of the incident, protective actions generally will be limited to operations in designated sectors; should the need arise, actions can be undertaken for the entire zone.

You should provide examples of your EPZs in a section that is an appendix to this plan.

The size of the zone is generally based primarily on the following considerations:

- Projected release estimates for most accidents will not exceed exposure *protective action guide (PAG)* levels outside the zone.

- Detailed planning within this area will provide a substantial base for expansion of response efforts in the unlikely event that this proves necessary.

- Planning within this area recognizes all the jurisdictional restraints imposed by the zone designation.

Incident Assessment

The initial response to any emergency condition should be based upon an assessment of its severity. All abnormal events observed in or near your facility should be immediately reported to a central location. Upon receipt of that telephone call, appropriate actions for response can be initiated.

Considerations for this section include the following:

Initial incident assessment: Initial incident assessment consists of

- Identification of the emergency condition
- Classification
- Notification (on site, off site, emergency response organization)
- Recommendation of initial protective actions

Ongoing incident assessment: Ongoing incident assessment may include, as appropriate,

- Computer assessment of incident conditions
- Meteorological data assessment
- Effluent release data assessment

- Atmospheric dispersion calculations
- Environmental pathway assessments
- Assessment of on-site conditions
- Assessment of off-site conditions
- Environmental and industrial hygiene monitor data

Protective Action Recommendations

Protective actions are measures taken to protect emergency workers, site personnel, and the public, based upon classification of the severity of the emergency and its potential effects with regard to health and safety. Protective action recommendations require prompt notification of off-site agencies and the public regarding the emergency situation.

Typical protective action recommendations may include but are not limited to the following:

- Evacuation
- Sheltering
- Respiratory protection
- Protective clothing
- Restrictions on foodstuffs and water

A good reference for assistance in developing your choice of protective action recommendations can be found in the EPA's publication entitled *Manual of Protective Action Guides and Protective Actions for Nuclear Incidents* (EPA-520/1-75-001).

Protective Action Decision Making

The protective action decision-making process requires an understanding of the emergency classification system as well as the types of protective actions you developed for this section.

Deciding which area requires protective actions will depend on several variables, each of which will have to be evaluated at the time of an incident. The most significant variables include the process conditions and existing meteorological conditions.

Evacuation

Evacuation of the population at risk is the most effective protective action. The decision to recommend an evacuation requires that several influencing factors be considered; these include but are not limited to the following:

- Timeliness of the recommendation
- Time required for evacuation to be complete
- Plume arrival and plume passage time
- Protection offered by buildings, shelters, or other structures

Considerations for discussion are as follows:

On-site evacuation procedures

- Areas to be evacuated
- Distance to be evacuated from the leak, spill, etc.
- Who, if anyone, will remain to take control of the emergency

Methods of notification

- The chemical released
- Quantity of the chemical
- Projected duration of release
- Wind direction and speed (if known)
- Potential impact area

Materials and situations

Routes of evacuation

- The quickest route may not be the safest.
- In the event of a toxic vapor release, always move upwind and/or at a 90° angle.
- Report to the assembly area designated by your supervisor. If no instructions are provided, select the safest preassigned area and proceed to that area.

Sheltering

Sheltering involves members of the population at risk seeking shelter in homes and/or buildings. Note that while evacuation (if accomplished before plume passage) minimizes chances of exposure, it also entails certain risks of injury and inconvenience. Consequently, serious consideration should be given to sheltering, if the desired result is reduction of population exposure to the hazard.

Sheltering is suitable as a protective action alone or may be used in lieu of evacuation for the following:

- Severe incidents in which an evacuation cannot be implemented because of inadequate lead time due to the rapid passage of the plume ("puff" release)

- When an evacuation is indicated, but local constraints such as inclement weather and road conditions dictate that directing the public to shelter is a more feasible and effective protective measure than evacuation

While evacuation is preferred, some buildings are capable of becoming secured facilities, allowing occupants to shelter in place *if evacuation cannot be accomplished in the available time.* A building is secure when the doors and windows are closed and ventilation/air conditioning systems, or other systems that would force or induce outside air into the building, are shut down.

EMERGENCY PLAN IMPLEMENTING PROCEDURES

ASSESSMENT OF EMERGENCY CONDITIONS, EMERGENCY CLASSIFICATION, AND PROTECTIVE ACTION RECOMMENDATION GUIDES EPIP - __ REVISION __ [DATE]

SUBMITTED BY: _____ DATE: _____

APPROVED BY: _____ DATE: _____

| All-Hazards | Issue Date | Procedure No. |
| Emergency Plan Manual | _/_/_ | EPIP-___ |

Assessment of Emergency	Rev. Date	Revision No.
Conditions and Emergency	_/_/_	0
Classification		Page __ of __ Pages

1.0 Purpose

This procedure provides guidelines for initial incident assessment and subsequent emergency classification, and it delineates responsibilities for activation of the [LOCATION] emergency management plan.

2.0 Applicability

This procedure applies to the affected area shift supervisor, field incident commander, and emergency manager. This procedure also serves as a reference for all personnel assigned to the [LOCATION] emergency management/response organization.

3.0 Definitions

3.1 *Emergency conditions*—situations occurring which cause or threaten to cause hazards affecting the health and safety of employees or the public, or which may result in damage to property

3.2 *Emergency classification*—a classification system of emergency severity based on operational and monitored conditions at or near the site

4.0 Instructions

4.1 Precautions

4.1.1 Specific actions required to mitigate the emergency condition are prescribed in standard operating procedures and are independent of any actions outlined in this EPIP.

4.1.2 Emergency management personnel classifying the event should consider the effect that combinations of events have upon the emergency classification; that is, events if taken individually constitute a lower emergency classification, but collectively may dictate the need for a higher emergency classification.

4.2 Initial actions

4.2.1 Upon recognition that an abnormal or emergency condition exists, the affected area shift supervisor should be notified. Recognition of the event can occur as a result of either

| All-Hazards | Issue Date | Procedure No. |
| Emergency Plan Manual | _/_/_ | EPIP-___ |

Assessment of Emergency	Rev. Date	Revision No.
Conditions and Emergency	_/_/_	0
Classification		Page __ of __ Pages

process operations or other personnel observing the abnormal or emergency condition.

4.2.2 The affected area shift supervisor should make an initial evaluation of conditions and request any needed assistance.

4.2.3 Process operators should initiate actions called for based upon the indicated symptoms and appropriate emergency operating procedures.

4.2.4 Upon notification of an emergency, the field incident commander (FIC), with input from the affected area shift supervisor, shall evaluate the event to determine the appropriate emergency classification level.

4.2.5 The FIC or affected area shift supervisor shall activate the EMRO as required for the type and classification of emergency.

4.2.6 The affected area supervisor, emergency manager, and FIC may use attachment 1 of this EPIP to help classify the incident.

4.3 Protective action recommendation guides

4.3.1 The emergency manager or field incident commander is responsible for selecting the protective action recommendations and ensuring that they are communicated to the county and state authorities in a timely manner.

4.3.1.1 The protective action recommendations generally concern the _____-mile EPZ. Protective action recommendations may be provided to county and state authorities for any potentially affected areas beyond the _____-mile EPZ.

4.3.2 The [COMPANY] has no authority with respect to imposing protective action response options beyond the boundaries of the [LOCATION].

4.3.3 Recommendations to the county will be made as appropriate to achieve the desired degree of protection for the public.

4.4 Protective actions: Initial actions

4.4.1 The initial protective action recommendation by the emergency manager or FIC to the county [applicable department] will be based upon operational conditions, meteorological data, and any exposure projection data available at the time.

| All-Hazards | Issue Date | Procedure No. |
| Emergency Plan Manual | _/_/_ | EPIP- __ |

Assessment of Emergency	Rev. Date	Revision No.
Conditions and Emergency	_/_/_	0
Classification		Page __ of __ Pages

The following factors will also be considered in making a protective action recommendation:

4.4.1.1 Population at risk, including special concerns in the area of release

4.4.1.2 Response time, including the time to assemble needed resources in order to implement the recommendation

4.4.1.3 Weather—current conditions, short-term and long-term forecasts, and changes in wind direction

4.4.3.4 Physical and environmental conditions, limiting factors which will affect the response time of the off-site agencies

Note: All precautionary considerations to ensure the safety of the public will be based upon available data to ensure the safety of the population at risk. The emergency manager/on-call emergency manager (OEM) and/or FIC will recommend the action to be taken, how much time is available to do so, and the potential affects of the recommended action.

4.5 Responsibilities

The emergency manager and/or FIC is responsible for protective action recommendations to off-site authorities and for ensuring that [LOCATION/COMPANY] personnel are properly protected. Information on [LOCATION] conditions to be considered concerning protective action recommendations is provided to the emergency manager and/or FIC by the field incident commander, incident support director, affected area personnel, and emergency operations center (EOC) personnel.

4.6 Subsequent actions

4.6.1 The FIC or emergency manager will continue to evaluate the incident and the potential of actual off-site consequences associated with the incident to determine the need for any change in the emergency classification.

4.6.2 The OSHA standard *Process Safety Management of Highly Hazardous Chemicals* (CFR 1910.119) requires that incidents which result, or could have resulted, in a catastrophic release be investigated within 48 hours.

For level 0 and level 1 incidents, the affected unit shift supervisor shall evaluate the incident and determine if it has catastrophic potential. If so, she or he shall notify the [POSITION/TITLE OF APPROPRIATE PERSON] as soon as possible.

4.6.3 As [LOCATION] conditions change or are projected to change or additional information becomes available, the protective action recommendations will be reevaluated and any changes will be transmitted to the county [AGENCY].

4.6.4 Additional information for evaluating subsequent protective action recommendations is located in reference 5.6 of this EPIP.

5.0 References

5.1 All-hazards emergency management plan, emergency classification section, hazard analysis—appendix _____ , evacuation routes—Appendix _____ , community maps—Appendix _____ .

5.2 EPIP-_____ , Duties of the Emergency Manager

5.3 EPIP-_____ , Duties of the Field Incident Commander

5.4 EPIP-_____ , Emergency Notification

5.5 [Applicable] process safety standard

5.6 EPA-520/1-75-001, *Manual of Protective Action Guides and Protective Actions for Nuclear Incidents,* U.S. Environmental Protection Agency, September 1975 (revised June 1980).

6.0 Attachments

6.1 Figure 8.9, EPIP-_____-__ , Emergency Classification System

INCIDENT REPORTING SYSTEM (IRS) FORM
Page 1 of 1

Message #:____

1) COMPANY NAME, FACILITY, INCIDENT LOCATION and BRIEF DESCRIPTION of EVENT:

_____

_____

_____

_____

_____

_____

_____

2) STATUS: Actual Event _____
            Drill   _____
            Terminated _____

3) CLASSIFICATION:

   (IRE) ____
   (UE) ____
   (A)   ____
   (SAE) ____
   (GE) ____

4) TIME DECLARED:_____(a.m./p.m.)

5) INCIDENT INFORMATION:
Hazardous Material Involved (Yes) (No)
Trade/Common Name:_____
_____
Chemical Name:_____

CLOSE OUT WITH LOG ENTRY

INCIDENT

INCIDENT CLASSIFIABLE — NO → ABNORMAL OPERATING PROCEDURES → CLOSEOUT — N

YES

CLOSEOUT — YES → END

INTERNALLY REPORTABLE EVENT | UNUSUAL EVENT | ALERT | SITE AREA EMERGENCY | GENERAL EMERGENCY

Activate EMRO   (EC) ____
Call Agencies   (EC) ____

EPA EXTREMELY HAZARDOUS SUBSTANCE LIST (Yes) (No)
PROTECTIVE ACTION RECOMMENDATION:(Evacuate) (Shelter) (Restrict Foodstuffs)(See DOT Emergency Response Guidebook)
HEALTH RISK/MEDICAL ADVICE: (Refer to MSDS)(See DOT Emergency Response Guidebook)
FATALITIES: (Yes) (No) Number:_____   INJURIES: (Yes) (No) Number:_____

TYPE OF RELEASE: (Gas) (Vapor) (Liquid) RELEASE MEDIUM: (Air) (Land) (Water) ESTIMATED QUANTITY:_____(Gal./Lb.

RELEASE TO ENVIRONMENT: (None) (Potential) (Occuring) (Terminated)

WIND DIRECTION (From): A: North B: Northeast C: Northwest D: South E: Southeast F: Southwest G: West H: East

AGENCIES NOTIFIED: REMARKS:_____
Facility EMRO:____ LEPC:____ MUTUAL AID :____   _____
Fire Dept.   :____ SERC:____ OTHER(list):____   _____
Police Dept. :____ NRC :____ _____

Initial Call:_____(Time) Print Name:_____ Title:_____

Follow-up Call:_____(Mins) Signature:_____ Date:_____

Figure 8.9 IRS form.

Response Facilities Considerations

This chapter will provide an overview of various considerations for *response facilities,* defined as any location designated and/or set aside for emergency operations. Criteria for response facilities include habitability factors, space allocation, and ability to support emergency operations.

Chapter organizer: What this chapter is about

- What are the considerations for a response facility? Communications interface is probably one of the most important considerations when response facilities are being set up. Other factors to consider are meeting rooms, rooms or space for external agencies, and meeting the requirements for relocation of critical operations.

    You must identify the facilities that can be set aside or easily converted for use by the emergency management/response organization (EMRO). Having viable facilities designated for use will greatly aid the transition from normal operations to emergency operations.

- What are the response facility considerations for spill situations, and how do they differ from fixed facility considerations? Because of the unpredictable nature of spills, with location being one of the key factors, it is difficult to identify and set aside facilities for response. Although it is difficult, it is not impossible. By identifying minimum acceptable standards for facility resources and planning for these contingencies, spill response management can be much more effective.

Response Facilities

Some basic considerations apply with regard to response facilities regardless of the size of the operation, type of operation, or location (corporate or field):

- *Basic organizational needs.* The basic organizational needs center on communications, shelter, decision-making support, and administrative support.

- *Basic operational needs.* How will the organization use the facilities or area? Is it a hardened site (buildings, structures)? Is it a mobile site (vans, etc.)? Is it an open site (staging area, etc.)? What types of operations are to be undertaken at the location?

- *Basic logistical considerations.* Once you have established the organizational and operational functions which the response facilities must meet, you need to address the logistical considerations. What kind of telecommunication capabilities will you require? What type of supplies will be stored for use? How long will it take to convert from normal to emergency operation? How long will the facility be used?

To begin the detailed consideration of response facilities, let's start with the incident scene and work our way back. The first response facility you will have to consider is the one at the incident scene. Generally speaking, this will be the easiest of all considerations. In order to begin and end your deliberations, simply ask, "Where will the first responder/person who discovers the incident be standing in relation to the incident?" The answer not only identifies your considerations for this initial response facility, but also tells you the type of equipment and staffing needs that you will have to address.

As you will have summarized, there is little you can do to plan for the initial near-scene response facility. However, once the response has begun, your options increase dramatically. For our purposes, however, we confine this discussion to the following areas:

Fixed facility: Mobile command center

Incident support center

Emergency operations center

Staging areas

Media center

Corporate location: Communications/notification center

Business unit/operating sector department

Executive management team

Crisis management organization

Media center

Spill scene: Command center

Staging areas

Media center

Canteen, rest areas

Decontamination areas

Demobilization areas

Fixed Facility

The considerations for all fixed facilities, regardless of size, are essentially the same. A careful analysis should be made of the development of facilities as stated in your plan. The first emergency facility we will discuss is the mobile command center. In essence, the first responding individual will be your mobile command center. For our purposes, however, we will discuss the equipping of a vehicle that can be used near the incident scene as a central point for information gathering, processing, and decision making. Several considerations need to be addressed in choosing the appropriate mobile command center. A good suggestion is to talk to the fire chief in your community. The fire chief should be quite happy to show you his or her command center. Another consideration concerns who will reside within the confines of the mobile command center? Do not be hasty with your answer. Remember, it might well have to accommodate external agencies and other representatives. A good rule of thumb is to plan for the following minimum staffing:

- On-scene incident commander (field incident commander)
- Assistant incident commander
- Communicator/driver
- Staff assistant/driver
- External agency and agency representative (Allocate two spaces—*external* means anyone not normally assigned a primary function in the mobile command center.)

Now that you have some concept of staffing, we need to consider communications hardware and support equipment (personal protective equipment, emergency response). Communications hardware is simple. Get the best you can, at the most reasonable price and within the constraints of your capabilities to use it. Radios, computers, cellular phones, pagers, hard-wired telephones, facsimile—all should be considered. Remember, in an incident your first line of communication will probably become overloaded, overworked, or overwhelmed. Backup communication systems are essential. Look at the local telephone services for assistance in establishing your options.

Other equipment considerations will depend on your circumstances. Do you need hazardous materials response equipment? Just remember, whatever equipment you procure, ensure that your personnel have been trained in its proper use and that appropriate documentation exists to verify the status of the equipment and the ability of the personnel to use it.

Command center considerations

The selection of a command center is critical. Will it be a dedicated facility? Will it be a temporary location, such as a hotel, warehouse, or other similar structure? First and foremost, the facility you choose as your command center should have the following characteristics:

- It must be large enough to accommodate your staff and those of external response organizations such as regulatory agencies and support organizations.
- It must be habitable for the duration of the incident or, at least must provide sufficient personal protection to ensure the safety of personnel assigned to work in the facility. This may mean stocks of personal protective clothing; special heating, ventilation, and cooling systems; and other protective barriers.
- It must have sufficient communications hardware capability to be effective as a command center.
- It must be capable of being subdivided to accommodate different working groups.
- It must be capable of being secure. That is, there is restricted access (egress and ingress).

Figure 9.1 shows an example of a command center layout. Figures 9.2–9.5 depict status boards for tracking emergency operations and other support materials for the command center and/or emergency response facilities.

The command post's primary function is to provide an area capable of housing those elements (emergency management organization) that support field operations (emergency response organization). In this aspect, the command post serves a clearinghouse function.

With the clearinghouse function in mind, you should consider the following items when preparing your command center:

- Status boards
    Incident status
    Sequence-of-events summary

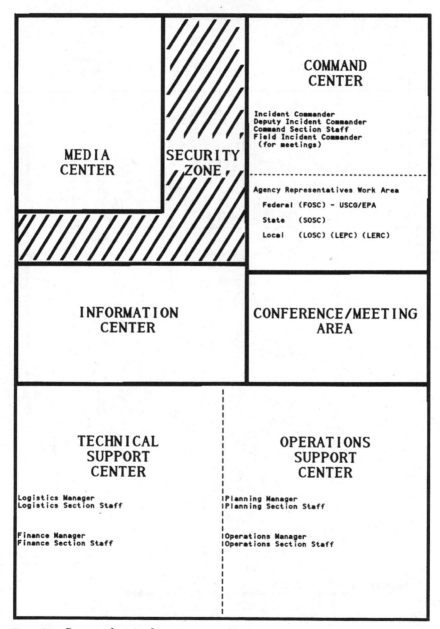

Figure 9.1   Command center layout.

OPERATIONAL PARAMETERS

PARAMETERS AS NEEDED	TIME					

Figure 9.2 Operational parameters.

INCIDENT RESPONSE WORKSHEET

INFORMATION	ACTION	FEEDBACK
IDENTIFY:		
* INCIDENT INFORMATION		

FACILITY STATUS
    GEOGRAPHIC AREA/LOCATION
    COMMODITY, QUANTITY (RQ),
    VOLUME & TOXICITY		

* INCIDENT ASSESSMENT		

SAFETY
    INJURY/FATALITY
    WHAT IS AT RISK
    ENVIRONMENTAL IMPACTS		

* SPECIAL CONCERNS		

METEOROLOGICAL CONDITIONS/
    CONSIDERATIONS
    POPULATIONS-AT-RISK		

* DECISIONS		
RESPONSE CAPABILITY/ACTIONS		
PROTECT:		
* PRECAUTIONS		
APPROPRIATE PERSONAL PROTECTIVE EQUIPMENT AVAILABLE		
* PROTECTIVE ACTION DECISION-MAKING		

ISOLATE AREA
    CONTROL SOURCE
    EVACUATION
    SHELTER
    OFFSITE PROTECTIVE ACTIONS		

ALERT:		
* DEFENSIVE RESPONSE ACTIONS		

SOUND ALARMS
    PROVIDE INSTRUCTIONS
    MOVE PEOPLE AWAY FROM SCENE
    ESTABLISH PERIMETER
    CONTROL ACCESS ROUTES		

* OFFENSIVE RESPONSE ACTIONS
    ERO ACTIVATED
    EMO ACTIVATED
    GO TEAM/CORPORATE SUPPORT
    OTHER SUPPORT		

COMMUNICATE:		
* INITIAL NOTIFICATIONS		

PERSONNEL IN IMMINENT DANGER
    REQUIRED INTERNAL NOTIFICATIONS
    REQUIRED EXTERNAL NOTIFICATIONS		

* FOLLOW-UP ACTIONS		

ADDITIONAL ASSISTANCE NEEDED
    SITUATION UPDATE
    ASSESS FACILITY/PERSONNEL
    STATUS
    ACTION/OPEN ITEMS
    CRITIQUE OF ACTIONS
    NEXT MEETING SCHEDULED (TIME)		

Figure 9.3 Incident response worksheet.

Key-parameter status (nonaffected operations)

Resource allocation

Emergency response organization incident objectives

Emergency management organization incident objectives

Field operations resources summary

Human resources information status

INCIDENT STATUS

INCIDENT NAME: _____

DATE: ___/___/___ TIME: _____ (latest update)

EMERGENCY CLASSIFICATION: DATE   TIME

Level 1   ____   ____

Level 2   ____   ____

Level 3   ____   ____

Level 4   ____   ____

PROGNOSIS: DATE   TIME

Stable   ____   ____

Escalating   ____   ____

De-Escalating   ____   ____

Terminating   ____   ____

PROTECTIVE ACTIONS:

Onsite:

Evacuation ____

Shelter   ____

PPE   ____

Offsite:

Evacuation ____

Shelter   ____

Monitoring ____

EMERGENCY PLANNING ZONE:

Sectors Affected ____

Distance   ____

DESCRIPTION OF EVENT: _____

_____

_____

_____

EMERGENCY ACTIONS UNDERWAY:

Notification:

Fire ____   National Response Center ____   Other (List) ____

Police ____   SERC ____

Contractors ____   LEPC ____

OPERATIONS: _____

_____

_____

METEOROLOGICAL DATA:

Weather _____   Wind Speed / Wind Direction ____

Temperature ____ (Fo)

Forecast next 24 hrs. ____   Stability Class ____

Figure 9.4 Incident status sheet.

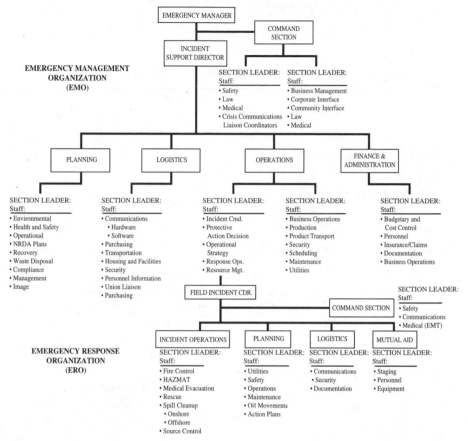

Figure 9.5 Emergency management organization.

Weather data

Media activities summaries

Notification status

Emergency planning zone

Maps

Charts

Aerial photographs

Command center

Evacuation flow diagram

■ Communications

Telephone

Cellular telephone

Facsimile

Computer
Satellite dish
Radio—handheld and commercial
Optional switchgear configurations
Video, television

- Accommodations
  Sleeping area
  Rest room, showers
  Canteen, kitchen
  Briefing room
  Quiet room, library
  Storage, supply
  Information center

You will also want to consider the habitability of the command post during an incident. Are you going to have to stay in the command post during severe weather? Under conditions requiring special protective considerations, such as toxic atmospheres or radioactive atmospheres?

Habitability is an important consideration and should not be taken lightly or given such a low priority that it is overlooked, as often happens. You would be surprised at the dramatic differences in level of productivity that can be achieved by having an emergency facility with adequate habitability considerations factored in. Several things should be considered:

- Working space
- Sound-deadening features
- Interior color scheme
- Exterior color scheme
- Equipment (desks, chairs, etc.)
- Ergonomic features
- Electrical outlets
- Lighting
- Heating, ventilation, and air conditioning (HVAC)
- Rest rooms

You will also need an adequate supply of preprinted forms and other supporting materials. You may wish to evaluate the following supplies:

Paper (lined, engineering, graphics, computer)	Cassette tape recorders, tapes
	Flip charts, flip chart paper
Pencils	Camera, film (35-mm and Polaroid)
Pens	Markers (permanent/erasable)
Stenopads	Staples
Forms (emergency)	Tacks
Forms (normal)	Pushpins
Maps	Tape (masking, packing, Scotch)
Telephone directories (in-house, commercial)	Rulers (of varying length)

As you can see, the list can be quite extensive. I am sure you will be able to add to this sample quite easily.

As you stock the emergency facilities, an area of consideration often overlooked, especially when the emergency facility is any distance from the incident scene or is to be staffed by more management organization personnel, is *personal protective equipment* (*PPE*). You should carefully analyze the need for PPE at each emergency facility. You may want to have a supply of the following personal protective equipment:

Safety glasses, side shields	Respirators
Helmets	Level A, B, C, and D protective clothing
Hearing protection	Gloves
Particulate masks	Boots (overshoes, safety shoes)
Fire-retardant clothing	Foul weather gear (seasonal)

As with the list of supplies, this list can grow dramatically. One important consideration, however, is to have an adequate supply on hand for your personnel and plenty of extras for any outside agency personnel who may be invited (or uninvited) into your emergency facility. This will include government, local response resources, executives, members of the media, etc.

Emergency Facilities at Nonfixed Site

Many companies operate over vast areas. A good example is the pipeline industry or the transportation and shipping industry. Predicting the exact location of an incident for these industries is nearly impossible. However, you can identify potential locations that could be used as emergency facilities for a long-term incident.

It is relatively easy to identify locations in the proximity of the right-of-way, along transportation routes, shipping lanes, ports, airports, and terminals. Signing up these facilities for adequacy as an emergency facility takes a little more time. These considerations pertain:

- Hotels
- Community colleges
- Auditoriums
- Meeting halls
- Churches
- Schools
- Salvation Army, Red Cross facilities
- Civil defense centers
- Industrial warehouses
- Office buildings
- Utility (gas, electric, telephone, etc.) facilities

In short, choose any location that will give you adequate space and that can be quickly converted for emergency use. I highly recommend that once you have identified these facilities, you approach the owners, managers, etc., and execute a letter of agreement for use of the facility during an incident. This may mean, say in the case of a hotel, that the hotel management will have to cancel meetings, relocate guests, and in general suspend its normal operations. Also make sure that the designated facility managers fully understand what is being asked of them.

As for equipment and the general setup and design, all the considerations for fixed facilities apply. However, you will be faced with higher costs, greater dependence on your logistics and finance sections for procurement (remember the telephone lines are not dedicated, as at a fixed facility) of support equipment. If faced with this situation, you will also want to prepare prepacked inventories of all consumables and PPE that may be needed for your response efforts.

Choosing an adequate emergency facility—whether it is a mobile command center, emergency operations center, command post, staging, or other support facility—is an important part of the planning process. People involved in emergency management/response activities are under a great deal of stress. Having a facility that is comfortable can reduce some of the stress. You will be surprised to see how small comforts can make a big difference in response operations.

The following section provides examples of the plan and emergency plan implementing procedures for emergency facilities.

Sample

EMERGENCY PLAN
IMPLEMENTING PROCEDURES

ACTIVATION OF THE
EMERGENCY OPERATIONS
CENTER
EPIP - __
REVISION __
[DATE]

SUBMITTED BY: _____ DATE: _____

APPROVED BY: _____ DATE: _____

Sample

1.0 Purpose

This procedure provides guidance and instructions for the activation of the *emergency operations center* (EOC).

2.0 Applicability

This procedure may be initiated following the declaration of an emergency classified as level 1—unusual event, or higher, at the discretion of the on-call emergency manager (OEM) and/or FIC. This procedure applies to all members of the emergency management organization.

This procedure becomes effective when issued.

3.0 Definitions

3.1 Emergency operations center

The EOC is the emergency facility from which the management of the overall [COMPANY] response, including coordination with federal, state, and local officials, will occur. Coordination of off-site support and assistance will also occur at the EOC. At the [LOCATION], the EOC is found [LOCATION].

4.0 Instructions

4.1 Initial actions

4.1.1 The incident support director (ISD), as part of assuming his or her responsibilities during a crisis, will verify that the EOC can perform the following functions at a minimum:

- Emergency management
- Administrative and communications support
- Safety, environmental, and health support
- Operations support

4.1.2 Facility activation steps:

- Call status board plotter and EOC assistant, if needed, for administrative support functions.

- Activate communication and video equipment.

- Contact the security and communications coordinator to dispatch a radio operator to the EOC, if one is needed.

Note: The first member of the emergency management organization to arrive at the EOC should activate the video recorder, but the ISD should assess the need for administrative staffing.

4.2 Minimum staffing requirements

The minimum staffing requirements for activation of the EOC and conference room are as follows:

- Management representative
- Operations support representative
- Safety and industrial hygiene representative
- Security representative
- Public affairs representative
- Environmental controls representative

Note: Each of the above indicates the primary position holder or qualified alternate.

4.3 Alternate EOCs

In the event that the primary emergency operations center is unavailable or must be evacuated, there are alternate locations from which emergency management operations may be conducted. The first alternate location is at [LOCATION], and the second is at [LOCATION]. A brief description of each, with access instructions, is provided below:

4.3.1 First alternate location. Insert your description.

4.3.2 Second alternate. Insert your description.

4.4 Subsequent actions

4.4.1 In the event of protracted emergency operations, the emergency manager may direct EOC staff to call for relief by their alternates, if necessary to maintain 24-hour operations capability.

4.4.2 Operation of the EOC will continue until such time as the emergency manager or the recovery manager directs its deactivation.

4.4.3 All emergency forms, checklists, or other written materials are to be saved, routed to the [POSITION TITLE], and subsequently filed in the emergency response and recovery activities record binder in the EOC.

5.0 References

5.1 All-hazards emergency management plan, emergency facilities and equipment section

5.2 EPIP-_____, Duties of the Emergency Manager

5.3 EPIP-_____, Duties of the Emergency Management/Response Organization during Emergencies

5.4 EPIP-_____, Access Control during Emergencies

5.5 EPIP-_____, Emergency Notification

5.6 EPIP-_____, Emergency Communications

6.0 Attachments

There are none.

Sample
Status Boards

Incident Operations Worksheet

Section: _____   Emergency Title: _____   Date: _____

Objective # and Description	Support Provided To Accomplish	Support Required To Accomplish	Est. Time To Complete(hrs)

214

INCIDENT OPERATIONS
DEBRIEF WORKSHEET

SECTION: _____   EMERGENCY TITLE: _____

VALUE ADDED PERFORMANCE: Things We Did Well

1. _____

2. _____

3. _____

PERFORMANCE IMPROVEMENT AREAS: Things We Need to Improve

1. _____

2. _____

3. _____

SUCCESS FACTORS: ASSISTANCE FROM OTHER SECTION(s)

1. _____

2. _____

3. _____

10

Public Information
Considerations

Establishing a practical public information program to respond effectively during an incident is an essential part of any emergency management system. An effective public information component offers a rare opportunity to illustrate your company's ability to handle the demands of an incident, especially with respect to community concerns. It is often referred to as the *crisis communication program,* but I prefer *public information program* because the former term seems to indicate that the only time you plan on talking to the community, media, employees, etc., is when there is an emergency or crisis. This perspective seems to beget a siege mentality. "Don't tell them anything!" is the old way of doing business. Today, you and your company need to be sure that your message is heard loud and clear and that the facts, as you know them, are effectively communicated through the media to your audience—the public and your employees. This chapter will provide an overview of various public information considerations. But first we offer a definition, in the context of the all-hazards emergency management system:

> The *public information* component of your system is designed to present incident-related information to the general public, including the media. The public information component forms a critical link with external audiences. This includes, but is not limited to, employees not directly involved in the incident, media management, rumor control, and outreach programs.

Public information considerations should reflect the policies of the company. Who should talk to the media as your spokesperson? What information will be released to the public? And how will you package that information?

Chapter organizer: What this chapter is about

What are the public information considerations for the emergency management/response organization (EMRO)? The public information policy and associated program define how you are to communicate with external and internal groups. It must ensure that all representative elements adhere to the policy and effectively implement the program. You must define the structure, functions, and operations for public information to work effectively throughout the organization. This is critical, as the field locations are generally your initial point of contact with external audiences.

Information: What the Public Wants

Today, more than ever before, effective communication plays an integral role in successful emergency response operations. Furthermore, the opportunities for communicating are vast. There are approximately 1200 television stations, 8400 radio stations, 1800 daily newspapers, 8500 weekly newspapers, and more than 12,500 magazines.

Getting information about an incident involving your company on the air or into print is not difficult. However, getting your message across to the right audience can be extremely difficult. Therefore, you must be a skilled communicator and deliver a message that is simple, attention-getting, and memorable. It is essential that your emergency management plan address the issue of public information. It is even more important that you address the focus of your public information program prior to an incident.

Your primary objective in the plan is to define the right message, identify audiences, and build an ongoing dialogue with them. Before you can deliver an effective message during a crisis, it is essential to complete the following steps:

- Identify and analyze your target audiences.
- Set your communications objectives.
- Develop your messages (prescripted statements).

In almost every instance where a company has successfully responded to a crisis situation, there is a common link. That link is *effective management/response operations*. Response operations save lives and property. Management operations ensure that the public, media, government agencies, and other interested audiences understand what is going on and that their concerns are being addressed. Public perception of your company's reaction to a crisis is as important as effectively responding and mitigating the incident.

Eight principles provide a basis for successful public information planning and response:

1. Accept responsibility.
2. Look like you care and mean it.
3. Do not worry about being sued.
4. Do the right thing.
5. Think in terms of broad defense.
6. Rely on research.
7. Beware of experts.
8. Understand that there is no "magic bullet."

If you keep these eight principles in mind, the public information portion of your plan and supporting materials should facilitate effective communications.

In my previous book, *It Can't Happen Here: All Hazards Crisis Management Planning,* I devoted a full chapter to the preparation of crisis communication materials. There are many volumes which speak in great detail on this subject. And you can—and your company probably does—find firms that specialize in public relations issues. As such, I will attempt not to belabor the issue of public information planning. Rather, I have provided some simple working guidelines, which you can use to create your own program or to evaluate your current program.

Prior to the Interview

Preparation, preparation, preparation! You must make the most out of every opportunity to communicate with external audiences during an incident. If you do not, the media will make the most out of every opportunity to ravage your image and your company's credibility.

Prior to your interview, you should be able to feel comfortable addressing the eight principles mentioned earlier. If you are not, contact one of your public affairs staff for advice and to talk about potential issues. "What if," you say, "I have no public affairs staff? What can I do?" Charles Webster, a colleague, works with many companies, preparing their personnel to deal with public information issues. In his brochure "Taking Control of Crisis Interviews," he outlines some steps he considers critical. I have modified them, condensing some and adding my own points on others. The following steps may be helpful!

1. Get the facts!

2. Develop a list of issues, and discuss them with key personnel.

3. Develop a list of questions you would ask, if you were a reporter.

4. Prepare your central message. This may comprise two or three points. Be sure you can back them up with facts. Have a clippings service tape the coverage of your incident.

5. Prepare, prepare, prepare. Have someone question you, and then review your answers.

6. Make your presentation brief, including key points and the central facts. Do not volunteer information!

7. Find out who else is being interviewed, consider their views, and be ready to respond.

8. Ask how the interview will be used: On its own? Part of a series? Local news? National news? International news? Documentary?

9. Eliminate complex terms, jargon, and acronyms. Make your answers simple.

10. Appearance is everything. How you are perceived is critical. Depending on your location, you should choose carefully how you will dress. Above all, do not present yourself as unapproachable to your audience. Do not wear colors that clash. And stay away from striped shirts and white shirts.

11. If possible, choose the setting for the meeting—know your ground.

12. Do not hang around after the interview.

13. Do not ever say anything to a member of the media *off the record*. (1) It is never off the record. (2) If you cannot tell it to your primary audience, it probably is best left unsaid.

14. Avoid anything that may impair your ability to think clearly, react quickly, or in general affect your alertness.

During the Interview

You have prepared, and now the moment of truth is upon you. What should you do? Prepare, prepare, prepare! Consider the following:

1. Accept responsibility. Be honest. A half-truth is one-half lie. Credibility is the key.

2. Think positively. Think in the present tense. Talk about what you are doing to deal with the incident.

3. Listen carefully. Do not be afraid to challenge the question or correct inconsistencies.

4. Each answer will be a story within itself. Make your points first, then seek to defend them.

5. Do not be lulled into a false sense of security. Remember, nothing is off the record.

6. Be prepared to refocus questions posed to you to your central points. Do not let the media get you off track or into a lengthy debate. Do not speculate.

7. Talk to the audience, not the camera. Your body speaks volumes. Body language can easily make you appear distrustful.

8. Do not be afraid to say, "I don't know." However, if you tell someone you'll find out, do and do it as fast as you can. Do not be afraid to have someone ask the question again.

9. Answer each question as if it were the first one. Reference to an earlier answer can make you appear uninterested, uncaring, or uninvolved.

10. Control your mouth. Stop speaking when you have finished your answer. Do not try to talk yourself out of a predicament—you will only get confused and look as if you are being less than truthful.

11. Stay away from wall building. Statements like "No comment" make you appear uncooperative, that you are hiding facts.

12. Document your conference. Record it, videotape it, or in some way ensure it is in your records. Make this a standing policy.

After the Interview

As mentioned earlier, when the interview is over, leave. You have work to do! Besides, the media will attempt to continue, informally, the interview process! You should always seek to correct any factual mistakes made by the media. Finally, review the tapes, recordings, etc., and contact your clippings service to get as much documentation as possible to go over and critique yourself with.

My colleague Charles Webster writes in his brochure "Taking Control of Crisis Interviews" about three steps to take control of the interview:

> Most people believe that reporters hold all the cards during interviews. Most people are wrong. Before commencing any interview, you can and must take control. In the process, you will educate the reporter, influence his or her line of questioning, have an opportunity to correct misinformation and secure agreement that you don't have to guess. At the

same time, you will calm down and lay the groundwork for a successful interview. Here's how:

Before Starting the Interview:

Step 1: Tell the reporter what you know about the situation. The reporter will appreciate your sharing the facts. You are likely the best source of information, and, by sharing, you have an opportunity to plant facts that can come back to you as interview questions.

Step 2: Ask the reporter what he/she has heard or wants to talk about. Reporters covering crisis events often have incorrect information masquerading as facts. After sharing facts, it is appropriate to ask what the reporter knows and wants to discuss. You can correct facts and gather useful intelligence about the likely course of questioning. Hearing the concerns of a reporter before the interview will allow you to formulate responses in advance of questions.

Step 3: Secure verbal agreement that you don't have to guess. Crisis interviews are often conducted long before all the facts are known. Tell the reporter there are some things that you don't know. Get the reporter to agree that you will stick to the facts. You might say, "If I know the answer I will tell you, but I think you will agree that it doesn't make sense for me to guess....Is that fair? Once the reporter agrees, you have a binding contract that you don't have to guess or speculate during the interview. You now control the information process.

Conclusion

Few crises will be as dramatic as Three Mile Island or the *Valdez*... unless it is your own. When your crisis occurs, the hardest part of dealing with it can involve answering the public call for information—a call personified by a television correspondent or newspaper reporter who shows up at your doorstep or on your telephone line to get the story. How well you respond depends on how well you have prepared.

Sample

All-Hazards Emergency Management Plan
Section __: Public Information

Sample

Guidelines

The purpose of this section is to provide an overview of the emergency management/response organization's responsibilities and managing actions and dealing with relations to the various publics. Specific procedures, guidelines, and policies have been established to support the general plan. (*Publics* include all employees, the community in which we operate, the general public, government agencies, and the media.)

Your guidelines should address the following:

- Employee notification
- Community notification
- Media notification
- Rumor control
- Press, news release statement information
- Public information
- Persons authorized to speak for the company

Media kits

The purpose of the media kit is to provide general assistance in responding to the media during an emergency. It is *not* intended to be used as a replacement for interaction and utilization of [RESPONSIBLE DEPARTMENT] services.

This media kit should be designed to provide you with basic information to be used in conjunction with your interview. The kit should provide important telephone numbers and some basic written materials on your facility and/or operational area to help you (1) in the earliest stages of an emergency and (2) in lieu of an available [RESPONSIBLE DEPARTMENT] representative.

Please note that in the event that the facility's [RESPONSIBLE DEPARTMENT] is *not* available, the first action should be to contact someone at the [LOCATION] office. That person will be able to provide you with valuable guidance and assistance in handling the press during an emergency. Your [RESPONSIBLE DEPARTMENT] coordinator and adviser will otherwise be on site to assist you as needed.

Example of a Preliminary News Release

LOCATION (date) — [COMPANY] EMRO is currently responding to an emergency at our _____ . The call came in around _____ a.m./p.m. today. At this time, our EMRO is on the scene and addressing the situation. We will have more information once we get word from our personnel at the scene.

We do not have any information about injuries at this point in time, but we will pass along any relevant information as it becomes available.

If you do have information on injuries and fatalities, you can inform the media, using general terms (no names, etc.).

[COMPANY] does have an emergency management plan, and we are implementing that plan at this time. We have notified local police about the incident and will keep them informed as the situation develops.

The _____ (facility/unit) makes _____

(product), which is used _____

_____

_____ .

Media Relations Guide

It is [COMPANY'S] policy to cooperate with the media in an emergency.

In an emergency situation, you may be the first contact a reporter has with [COMPANY].

Plan on the media showing up at the scene or calling your office for details of the emergency.

Remember, in the first hours of an emergency, the reporters want the who, what, where, when, why, and how of the story. They are not out to make [COMPANY] look bad. As you assess the emergency from an operational point of view, prepare some key points about the situation that you want to make with reporters when they show up.

Quickly prepare for the interview. Have your media relations objectives ready. Your media relations objectives concern

- The actions you are taking to contain the emergency
- Whether the situation is a danger to the community
- Information about the emergency

Stay cool. You're the expert.

Hints for the interview

Talk to the real audience. The real audience is the people at home, not the reporters or the camera crew.

Remember the editorial process. The reporter is looking for a 20-second sound bite containing our actions and concern about the incident.

Refer to your media relations objectives at every opportunity.

State the most important facts first. State who, what, where, when, why, and how. Speak directly and concisely.

If you don't know, say you don't know. Do not try to snow the reporter. The reporter will have greater respect for you (and the company) if you don't waste time trying to dance around an issue ("I don't know...but as soon as I do, I'll get back to you."). Then do.

Never say, "No comment." The reporter will think you are trying to hide something. If you cannot discuss something because it involves matters of a confidential nature, or you if don't know, say so.

Do not speculate or guess. Reporters will understand that in the early moments of an emergency not all the facts are known.

Be responsive, but maintain control. Do not lose your cool with reporters if they seem uninformed or get a little pushy. They are trying to obtain information to file a credible story. Help them.

Do not release names. Do not give out the names of injured personnel until their families have been notified. Explain that to the reporters. They will understand.

Never lie. Be honest and factual. Tell the reporters where they can safely get pictures or a videotape of the scene. *If it is safe,* show them what you are doing to contain the emergency, and *let them take photographs or videotapes* of your actions.

Short answers are better than long ones. They are most easily understood and more likely to be used unedited.

Keep it simple. Do not be technical. Remember, you are talking to people who do not share your knowledge of the industry. Do not use jargon or acronyms.

Look at the reporters, not the camera. Assume that TV cameras and microphones are always on...and possibly recording your words, actions, and expressions.

Be serious. Any attempt at humor will fail with some readers, viewers, or listeners and may embarrass you and the company.

EMERGENCY PLAN
IMPLEMENTING PROCEDURE

RELEASE OF EMERGENCY
INFORMATION TO THE PUBLIC
EPIP - __
REVISION __
[DATE]

SUBMITTED BY: _____ DATE: _____

APPROVED BY: _____ DATE: _____

1.0 Purpose

This procedure describes corporate policy and provides guidance regarding the release of information about an incident to the public.

2.0 Applicability

This procedure applies to all [COMPANY] personnel with a role in the response to an emergency incident.

3.0 Definitions

There are none.

4.0 Instructions

4.1 Public information

[COMPANY'S] objective is to see that all reports of any emergency are factual and represent the company's position fairly and accurately. Cooperation with news media representatives is the most reliable guarantee that this objective will be met.

4.1.1 Personnel authorized to speak to the media

Personnel authorized to speak to the media in a terminal emergency shall be restricted to [RESPONSIBLE PERSON'S TITLE].

For transportation incidents the [RESPONSIBLE PERSON'S TITLE] or designee is authorized to be [COMPANY'S] sole on-scene spokesperson. All other personnel at the site of the incident will respond to reporters' questions by referring them to the current spokesperson.

Where practicable, designate (or suggest to off-site response agencies that they designate) a news center/media briefing area to ensure safety of the media and to provide a centralized point for the dissemination of press releases.

4.1.2 Spokesperson's attitude

Show [COMPANY'S] ability and willingness to respond to the incident.

Be courteous and responsive. Do not lose your temper.

Speak clearly and deliberately.

All-Hazards	Issue Date	Procedure No.
Emergency Plan Manual	_/_/_	EPIP-___

Release of Information	Rev. Date	Revision No.
to the Public	_/_/_	0
		Page __ of __ Pages

4.1.3 Release guidelines

Release only verified information to the media.

Be positive of the facts. If you do not know the answer to a question, say so. An inaccurate or misleading answer is worse than no answer at all. Indicate that you will try to get an answer and get back to them. Remember to follow through on all such promises.

Reduce speculation about future effects of the incident or spill.

Reassure the public that appropriate corrective actions are being taken.

All statements to the news media shall be limited to known facts that are not in dispute. Facts will usually include

- Location, time, date of incident
- Type of incident
- Steps that have been taken to contain, control, or handle the emergency
- Emergency response personnel who have been called to the scene
- Current emergency classification. Initially, the full extent of the incident may not be known. Explain that people will be advised if and when the classification is changed due to new information.
- The state and federal agencies that have been informed

Do not release any information that may violate an individual's privacy. Names of injured individuals and/or fatalities should not be released, although the name of the hospital where the injured or fatalities have been taken may be given if appropriate.

4.2 Precautions

All statements to the news media shall be limited to known facts that are not in dispute.

No statement regarding any incident will be made by any company employee, except those authorized as described above.

As soon as possible after classification of incident conditions into one of five emergency groups as prescribed in EPIP-____,

All-Hazards	Issue Date	Procedure No.
Emergency Plan Manual	_/_/_	EPIP-___

Release of Information	Rev. Date	Revision No.
to the Public	_/_/_	0
		Page __ of __ Pages

ensure that the appropriate local and state agencies are notified, as required in accordance with EPIP-____. Public alerting and notification within the ____ emergency planning zone (EPZ) will be accomplished through ____ .

Whenever possible, direct reporters' inquiries to public safety agency personnel who are on the scene.

As soon as possible, relay information concerning the incident to the local [RESPONSIBLE DEPARTMENT] representative who will then handle all media inquiries in the aftermath of the incident.

No statements will be made regarding the following. All such speculative issues shall be addressed only by [COMPANY] [RESPONSIBLE DEPARTMENT].

- Estimates of amounts of released materials
- Estimates on resumption of normal operations
- Circumstances that might have led to the incident
- Possible off-site effects
- Estimates of dollar value of losses
- Liability for the incident
- Estimates of how long it will take to clean up
- Appropriateness of government or other agency's response efforts.

5.0 References

Emergency management plan, section ____ , appendices ____ , ____ .

6.0 Attachments

Public information checklist.

Public Information Checklist

Location:_____

Time of incident: _____ Date of incident: _____

Type of incident: _____

Steps [COMPANY] has taken to contain, control, or handle the incident.

_____

_____

_____

_____

Emergency organization personnel who have been called to the scene ([COMPANY], other).

_____

_____

_____

The current emergency classification. Initially, the full extent of the incident may not be known. Explain that people will be advised if and when the classification is changed due to new information. _____

_____

The state and federal agencies that have been informed: _____

_____

11

Postincident Operations Considerations

Postincident operations are an integral part of the planning process. Postincident operations planning considerations are often overlooked when the basic plan is being developed. You cannot afford to overlook any postincident planning issues and still expect to ensure that your plan can be adequately executed.

In the context of the all-hazards emergency management system, *postincident operations* are all operations designed to support the termination, reentry, recovery, and humanitarian assistance requirements arising from an incident. This may include, but is not limited to, establishing a recovery organization, addressing the transition of the management/response system structure to an organization focused on reestablishing fundamental business operations.

Chapter organizer: What this chapter is about

What are postincident operations considerations? Key to the organization of an effective all-hazards emergency management system is the structure of a recovery organization representing key support elements. Within this context, you must address the composition, functions, and span of control of the recovery organization.

The recovery organization may have to draw upon more external resources and expertise than the emergency management/response organization (EMRO). How the recovery organization and augmentation resources interface is important. A well-defined plan and supporting materials will address this issue.

Dealing effectively with the complexities of a catastrophic incident requires a well-thought-out plan and trained staff able to execute the plan. Of the 11,000+ industrial-related injuries and deaths that occurred between 1980 and 1988, most were the result of small-scale industrial accidents. However, even in accidents involving only a few workers, providing assistance can require a lot of resources. For example, a colleague who was a refinery manager told me of an incident involving one of his employees. The man was involved in an accident and received burns over a substantial portion of his body. The refinery manager activated the humanitarian assistance plan to notify next of kin, provide transportation to the hospital, and offer temporary housing for out-of-town family. He said it took almost twenty of his human resource department staff (augmented) to respond. His closing comment is worth documenting. "Can you imagine how many people it would have taken, if we had a major incident, with more casualties? I'm thankful we had a plan in place to address the issue."

What if? What if the refinery manager in this example did have a major incident and did not have a plan to activate? The sheer magnitude of simply identifying victims and notifying family members could have been a logistical nightmare!

Current Issues in Postincident Planning

Postincident operations begin when the emergency situation has been brought under control. Notice, I did not say mitigated or terminated. *Control* is the operative word. Once you have gotten ahead of the incident, you can begin to refocus your resources and channel them to postincident-related issues. These include

- Assessments, including incident investigation
- Business recovery considerations, including reentry operations and full-scale recovery operations
- Human factors including humanitarian assistance, community outreach, financial aid, and altered work schedules
- Safety, environmental, and health issues including waste management planning, environmental impact assessment (natural resource damage assessment), environmental reporting, safety reporting, and planning for the safety, environmental, and health aspects of the postincident recovery phase

An important consideration, often overlooked in the planning process, is the communication of expectations. As a planner, you need to effectively communicate your expectations to all personnel who may be potentially involved in the response to an incident. You also have to communicate your expectations to the community. Consider for a moment, as you are developing the plan, this question: What would I do if we had a catastrophic incident that had the potential to affect the community? Would I stay at my post? Or would I look to help my family?

If you expect people to perform certain functions, you must communicate your expectations to them. You should also plan to assist them by providing the support necessary to allow them to focus on their emergency role. For example, in a severe weather situation such as a hurricane, you want to ensure that those in response roles have the time and necessary support to secure their family and personal possessions prior to assuming a full-time emergency role. If you do not communicate your expectations, you could be in for a rude awakening.

One area often neglected is human resource considerations. We plan for primary position holders and generally train and drill these personnel. But you should plan for, train, and drill alternate position holders. Qualified alternates are critical to any response and postincident operations. Consider these issues:

- Altered work schedules
- Communicating with and accounting for personnel
- Finding personnel
- Assisting personnel
- Extended benefits
- Leave forgiveness
- Financial assistance
- Temporary housing and other logistical support

Obviously, the above list is not meant to be comprehensive. You have to look at your hazard analysis, capabilities, and basic plan and determine how you intend to address these and other issues.

You may wish to consider the following points as a checklist against which you can judge the adequacy of your plan to address postincident operations. The examples that follow may also assist you in developing this portion of the plan.

- Staffing of the emergency operations center
- First actions
- Resources required, diminished work force
- Expectations of management and employees
- Communicating with employees and the community
- Resumption of normalcy
- Establishing trauma teams

- Planning for the worst
- Ongoing needs of employees
- Recordkeeping, documentation
- Personnel files
- Job descriptions
- Insurance
- Emergency contacts
- Support services
- Psychological counseling
- Basic support needs such as electric generators, building supplies, loans, and cash advances

Conclusion

Postincident operations planning must be part of your all-hazards emergency management system. It is a part that should be periodically validated through drills. There are many management functions in the postincident phase that need to be validated. Such things as incident investigation, preparation for litigation, and collecting and reviewing the data generated during an incident are but a few of the areas we often overlook, but that can have a significant impact, even to the point of creating a new crisis!

Sample

Forms

Sample

EMERGENCY MANAGEMENT/RESPONSE ORGANIZATION (EMRO) DATA

EMRO MEMBER:	PHONE #s:
	OFFICE _____
	HOME _____
BASIC ASSIGNMENT:	EMERGENCY _____
	OTHER _____

ALTERNATE POSITION HOLDERS:	PHONE #s:
	OFFICE _____
	HOME _____
	EMERGENCY _____
	OTHER _____

RESPONSIBILITIES & ASSIGNMENTS:

KEY DATA:

REGULAR JOB TITLE –	IMMEDIATE SUPERVISOR –
DEPARTMENT –	NORMAL HOURS –

AREAS OF EXPERTISE –	ASSISTANTS AND SUBORDINATES –

HOME ADDRESS –	HOME PHONE –
SPOUSE'S NAME –	CHILDREN
YEARS WITH COMPANY –	PRIOR ASSIGNMENTS –
QUALIFICATIONS –	

REVISION DATE _____

PERSONNEL DIRECTORY

FACILITY	Name	Home Address	Office Phone Home Phone
Manager	_____	_____	_____
		_____	_____
Assistant Manager	_____	_____	_____
		_____	_____
Operations Manager	_____	_____	_____
		_____	_____
Safety Manager	_____	_____	_____
		_____	_____
Technical Manager	_____	_____	_____
		_____	_____
Human Resources Manager	_____	_____	_____
		_____	_____
Environmental Manager	_____	_____	_____
		_____	_____
Division Manager	_____	_____	_____
		_____	_____
Marketing Manager	_____	_____	_____
		_____	_____
Public Affairs Manager	_____	_____	_____
		_____	_____

REVISION DATE _____

CLEANUP, CONTRACTOR, CONSULTANT DATA

SERVICE:

COMPANY OR AGENCY & ADDRESS:			PHONE #s:
PERSONNEL –	TITLE –	HOME PHONE –	OFFICE _____
			HOME _____
			EMERGENCY _____
			OTHER _____

BACKUP & ADDRESS:			PHONE #s:
PERSONNEL –	TITLE –	HOME PHONE –	OFFICE _____
			HOME _____
			EMERGENCY _____
			OTHER _____

CAPABILITIES & ASSIGNMENTS:

AREAS OF EXPERTISE:	CRITICAL SUPPLIES & EQUIPMENT:

REVISION DATE _____

PUBLIC OFFICIALS MASTER LIST

EMERGENCY DIAL:		

CITY OF:	CITY #	PHONE #s
Mayor		
Civil Manager		
Police Chief		
Fire Chief		
Health Officer		
Civil Defense/EMA		

COUNTY OF:	COUNTY #	PHONE #s
County Administrator		
County Supervisor		
Sheriff		
Health Officer		
Fire Chief		

STATE OF:	STATE #	PHONE #s
Governor		
Chief of Staff		
Attorney General		
State Senator		
State Representative		
State Police		
Environmental		

FEDERAL:	FEDERAL #	PHONE #s
Congressman		
Con. Administrative Assistant		
Sen. Administrative		
EPA Reg. Director		
Disaster Officer		
Civil Defense/EMA		

For Additional Details, See Public Official's Individual Data Sheet

REVISION DATE _____

PUBLIC OFFICAL INDIVIDUAL DATA

BRANCH OF GOVERNMENT:

OFFICIAL		PHONE #s:
NAME:	OFFICIAL TITLE:	OFFICE _____
		HOME _____
		EMERGENCY _____
		OTHER _____

BACKUP OFFICIAL		PHONE #s:
NAME:	OFFICIAL TITLE:	OFFICE _____
		HOME _____
		EMERGENCY _____
		OTHER _____

STAFF:	POSITION:	PHONE #s:

RESPONSIBLE FOR SERVICE:	PHONE #s:

RESOURCES	EQUIPMENT

RESPONSE UPDATE

INCIDENT:	EMERGENCY CALLED:
	Date: _____ Time: _____

CALLER NAME:	AFFILIATION:	PHONE #s:
		OFFICE _____
RESPONDENT:		HOME _____
		EMERGENCY _____
		OTHER _____

INCIDENT DESCRIPTION: (Known Facts Only)

CURRENT SITUATION:

Injuries: _____ Yes _____ No   If yes, list below   Property Damage: _____ Yes _____ No

NAME:	AFFILIATION:	NATURE OF INJURY:

Received By:	Distribution:

REVISION DATE _____

PUBLIC AGENCY CONTACT REPORT

INCIDENT:	Date: _____ Time: _____

GOV'T AGENCY:	Time of Contact:	Key Questions:
CONTACT:		
		Response:
Phone:	Reply Deadline:	
Spokesperson:		
		Follow-up:

GOV'T AGENCY:	Time of Contact:	Key Questions:
CONTACT:		
		Response:
Phone:	Reply Deadline:	
Spokesperson:		
		Follow-up:

GOV'T AGENCY:	Time of Contact:	Key Questions:
CONTACT:		
		Response:
Phone:	Reply Deadline:	
Spokesperson:		
		Follow-up:

GOV'T AGENCY:	Time of Contact:	Key Questions:
CONTACT:		
		Response:
Phone:	Reply Deadline:	
Spokesperson:		
		Follow-up:

Revision Date: _____

12

Training Considerations

It is essential to establish and develop an effective organization that can respond and manage during an incident. Ensuring that the appropriate training is provided and documented is paramount. This chapter will provide an overview of various training considerations. Everyone who works at, visits, and/or provides services to your organization requires some kind of training. This may range from basic introductory information to detailed operations-based training for external people with a response role. The following definition clarifies the meaning of training, as used in the all-hazards system.

> *Training* involves any and all activities related to the transfer of knowledge about the functions of components of the all-hazards system. This includes, but is not limited to, formal classroom-type training, hands-on training, discussions, meetings, conferences, and so on. In order to qualify as training, the session must be properly documented. Training considerations address both the response and the management parts of the system. A trained emergency management/response organization (EMRO) functions more efficiently. Training reduces the potential for panic, chaos, and confusion that so often are a part of the reaction to a crisis.

**Chapter organizer: What this chapter
is about**

What are the training considerations for the emergency management/response organization? You must define the structure, functions, and span of control of the emergency management/response organization (EMRO). Training equals learning. The approach to developing the EMRO must carry with it a vesting of interest for the participants. Adults learn differently than children, so your training methods have to be geared toward effective learning (adult learning), or else the training will not be successful.

Training: An Approach

Training should consist of classroom and hands-on practical applications. In my previous book, I devoted a chapter, entitled "Training: The Critical Process," to this subject. For our purposes, I will not restate this information. Rather, I will talk about how to approach the training process and what constitutes effective training.

A systematic approach to preparing effective training programs consists of the following:

1. *Task analysis.*   When designing an integrated program, we determine the skills, knowledge, and procedures required for satisfactory task performance.

2. *Program development.*   Objectives are defined from the skills, knowledge, and procedures identified during task analysis. Plans are then prepared to support objectives.

3. *Instruction.*   The program is systematically presented by using appropriate instructional methods. These may include lecture, self-paced or group-paced mediated instruction, simulation, and team training.

4. *Evaluation.*   Performance standards and evaluation criteria are developed from the objectives. Each element is evaluated to ensure the program is appropriately designed.

One of the first steps toward developing an effective training component for the all-hazards emergency management system is to conduct a task analysis to determine the skills, knowledge, and procedures required for satisfactory performance. In essence, you have to outline what you expect from people after they have been trained. This process is also an excellent way to check the plan for commitments and to determine your ability to fulfill them.

Upon completion of the task analysis phase, you will want to design and develop training materials. Generally, lesson development will consist of defining learning objectives from the task analysis. Instructional plans will then be prepared to support the learning objectives. To ensure appropriate documentation, materials should include

Lesson plans

Audiovisual aids

Presentation notes

Student materials (readings and handouts)

Tests

Training documentation forms

As each milestone is reached, you should conduct a review and seek approval of the training materials (at a minimum this should be a first-draft review and comment and a final-draft review and comment by key personnel).

Focus on ways to assist your organization in the development of its human resources:

- Customized education and training programs, seminars, and workshops
- Supervised on-the-job training
- Group-paced and self-paced mediated instruction
- Management development training
- Train-the-trainer programs
- Drills and exercises (Chap. 13)

In your all-hazards emergency management system, key topics for training should include elements for the implementation of emergency management, incident command, and response systems. Other pertinent topics should include the following:

1. Emergency management/response planning
   Development of plans for fixed sites, transportation operation spills, and support organizations
   Selecting the planning team
   Four phases of emergency management/response planning and operations
2. Emergency management/response organization (EMRO)
   Developing the organization structure
   Incident command systems
   Functions, duties, and tasks
3. Emergency preparedness, train the trainer
   Effective instructional systems development
   Testing and performance evaluation
4. Emergency response facilities and equipment
   Design and function of key emergency response facilities
   Essential equipment for emergency management and response

Emergency management/response hazard analysis

   Hazard operability studies
   Job hazards analysis
   Developing most-probable-case and worst-case scenarios

Documentation: Key to the Program

One of the most critical elements of your training program is documentation. Beyond assigning responsibility to someone for the management of training, you must consider the training and information needs of the end users of the plan and supporting materials.

Have employees been trained to know what to do in the event of an incident? What about contractors, vendors, visitors, managers, and external responders (agencies, other resources)? You must be able to comfortably answer these questions and rest assured that your documentation process adequately addresses these groups.

Your documentation should provide historical information on training and answers to the following questions:

What is the schedule for the next 12 months?

Who will be trained?

Who will do the training?

What type of training will be implemented?

What is the schedule for specific training offerings?

What will be done to update the program?

How will the trainees be evaluated?

What are the applicable regulatory guidance and company policy and procedure requirements?

The above list is not meant to be all-inclusive. Rather, it should illustrate the importance of the training program's documentation requirements. The following examples illustrate how you might develop the training portion of your plan, forms for documentation, and examples of training materials. Since each facility, operation, and location is unique, you will have to fit the examples to your specific case.

Sample

IPAC is a program developed by Logical Management Systems, Corp. It is designed to assist in the preparation of personnel to meet the required OSHA awareness-level and operations-level emergency training requirements, as set forth in OSHA 1910.120, *Hazardous Waste Operations and Emergency Response* (HAZWOPER).

Each entity with a HAZWOPER requirement may wish to consider this material for incorporation with site-specific training that would further address the regulatory requirements. The material presented here is intended to provide an example, not meant to be comprehensive. Any use you make of it should be evaluated against the appropriate regulatory and other requirements you must adhere to.

Sample

IPAC

IPAC is an acronym developed by Logical Management Systems, Corp. IPAC is used to assist personnel to take action in the event of an incident in the workplace. The letters mean

I = Identify the incident in progress.

P = Protect yourself by getting out of danger.

A = Alert others.

C = Communicate, call for help.

OSHA 1910.120, *Hazardous Waste Operations and Emergency Response,* requires that you establish emergency response operation capabilities for releases of, or substantial threats of release of, hazardous substances without regard to the location of the hazard. A site-specific *incident command system* (ICS) consisting of trained personnel must be established. Two of the designated categories of personnel are

- First responder awareness level
- First responder operations level

IPAC is designed as a practical aid to help the first responder awareness-level and first responder operations-level personnel accomplish emergency response tasks as defined in OSHA 1910.120.

Awareness-Level Personnel

Awareness-level personnel are not asked to do anything more than they would normally want to do (protect themselves, warn others, call for help).

An overall objective of awareness-level training, and one of the intentions of OSHA 29 CFR 1910.120, is to make sure that you have the information, procedures, and skills you need in order to respond during an incident and perform the above awareness-level functions efficiently, effectively, and *safely*.

The following pages will explain each of these awareness-level functions.

Identify

Recognize an incident in progress. Be familiar with the hazardous materials that are used in your workplace.

- What substances are present in the workplace?
- What are the characteristics of these substances?
- What are possible signs of a release of substances such as these?

Be familiar with "normal" conditions in your workplace.

- What are the normal day-to-day sounds?
- What are other normal signs (vent plumes, flashing lights)?

Be familiar with your facility's emergency warning systems.

- What type(s) of warning systems are provided?

Do not be afraid to ask questions!

Protect

Remove yourself from areas that may be affected by the incident. Be familiar with all exits from your work area.

- Do not allow exits to become blocked.
- Keep paths to exits clear.

Know the evacuation routes and assembly areas.

- What are the primary routes of evacuation from the facility?
- Are alternate routes of evacuation available?
- What are the designated assembly areas?

When necessary, or when told to do so, safely evacuate to a predesignated assembly area so that your safety may be accounted for and so that others will not endanger themselves unnecessarily while searching for you.

Alert

Alert others to danger. Notify your supervisor, the facility manager, or operations-level responder personnel if they are available.

- Know who these people are.

Be familiar with your facility's emergency warning systems.

- What type(s) of warning systems are provided?
- Know the warning signals.
- Know how to activate these systems.

Know where others are working in the facility.

- Where do your fellow employees work?
- Are there outside personnel present (contractors, visitors)?

Never put yourself in danger. You are not trained to perform search and rescue operations at the awareness level.

Communicate

Call for help. Know your facility's emergency notification procedures.

- Is there a "lead" agency (such as the local fire department) that has been designated to handle all emergency calls and coordinate fire, police, and medical response in the community?
- Where are the phone numbers posted?

Know when to call for help.

- What are the capabilities of on-site personnel to deal with each type of emergency?
- When should an incident be reported to outside agencies?

When in doubt, call for help! It is better to be safe than to be sorry.

Operations-Level Personnel

Operations-level personnel are asked to take defensive actions to stop or control the incident. The following pages will explain each of these operations-level functions.

Identify

There are many means that you can use to identify hazardous situations or incidents in your workplace. We have discussed several in this module. These include, but are not limited to, the following:

Your senses	Placards and labels
Location	Shipping papers
Container shapes	Material safety data sheets
Container markings and colors	Detection devices

There are several things you should do when you *identify* a hazardous situation or incident.

Protect

After you *identify* a hazardous situation or incident, you want to *protect* yourself and others. Some basic protective actions you can take include, but are not limited to, the following:

Time: Reduce your exposure time.

Distance: Remove yourself from the area.

Shielding: Put a protective barrier between you and the hazard.

Often referred to as *protective actions,* the following are ways to implement time, distance, and shielding:

Evacuate the area.

Shelter in place.

Use personal protective equipment.

If you *evacuate* an area, you should consider the following:

- You should exit the area, using designated evacuation routes. Assess the situation to determine the safest route.

- Evacuation routes will be determined by the incident or circumstance. Determine the appropriate egress route, and tell others in your work area.

- Report to a designated assembly area to ensure you are properly accounted for.
- Prior to evacuating your work area, place your equipment in a safe shutdown condition if practicable.

The following sample evacuation checklist provides an example of the typical actions you can take to *protect* yourself by evacuating an area.

Sample

Evacuation Checklist

1. Sound unit evacuation alarm.
2. Account for all personnel and report this information to one of the following:

   - Field incident commander
   - Incident support director
   - Your operations manager

3. Assess safety of primary assembly area.
4. Ensure all personnel remain at designated assembly areas.
5. Ensure accountability of outside operators via radio contact. Maintain radio contact with the outside operators (if not at the assembly area) until all personnel are released by the field incident commander and/or incident support director.

You may not be able to evacuate the area in a timely manner. In this instance, *sheltering in place* may be your best option. Sheltering-in-place involves *shielding* yourself from the effects of the hazardous situation.

Sheltering involves members of the population at risk seeking protection in areas (generally buildings or special rooms) that can be made relatively airtight.

If you are ordered to shelter in place, you should consider the following:

1. Look for a designated shelter-in-place area or for your assigned area.
2. Place your equipment in safe shutdown, if time permits.
3. Once in the shelter-in-place location, do not exit until you receive specific authorization.

The following sample shelter-in-place checklist provides an example of typical considerations of sheltering in place.

Sample

Sample

Shelter-in-Place Checklist

1. Close all doors to the outside, and close and lock all windows (windows sometimes seal better when locked).

2. Set all ventilation systems to 100 percent recirculation so that no outside air is drawn into the structure. Where this is not possible, ventilation systems should be turned off.

3. Turn off all heating systems.

4. Turn off all air conditioners, and switch inlets to the *closed* position. Seal any gaps around window-type air conditioners with tape and plastic sheeting, wax paper, aluminum foil, or other available materials.

5. Turn off all exhaust fans.

6. Close as many internal doors as possible.

7. Use tape and plastic food wrapping, wax paper, aluminum foil, or other available material to cover and seal vents and other openings to the outside to the extent possible (including any obvious gaps around external windows and doors).

8. If the gas or vapor is soluble or even partially soluble in water, hold a wet cloth or handkerchief over your nose and mouth if gases start to bother you. For a higher degree of protection, go into a bathroom, close the door, and turn on the shower in a strong spray to "wash" the air. Seal any openings to the outside of the bathroom as best as you can.

9. If an explosion is possible outdoors, close drapes, curtains, and shades over windows. Stay away from external windows to prevent potential injury from flying glass.

10. Minimize the use of elevators in buildings. These tend to "pump" outdoor air in and out of a building as they travel up and down.

11. Await instructions from EMRO personnel, field incident commander, and/or incident support director.

Sample

Another way to protect yourself is by using *personal protective equipment (PPE)*.

Protecting Your Body

In the event of an incident, you must make sure that you are protected from chemical exposure. This means protecting any vulnerable route of entry into your body. To be safe, assume the worst. If you do not have the right protective equipment, stay away from the spill.

Some chemicals are most hazardous when they are inhaled. You may need equipment to protect your nose, mouth, and lungs. Such respiratory protection may include a respirator or a full-scale, self-contained breathing apparatus. You need to be physically able and trained to use this equipment, if the need arises.

A warning label on the chemical container or the material safety data sheets for that chemical can tell you whether and what respiratory protection is necessary.

Personal protective equipment comes in many forms. These include, but are not limited to:

Protective clothing

Protective clothing is meant to keep dangerous materials from coming into contact with skin, eyes, and other parts of the body. Due to the wide range of chemicals you may encounter, the selection of protective equipment should be based on three factors:

- Flammability
- Corrosivity
- Toxicity

Special protective clothing is categorized as follows:

- *Level A:* fully encapsulated suit
- *Level B:* special protective clothing with *self-contained breathing apparatus (SCBA)*
- *Level C:* special protective clothing with filter mask
- *Level D:* no protective clothing

Respiratory protection devices

Respiratory protection devices should be supplied to your personnel as appropriate:

Filtering devices. Filters are useful where there is adequate air to breathe. There are many different kinds of filtration devices, ranging from simple dust or mist masks for keeping out dust to full-face, powered, air-purifying masks capable of filtering out specific chemicals.

Supplied air-breathing devices. A supplied air-breathing device may be a mask hooked up by hose to a stationary air supply. It may also be a self-contained device with a portable air supply. A self-contained breathing apparatus is an example of this type of self-contained unit.

Alert

Now that you have protected yourself, you need to *alert* others to the potential danger or situation. This can be accomplished through a variety of methods. Typical examples include

- Sounding an alarm
- Physically warning others
- Using special signs, signals, and banners
- Visual indicators

Although we could continue to list the various means you can use to alert others, the above should provide sufficient examples for you to consider as you think about your options for alerting others.

Communicate

Once we have alerted others, we will need to *communicate* information to the appropriate authorities. This may be your immediate supervisor, or it could be regulatory agencies, local community officials, or anyone in authority who has a need to know about your situation or may be responsible for taking further action to notify and protect others.

You should consider the following when communicating with others:

Communication basics. *Communication* may be defined as the transmission of information, ideas, emotions, skills, etc., by the use of symbols, words, pictures, figures, graphs, etc. Transmission is the ability to convey your message in a clear, concise, and understandable manner. How you convey your information in many respects is more important than the actual content of the information.

The property of transmission in the communication process is probably the most prevalent property of communication, as is the use of symbols (verbal and nonverbal cues) in the transmission process.

Communication includes all the procedures by which one mind may affect another.

Effective communication within groups as well as between pairs of individuals always requires a correct reading or interpretation of both explicit verbal cues and the more subtle nonverbal cues. In an emergency, the ability to communicate quickly, accurately, and effectively is of unparalleled importance, because many communications must be made over radio or telephone without benefit of nonverbal cues.

Emergency communications should be a natural extension of the normal operating communication procedure. Before you begin, know your data. Work with key technical and management resources to analyze and assess relevant plant information. Crisis communications can be successful when focused on

- Personalizing the message—do not use jargon
- Knowing your audience
- Controlling the size of the audience
- Involving community leaders
- Being conservative—do not overstate or understate the facts
- Working with the media
- Accessing outside resources
- Being organized

Accurate, timely, and complete communications form the basis for all emergency actions. More problems result from poor communications than from any other single factor during emergency situations. Standard terminology and formality are important considerations regarding communications during normal plant operations and in emergency situations.

All your communications should be as follows:

F: *Formal*   Treat the person on the other end of the line as an official rather than a friend. Experience has shown that formality in communications eliminates confusion during emergency situations and adds to overall efficiency of the response.

A: *Accurate*   Ensure the facts are accurate and complete and that all units are provided. To ensure that communications are *accurate,* give only the facts, be sure the information is complete, and provide all measurement units. Get a complete repeat-back of the message. Request a repeat-back if one is not given immediately.

C: *Concise*   Get your message across with as few words as possible.

T: *Timely*   Late information can expand the problem. Timely information is essential. The quality of a task should not be sacrificed just to do it quickly. Poor or wrong information can be worse than late information. When you are making initial contact, especially with off-site organizations, identify yourself and ensure that you are speaking to the correct person.

The following suggestions are provided to assist you when you have to communicate during an emergency. Develop and practice these skills in nonemergency situations, and you will find that you can respond more efficiently during an emergency. Here are aids to help you:

Prepare	Think ahead and plan your communication. Give your communication a beginning, middle, and end. If you are briefing and time permits, prepare good visual aids and arrange the briefing room in advance.
Clarify	Make the communication clear and understandable. Unravel the difficulties in your own mind first. Evaluate the competencies of the person who is receiving the communication—is she or he technically knowledgeable? Avoid obscure ways of putting things. Seek clarifying questions—ensure accurate communications. Avoid acronyms and the use of jargon.
Simplify	Put complex matters in simple form. *Avoid complicated terminology*. Give an overview or outline first. Summarize the key points at the end of the communication.
Animate	Make the subject come alive. Be enthusiastic regarding the communication. Treat all communications as if they were the single most important thing to be accomplished at the time.
Be yourself	Foster the ability to cope with stress, nerves, and tension; and behave naturally. Breathe deeply, eliminate nervous habits, and think confidently.

Sample

TRAINING MATERIALS
DOCUMENTATION FORMS

Sample

The following are provided as examples (with explanations as to their use) of the types of training documentation forms, tools, and accessories you can use to enhance your training efforts. Where appropriate, each contains or is followed by an explanation.

- Position analysis information form
- Lesson plan format and continuation sheet
- Lesson note form(s)
- Instructor checklist
- Keys to effective presentation
- Critique checklists
- Training evaluation forms

The position analysis information form should be used to document the training requirements for each position in the emergency management/response organization (EMRO). Key information would include position staffing requirements and prerequisites (block 2) where you would designate the skill level requirements for the position.

Item B describes the training requirements for the position including the date trained and the date retraining should be accomplished by. Ten examples of the type of training that can be provided are highlighted in the *Position Analysis Information Form* shown below.

The lesson plan format provides an effective means for ensuring that preparation is accomplished prior to instruction and that key points are brought out during training. Our example is broken down as follows:

1. *Lesson plan module.*   Here you should put the course number of the module to be presented, for example, MX-1.

2. *Time.*   Here you insert the length of time it will take to present the lesson, for example, 3 hours.

3. *Month/year.*   Here you insert the applicable date when the lesson/module was current, for example, 7/94.

4. *Class code.*   This indicates the classification of the level of the presentation, for example, M-1 = management level 1 and T-5 = technical level 5.

5. *Page ____ of ____.*   This indicates the current page and total page count.

6. *Lesson title.*   This indicates the formal title for the lesson, for example, "Overview of the Emergency Management System."

7. *Level of instruction.* Cognitive indicates classroom-type instruction, theory, etc., while practical would indicate interactive or hands-on instruction.

8. *Behavioral objectives.* Here you list the terminal module objectives. These are the key points or learning skills that would be transported to the student. For example, upon completion of this module, the attendees will be able to complete the notification forms for emergency notification of external agencies.

9. *Training aids and equipment.* Here you list all appropriate and required training aids and equipment, for example, pointer, flip chart, 35-mm projector.

10. *Reference material.* Here you list any reference material that instructors should familiarize themselves with or use in the presentation.

11. *Preparation.* Indicate the necessary review and preparation steps. For example, review EMP, sections 5, 7, 9, Appendices B, D, G, and EPIPs 110, 210, 250. Also review overhead foils and video, "All-Hazards Emergency Management."

12. *Presentation.* The presentation section should outline key points, objective, and brief statements to facilitate the instructor's presentation.

13. *Instructor notes.* This section should correlate to the presentation section, indicating what activity is to take place, for example, what slide or overhead is to be shown. Instructors may also write in any prompts that they wish to include for themselves.

Page 2 of this form is merely a continuation of the presentation and instructor notes sections.

Lesson notes can be varied according to preference. Some instructors prefer to hand out reading material supported by blank note forms. Others will hand out copies of overhead transparencies or slides or a combination of these. I have prepared some examples of various types from simple to more complex.

The next example is a checklist form from my first book. I have found it useful in making the presentation for the class and training work efficiently. I hope you find it useful. It consists of three pages and can be modified to fit your needs.

Following the checklist is another set of helpful hints entitled, "Keys to Effective Presentation." I hope they will help you with reminders and prompts to consider when you are preparing your training presentation.

Last, I have included a set of critique checklists and forms, focused on student evaluation type of information. You should consider them a valuable part of your documentation package. Remember, good feedback will facilitate improvement of the system.

Final Check Before Start of Session

Classroom management

____ **Item A: Personnel and logistics**

    ____ Structure training hours.
    ____ Schedule times with participants and managers.
    ____ A list of participants is available.
    ____ Beverages and/or food arrangements have been made.
    ____ There are extra pencils, pens, and pads of writing paper.
    ____ Training facility instructions are available (e.g., location of restrooms).

____ **Item B: Room appearance**

    ____ The room has been reserved.
    ____ The classroom is clean.
    ____ Desks and/or tables are arranged neatly.
    ____ There is adequate seating.
    ____ There are adequate writing surfaces.
    ____ Class-in-session lights are turned on.

____ **Item C: Audiovisual equipment**

    ____ Ensure that equipment works.
    ____ Set audio level.
    ____ Videotape(s) should be advanced to appropriate segment(s).
    ____ Videotape player, monitors, and extension cords should be compatible.
    ____ Monitor stand is available.
    ____ Flip chart (or chalkboard) is available.
    ____ Marker (or chalk) is available.

____ **Item D: Lesson plan**

    ____ Lesson plan is arranged in current order.
    ____ Lesson plan is customized.
    ____ Copies of tests are available.

___ **Item E: Lighting**

    ___ Lights can be turned up when the instructor is the focus of attention or when the students are working on a particular module.

    ___ Lights can be turned down when modified lighting is necessary to highlight a film, slide, or some other training aid.

___ **Item F: Curtains**

    ___ They are to be kept closed except when opened for a video presentation or to expose a training aid.

    ___ When they are open, only the necessary area is exposed, that is, only the chalkboard or screen in use.

___ **Item G: Sound**

    ___ The sound is adjusted so that all personnel in the classroom can hear the presentation clearly.

    ___ The sound level is adjusted so that there is no feedback (high-pitched squeak) in the system.

___ **Item H: Special effects**

    ___ Special effects can be used to add emphasis to a key point or retain attention without creating a "dog and pony show" atmosphere.

Remarks:

_____

_____

_____

Keys to Effective Presentation

Control of interest

    ___ Item A: Student involvement. The students are involved in the teaching process through maximum use of questions and practical exercises.

    ___ Item B: Humor. Humor used in the presentation is appropriate (no religious, racial, or sexual overtones).

    ___ Item C: Training aids. Training aids are used where the subject requires visual or audio support.

    ___ Item D: Interest factors. Interest factors are used to contribute to the class.

Lesson organization

____ Item A: Introduction
    ____ A gain-attention step is used.
    ____ The subject is tied in to previous and subsequent instruction.
    ____ The training objectives are fully explained.

____ Item B: Body
    ____ The class is broken into meaningful segments.
    ____ The segments of the class are presented in a logical sequence.
    ____ Transitions are used to move from one segment to another.

____ Item C: Conclusion
    ____ The students are alerted for the review.
    ____ All main points are reviewed in a logical sequence.
    ____ There is a strong concluding statement.

Establish a good learning environment

____ Item A: Communicate an optimistic, high standard of expectation to the group.
____ Item B: The lesson objectives are explained until all the students see them as valid, important, attainable, and personally valuable.
____ Item C: Provide at least one incentive (tangible or intangible) for good performance.
____ Item D: Reinforce any (and all) behavior(s) in the lesson objective(s) occurring during the practice portion of the lesson.
____ Item E: Extinguish any (and all) inappropriate actions of the group.

Training aids

____ Item A: The training aid(s) used:
    ____ Reinforce the spoken word.
    ____ Make things clearer.
    ____ Aid in retention.

____ Item B: The training aid(s) are:
    ____ Appropriate, simple, accurate, necessary, attractive
    ____ Not a distraction
    ____ Large enough to be seen by everyone in the classroom

_____ Not used as a crutch by the instructor
_____ In the proper position on the platform
_____ Removed or covered when no longer required

_____ Item C: If an overhead projector is used,
     _____ The slides are neat and attractive.
     _____ Slides do not contain too much material.
     _____ The lettering is large enough to be seen by all learners.
     _____ The projector is turned off when no longer required.

_____ Item D: If the chalkboard is used,
     _____ The lettering is of proper size to be seen by all learners.
     _____ The lettering is neat.

_____ Item E: If a flip chart is used,
     _____ The lettering is of proper size to be seen by all learners.
     _____ The lettering is neat.
     _____ Color of markers is appropriate to distinguish key points.

_____ Item F: If a 35-mm projector is used,
     _____ The projector is of the type needed for presentation (sound/silent).
     _____ The lens is of sufficient size to enable all personnel to see the slides.
     _____ Slides used are,
         _____ Professionally done
         _____ Created in-house
         _____ Other

_____ Item G: Videotape/projector
     _____ Projector is easily seen by all personnel.
     _____ Sound is adjusted to meet the size of the room.
     _____ Professional tapes are used.
     _____ In-house tapes are used.

_____ Item H: Demonstrations
     _____ Actual item or equipment is used.
     _____ Safety precautions are provided.
     _____ Item and equipment check is accomplished prior to demonstration.
     _____ Simulation and model are used.
     _____ Comparison to actual items is provided.

Critique Checklists and Forms

[YOUR COMPANY]
Emergency Management Program (EMP)
Training Postevaluation

For each of the items in the following, please indicate your opinion by circling a number from 5 to 1. Space is also provided for any comments you may have which will assist us as we plan for future training sessions.

5 = Strongly agree with statement

4 = Agree

3 = Uncertain

2 = Disagree

1 = Strongly disagree

Program content, structure

1. The program was well organized.   5   4   3   2   1
2. The purpose of the program was clear.   5   4   3   2   1
3. The program achieved its purpose.   5   4   3   2   1
4. The program had real-life applications.   5   4   3   2   1

Additional comments:

_____

_____

_____

Course manual

5. Course materials supplemented the   5   4   3   2   1
   instruction.
6. The course materials were well organized. 5   4   3   2   1

Additional comments:

_____

_____

_____

Facilities

7. The classroom arrangement was good.   5 4 3 2 1

8. The number of participants was   5 4 3 2 1
   manageable.

Additional comments:

_____

_____

_____

Instructors

9. The instructors were knowledgeable about   5 4 3 2 1
   the subject matter.

10. The instructors encouraged participant   5 4 3 2 1
    input.

11. The instructors tailored their presentations   5 4 3 2 1
    to meet the needs of the audience.

12. The instructors interacted well with the   5 4 3 2 1
    participants.

Additional comments:

_____

_____

For each statement below, please respond yes or no and briefly
explain your response.

13. I found particular topics of the course more useful than others.

    Yes_____   No_____

    Please list below:

_____

_____

Comments: (Which ones and why?)

_____

_____

_____

14. I would recommend particular topics to be added to the course.

   Yes_____ No_____

Comments: (Which ones and why?)

_____

_____

_____

15. I think the program could be improved in the following ways:

_____

_____

_____

_____

Training Evaluation Form

Location: _____

Date: _____

Instructor: _____

Now that you have completed this block of instruction, we would appreciate your assessment of the course, the support material, and the instruction.

For each item listed below, please circle the number (5 = strongly agree, 4 = agree, 3 = uncertain, 2 = disagree, 1 = strongly disagree), under the heading that best expresses your opinion. Space is provided under each section for any additional comments you might wish to offer.

Course content and structure

1. The course was well organized.   1 2 3 4 5
2. The purpose of the course was clear.   1 2 3 4 5
3. The course achieved its purpose.   1 2 3 4 5
4. The activities and exercises were useful. 1 2 3 4 5
5. The course had real-life expectations.   1 2 3 4 5

Comments: _____

_____

Course materials

6. The slides, video, and overheads (other) made the material clear and understandable.   1 2 3 4 5

7. The trainee manual is helpful and easy to read.   1 2 3 4 5

8. The overhead transparencies were clear and helpful.   1 2 3 4 5

9. Overall, the support materials worked well together.   1 2 3 4 5

Comments: _____

_____

_____

Facilities

10. The classroom arrangement was good.   1 2 3 4 5

11. The number of trainees was manageable.   1 2 3 4 5

Comments: _____

_____

_____

Instructors

12. The instructor(s) knew the subject matter.   1 2 3 4 5

13. The instructor(s) encouraged class participation.   1 2 3 4 5

14. The instructor(s) tailored the topic to my needs.   1 2 3 4 5

15. The instructor(s) interacted well with the class.   1 2 3 4 5

16. The instructor(s) kept the class running smoothly.   1 2 3 4 5

Comments: _____

_____

_____

For each statement below, check yes or no.

17. I found particular sections of the course more useful than others.

    Yes_____   No_____

    If yes, which ones and why? _____

    _____

    _____

    _____

18. I would recommend particular information be added to the course.

    Yes_____   No_____

    If yes, what and why? _____

    _____

    _____

    _____

19. I would recommend that the video and written materials be improved.

    Yes_____   No_____

    If yes, how? _____

    _____

    _____

    _____

POSITION ANALYSIS INFORMATION FORM

DATE _____

A. Primary Identification Information:

1. Emergency Title_____

2. Position Requirements/Prerequisite Skills:_____

3. Primary Duties _____

   _____

   _____

4. Secondary Duties: _____

   _____

   _____

B. Training Requirements:

	Date Trained	Retraining Due Date
1. Awareness Level Training:	_____	_____
2. Operations Level Training:	_____	_____
3. Specialist Level Training:	_____	_____
4. Technician Level Training:	_____	_____
5. Incident Commander Training:	_____	_____
6. Emergency Manager Training:	_____	_____
7. Crisis Media Training:	_____	_____
8. Incident Investigation Training:	_____	_____
9. Community Outreach Training:	_____	_____
10. Litigation (Witness) Training:	_____	_____

LESSON PLAN MODULE: (1)	TIME _(2)_	MONTH/YEAR _(3)_/_____	CLASS CODE ____(4)___	PAGE _(5) OF ____

LESSON TITLE
(6)

LEVEL OF INSTRUCTION   COGNITIVE   PRACTICAL

(7)   _____   _____

BEHAVIORAL OBJECTIVES

(8)

TRAINING AIDS AND EQUIPMENT (9)	REFERENCE MATERIAL (10)

PREPARATION
(11)

PRESENTATION	INSTRUCTOR NOTES
(12)	(13)

PRESENTATION	INSTRUCTOR NOTES	PAGE ____ OF ____

LESSON NOTES

SLIDE #

SLIDE #

SLIDE #

13

Plan Validation (Drills) Considerations

Establishing and developing an effective drill and exercise program that serves to validate your emergency management system (EMS) is one of the final steps in program development. This chapter will provide an overview of various types of drill and exercise considerations. First a definition:

> *Plan validation* is the process of ensuring that you can validate the ability of your emergency management/response organization (EMRO) to perform a set of critical tasks under simulated emergency conditions. This includes, but is not limited to, management initiatives, response activities, direction, control, mitigation, and postincident activities.

Chapter organizer: What this chapter is about

What are the validation considerations for effectively ensuring emergency management/response capability? Your EMS defines the course of action your organization intends to take in responding to, managing, and mitigating an incident. To verify its accuracy, you must have a means in place to substantiate performance. You must set minimum acceptable standards of performance and adhere to them. The drill and exercise program should reflect how your organization will perform under actual emergency conditions.

Drills and Exercises

An integrated drill and exercise program provides the basis for assurance that the organization can successfully assume emergency roles and functions in accordance with the emergency management plan.

This program is, by its very nature, multifaceted. Drills and exercises can be broadly classified in four major categories:

- Orientation and walk-through (tabletop)
- Mini drill (interactive tabletop)
- Functional drill (interactive)
- Full-scale (full-scale interactive exercise)

Each of these categories requires different resources and skill sets to implement. Some require minimal preparations and are simple to execute, while others may be more complex and require greater efforts and resources. Each provides its own benefits. The following summaries provide an overview of each type.

Orientation and walk-through (tabletop)

Orientations and walk-through drills are generally used to acquaint personnel with policies and procedures developed in the planning process, by providing a general overview of the emergency management plan and its components. An orientation and walk-through are especially effective in ensuring that emergency management/response personnel understand their roles and responsibilities and help to clarify nebulous plan elements. While an orientation and walk-through do not normally involve any overt simulation or role playing, they can be used to review the emergency management plan (EMP) and its components in a nonthreatening setting, allowing you to apply them to potential emergency situations or past events familiar to everyone. The following breakdown characterizes the orientation and walk-through.

Definition: A scenario-based discussion presented in a structured, classroom-type setting

Goal: Assessment of knowledge of plans, procedures, and job functions related to simulated emergency events

Designed to: Facilitate interaction; promote discussions on anticipated actions, decision-making processes, response options, and impacts of actions; and identification of issues versus problem solving

Characterized by: - Discussion-based
                      - Individual and team training
                      - Team-building focus
                      - A conference room or small group setting
                      - Interactive discussions among participants

- No mobilization of resources
- No simulation except as necessary to prompt consideration of issues as appropriate
- Dialogue guided by a moderator
- Documentation of participant discussions
- Evaluation of knowledge as compared to performance in relation to a set of training objectives by the moderator

Critique: Focused on issues and concerns raised during discussion and as identified by the moderator.

Evaluation: Letter report highlighting issues and concerns raised during the scenario-based discussion. Recommendations provided are broader in scope and are designed to encourage further development of the emergency preparedness system. There is limited data collection, analysis, documentation, and presentation of findings.

Mini drill (interactive tabletop)

A mini drill is primarily a learning exercise that involves limited simulation. Predesigned situations and problems are combined with limited role playing to generate action and discussion of the plan, its procedures, policies, and identified resources.

Mini drills are especially good for familiarizing groups and organizations with their roles and for practicing proper coordination under a highly controlled setting. They also provide a good environment in which to reinforce the logic and content of the plan and to integrate new policies into the decision-making process.

Mini drills allow participants to act out critical steps, recognize difficulties, and solve problems in an interactive format. The following breakdown describes the key features of the mini drill format:

Definition: A scenario-based validation of specific elements of the emergency plan presented in an interactive format, generally at or near the actual location of occurrence and/or designated emergency facilities

Goal: Validation of specific elements of the emergency plan, procedures, and job functions under simulated emergency conditions with limited facilitation of actions and decision-making processes

Designed to: Validate emergency plan and supporting materials, ensure specific capabilities, and assess operability of designated emergency-related equipment

Characterized by:
- Practice and validation of a specific functional response

- Focus on demonstration of knowledge and skills as well as management/response element interaction and decision-making capability
- Actual or simulated response locations and/or facilities
- Involvement and interaction of a limited number of management/response elements, with optional involvement of external organizations
- Mobilization by limited elements of the EMRO
- Varying degrees of actual, as opposed to simulated, notification and mobilization of resources
- Simulation, directed through a drill support organization, of nonparticipating essential activities that impact management/response efforts
- Use of controllers to ensure that activity remains within intended parameters
- Evaluation of performance against a set of drill objectives by the drill support organization or an evaluator

Critique: Focused on performance observations of the drill control organization and specific objective-related items as contained in the drill evaluation guide.

Evaluation: A report focusing on specific objective-related issues and related performance. Recommendations provided are designed to focus on options for corrective actions as well as to encourage further development of the emergency preparedness system. Data collection, analysis, documentation, and presentation of findings are more in-depth.

Functional drill (interactive)

A functional drill involves emergency simulation designed to provide training for, and evaluation of, the EMRO. More complex than the two previous types of drills, it focuses on interactive decision making and coordination in a controlled free-play environment. While some field operations may be simulated activities, messages and information are typically exchanged by using realistic communications via radios and telephones. The functional drill permits decision makers, responders, and coordination and operations personnel to practice emergency management/response actions in a realistic setting with real-time constraints and stress. It typically includes the EMRO and limited external agencies performing a series of interactive emergency functions for the purpose of validating all plan linkages. The following breakdown provides more detail on the functional exercise format.

Definition:	A scenario-based validation of all elements of the emergency plan presented in an interactive format, generally at or near the actual location of occurrence and at all designated emergency facilities
Goal:	Validation of all elements of the emergency plan, procedures, and job functions under simulated emergency conditions with observation and evaluation of actions and decision-making processes by an evaluation team
Designed to:	Validate emergency plan and supporting materials, ensure all capabilities, and assess operability of designated emergency-related equipment.
Characterized by:	■ Validation of functional response by EMRO; focus on demonstration of knowledge and skills as well as management/response element interaction and decision-making capability

- Actual response locations and/or facilities
- Involvement and interaction of all levels of management/response elements, with limited involvement of external organizations
- Mobilization by all elements of the EMRO
- Actual, as opposed to simulated, notification and mobilization of resources
- Limited simulation of nonparticipating external elements and agencies
- Use of controllers to ensure that activity remains within intended parameters
- Evaluation of performance against a set of drill objectives by the drill evaluation organization

Critique:	Focused on performance observations of the drill evaluation organization and objective-related items as contained in the drill evaluation guide.
Evaluation:	A formal evaluation presentation is followed by the written report on specific objective-related issues and performance. Recommendations provided are designed to focus on options for corrective actions as well as to encourage further development of the emergency preparedness system. Data collection, analysis, documentation, and presentation of findings are very detailed.

Full-scale exercise

A full-scale exercise evaluates all components of the EMRO, and internal and external support organizations simultaneously. It exercises the interactive elements of the community emergency program. It is similar to the functional exercise, but it is more complex, because it has more participating groups. A detailed scenario is used to simulate an emergency which requires on-scene direction, control, and operations and includes coordination and policy-making roles at various emergency facilities. Direction and control, mobilization of resources, communications, and other special functions are rigorously exercised. The following breakdown provides more detail on the full-scale exercise format.

Definition: A scenario-based validation of all elements of the emergency plan and associated external emergency plans, presented in an interactive format, at or near the actual location of occurrence with full activation of all emergency facilities

Goal: Validation of all elements of the emergency plan, procedures, job functions, and associated emergency plans under simulated emergency conditions by all participating entities

Designed to: Validate emergency plans and supporting materials and external linkages; ensure all capabilities; and assess operability of all emergency-related equipment.

Characterized by: ■ Validation of emergency management/response functions. Focus on demonstration of knowledge and skills as well as management/response element interaction and decision-making capability.

■ Actual response locations and/or facilities

■ Involvement and interaction of all internal and external management/response elements, with full involvement of external organizations

■ Mobilization of all elements of the EMRO

■ Actual, as opposed to simulated, notification and mobilization of resources

■ Limited simulation, directed through a drill support organization

■ Use of controllers to ensure that activity remains within intended parameters

■ Evaluation of performance against a set of drill objectives by the drill support organization evaluation team.

Critique: Focused on performance observations by the drill control organization evaluation team and specific objective-related items as contained in the drill evaluation guide.

Evaluation: A formal oral presentation followed by a detailed written report focusing on specific objective-related issues and performance. Recommendations provided are designed to focus on options for corrective actions as well as to encourage further development of the emergency preparedness system. Data collection, analysis, documentation, and presentation of findings are very detailed.

Progressive Exercise Program

Recognizing that the drill and exercise types described in this book and my previous book are intended to build on one another, each one becoming more complex and comprehensive, you will have to develop a progressive exercise program which first schedules basic orientations for personnel. These orientations, often referred to as *tabletop drills,* introduce the plan, its components, and specific policies and responsibilities which apply to the conduct of emergency management/response operations.

Mini drills are then conducted to practice actual coordination and leadership provisions of the plan, including those emergency operation concepts which may be new to many personnel. These should be followed by functional exercises to integrate the emergency plan's more complex sections under simulated-emergency conditions, culminating in a full-scale exercise designed to validate the entire program.

When developing the scenario for the full-scale exercise or any other drill format, you should consider the following as the minimum elements:

- The basic objectives of the drill and exercise
- Appropriate evaluation criteria
- The date, time, place, and participating organizations
- Simulated events
- A time schedule of real and simulated initiating events

Your drill and exercise scenarios should vary from year to year to ensure that all major elements of your plan, including appendices and EPIPs, are tested within a 5-year period.

Coordination with state and local officials should be accomplished to ensure that these authorities are prepared to mobilize and provide off-site emergency response resources adequate to respond to your exercise accident scenarios and to coordinate the activities of their respective agencies in accordance with established plans and protocols.

A news media orientation should be conducted prior to conducting any large-scale exercise, to inform the press of the basic content of the emergency preparedness program and the purpose of the exercise.

Sample

EMERGENCY MANAGEMENT PLAN IMPLEMENTING PROCEDURE EMERGENCY PREPAREDNESS DRILLS AND EXERCISES EPIP - __ REVISION __ [DATE]

SUBMITTED BY: _____   DATE: _____

APPROVED BY: _____   DATE: _____

Sample

1.0 Purpose

The purpose of this procedure is to establish the requirements to successfully implement drills. The drill and exercise program is designed to train and test personnel assigned to the EMRO. The program is designed to ascertain that the organization is capable of executing the tasks necessary to quickly identify an emergency, assess the consequences, notify personnel and regulatory organizations, make protective action decisions, and respond to the situation.

2.0 Applicability

This procedure applies to the emergency management and response personnel who are responsible for maintaining sufficient preparedness for responding to an emergency condition.

3.0 Definitions

3.1 Drill

A drill is a supervised instructional period aimed at validating, developing, and maintaining skills in a particular operation. All drills will be supervised and evaluated by a qualified drill controller. The designated drill controller should possess the necessary expertise in his or her functional area of responsibility.

3.2 Exercise

An exercise is an event that validates either a major portion of the basic elements of the emergency management plan and the implementation capabilities of the EMRO and/or other associated entities' plans. The exercise may include validation of the implementation of the local emergency management agency plans and the mutual aid organizations involved. The exercise will simulate an emergency condition that would require the response of appropriate authorities. Exercises will be evaluated and critiqued.

3.3 Scenario

A scenario is a script which describes various simulated emergency events in an exercise or drill. The specific elements that will be incorporated into the scenarios are described in section 4.2.2.

3.4 Players

Players are those participating emergency plan position holders and other personnel who have been assigned active roles in the response to any emergency.

3.5 Controllers

Controllers are those predesignated personnel who have been assigned responsibility for providing drill and exercise messages and scenario-specific data to the players. Controllers also may initiate certain actions to ensure continuity in the developing drill and exercise scenario.

3.6 Evaluators

Evaluators are those predesignated personnel who have been assigned responsibility for documenting and evaluating the actions of the players in response to the developing drill/exercise scenario. Evaluators are a source of input to the drill/exercise critique process.

3.7 Observers

Observers are those personnel invited to view a drill or exercise, but who serve no evaluation, control or participatory function in that drill or exercise.

3.7.1 Observers also do not possess any authority to control or alter the scenario during a drill or exercise.

3.7.2 Observers shall not interfere with the actions of the players, controllers or evaluators. Any questions or concerns on the part of an observer during a drill or exercise should be communicated to a controller, who will then decide if further action is required.

4.0 Instructions

4.1 Precautions

4.1.1 Initial messages and communications which are transmitted during any drill or exercise should be preceded and terminated by the statement *"This is a drill."*

4.2 Exercises

4.2.1 The [DEPARTMENT, POSITION, TITLE] will be responsible for coordinating the annual emergency preparedness exercise.

4.2.2 The [DEPARTMENT, POSITION, TITLE] will be responsible for developing the annual emergency preparedness drill and exercise scenarios which will include, as a minimum, the following elements:

- The basic objectives and appropriate evaluation criteria
- The date, time, place, and participating organizations
- The simulated events
- A time schedule of real and simulated initiating events
- Arrangements for advance information and materials to be provided to evaluators
- A narrative summary describing the conduct of the exercise and drill. As appropriate, the summary should include descriptions of simulated casualties, off-site agency assistance, rescue of personnel, use of protective clothing, deployment of industrial hygiene teams, and public information participation.

4.2.3 The annual exercise scenario will vary each year to ensure that all major elements of the emergency response plans and procedures for the organizations involved are tested within a 5-year period.

4.2.4 Provisions will be made to start an exercise between 4:00 p.m. and 11:00 p.m. and another between 11:00 p.m. and 7:00 a.m. once every 6 years.

4.2.5 Exercises should be conducted under various weather conditions, when possible.

4.2.6 Some exercises should be unannounced.

4.2.7 The [DEPARTMENT, POSITION, TITLE] will coordinate with mutual aid organizations and other local agencies to ensure that they are prepared to mobilize and provide off-site emergency adequate to respond to the scenario as set forth in the exercise guidelines.

4.2.8 The [DEPARTMENT, POSITION, TITLE] will appoint controllers for the exercises.

4.2.9 Evaluators (internal) and personnel from regulatory agencies will observe, evaluate, and critique the exercise. Oral critique will be conducted at the conclusion of the drill exercise as soon as practicable to assess and evaluate the performance of the participants.

4.2.10 The [DEPARTMENT, POSITION, TITLE] will be responsible for recording and documenting items identified in the critique and the names and positions of personnel participating in the drill and exercise. This information will be documented and distributed as appropriate.

4.2.11 A news media orientation will be conducted prior to any large-scale drill or exercise to inform them of the basic content of the emergency preparedness program and the purpose of the exercise.

4.3 Critiques

Drills and exercises provide the principal means for assessing the effectiveness of the emergency management plan (EMP), its associated implementing procedures, and the state of emergency preparedness of personnel and equipment. To evaluate the performance and lessons learned, a critique will be conducted in a timely manner following each drill or exercise. The objectives of the critique session will be to evaluate the emergency response of participating personnel, to assess the adequacy of dedicated emergency equipment, and to identify deficiencies in the EMP and emergency plan implementing procedures (EPIPs).

The purpose of a critique is to compare the observed response of the participants with the response anticipated in the scenario. Each evaluator will use an evaluator's checklist to assess the observed response and compare it with the anticipated response. Each evaluator's checklist (attachment 1) will be unique to the drill or exercise and to the facility or personnel being evaluated. In addition, each evaluator will keep a chronological log, using the evaluator's or controller's log sheet (attachment 2).

The critique will include a discussion of both acceptable and unacceptable emergency responses. Observed deficiencies, as well as recommended corrective actions, will be recorded and documented.

A written summary of the exercise critiques will be prepared. This summary will include the objectives of the drill or exercise and a list of participants, controllers, and observers. This summary will also include a list of any identified deficiencies as well as recommendations for resolution. This information will be provided to the appropriate EMRO representatives for action.

5.0 References

5.1 Emergency Management Plan, section _____.

6.0 Attachments

6.1 Attachment 1, Evaluator's Checklist

6.2 Attachment 2, Evaluator's/Controller's Log Sheet

EVALUATOR'S CHECKLIST

EPIP-	ATTACHMENT 1	PAGE	of	PAGES

LOCATION/POSITION BEING EVALUATED:_____

TIME	EXPECTED RESPONSE	ACTUAL RESPONSE

SIGNATURE:_____   DATE:_____

EVALUATOR'S/CONTROLLER'S LOG SHEET

EPIP-   ATTACHMENT 2   PAGE   of   PAGES

LOCATION/POSITION BEING EVALUATED:_____

TIME   SUMMARY OF ACTIVITIES

SIGNATURE:_____   DATE:_____

Sample

DRILL AND EXERCISE FORMS AND ASSOCIATED MATERIALS

Sample

The following are provided as examples, with explanations as to use, of the types of drill or exercise documentation forms, tools, and accessories you can create to facilitate the design, implementation, and tracking of your drill and exercise program efforts. Where appropriate, each form contains or is followed by an explanation.

Included are the following:

- Message form
- Simulation problem input form
- Tabletop problem input form
- Controller checklist form

The message form can be used for a variety of drill or exercise type of activities. The following explanation is provided for the numbered items appearing in the form.

1. *(Type) message.*   This is the header for the form. As indicated by the underscore, you insert the type message appearing on the form, for example, drill or exercise message, contingency message, supplementary message, information message.

2. *"This is a drill. These events did not occur."*   This header should appear at the top and bottom of each message, ensuring that anyone will readily recognize the information as drill- or exercise-related.

3. *To.*   This indicates the position or title or person who is the recipient of the information.

4. *From.*   This indicates the simulator and initiator of the message.

5. *Time.*   The approximate time at which the information should be introduced.

6. *Message.*   This encompasses text and/or data that the recipient must act on.

7. *Related information.*   This portion of the form can be used to supplement the message block 6 and/or provide prompts for evaluation and control personnel. For example, if your plan calls for activation of an alarm based on the receipt of certain information, you would want to evaluate that this occurs without prompting.

If you include related information, do not provide the hard copy of the message form to the player for obvious reasons.

8. *Drill master number _____ key code.*   This section of the form contains the code for sequence of or order in which the message appears. For example, T-5 may indicate tabletop message number 5, where T=tabletop and 5=fifth message to be passed. This system is particularly useful if related messages are separated by a number of

other messages or if you have supplementary or contingency messages related to the primary message.

This form is generally used when you employ a simulation group or are operating from remote locations where input must be transmitted via telephone, radio, etc.

"This is a Drill"
"These Events Did Not Occur"

SIMULATION PROBLEM INPUT SHEET

EXERCISE:	**(1)**
TIME:	**(2)**
SIMULATOR:	**(3)**
INPUT TO:	**(4)**
CONTACT:	**(5)**
ROLE PLAYED:	**(6)**

PROBLEM
THIS IS AN EXERCISE.

(7)

THIS IS AN EXERCISE.

PERTINENT INFORMATION

RESPONSE   **(8)**

FOLLOW-UP   **(9)**

"This is a Drill"
"These Events Did Not Occur"

Drill Master #_____ Key Code

TABLETOP PROBLEM INPUT FORM

Information	Issues	Priority	Action	Resp.	
(1)	(2)	(3)	(4)	(5)	

Controller Checklist

Time	Message #	Expected Action	YES	NO	Controller Action
(1)	(2)	(3)	(4)		(5)

Evaluator Checklist

(1) Evaluator Assignment:_____

(2) Evaluation Objective: Initial Activation/Response

(3) EVALUATION ITEM   **(4) ACHIEVED**   **(5) EVALUATOR COMMENTS**

Facility Activation

    Timely   VG   G   P N/A

    Organized   VG   G   P N/A

Clear Lines of Authority
Established

    Incident Commander   VG   G   P N/A

    Command Section   VG   G   P N/A

    Planning Section   VG   G   P N/A

    Logistics Section   VG   G   P N/A

    Finance Section   VG   G   P N/A

    Operations Section   VG   G   P N/A

    Remainder of Business   VG   G   P N/A
    Operations

SAMPLE

(Type) (1) Message

(2)
"This is a Drill"
"These Events Did Not Occur"

TO: (3)   TIME: (5)

FROM: (4)

_____

MESSAGE: (6)

_____

RELATED INFORMATION: (7)

(2)
"This is a Drill"
"These Events Did Not Occur"

(8) Drill Master no. _____ key code

SAMPLE

The simulation problem input form is another example of the message form. You will notice some variation with regard to information on the form and the response and follow-up blocks. The following explanation applies to this form:

1. *Exercise.* You may wish to name your exercise or drill. If you have multiple drill commitments, this is a good way to track the associated documentation.

2. *Time.* This is the time when the message or information should be introduced into play.

3. *Simulator.* This indicates who passes or introduces the message.

4. *Input to.* This indicates to whom the message is input. An effective way of evaluating communications within your EMRO is to pass a message to one person which would actually be handled by another person, for example, a message input to the logistics director that should be handled by the media relations director.

5. *Contact.* This indicates the primary contact for your EMRO, who should be handling the input.

6. *Role played.* This indicates the role your simulator is playing, for example, someone from a regulatory agency.

7. *Problem.* In this section, like the other message form, you input the pertinent data and problem information.

8. *Response.* This section is provided for the simulator to note any actions to be taken or that the player indicates will be taken.

9. *Follow-up.* This section is also a notation space for the simulator to highlight any actions that are to be taken. For example, if a player says he will call back in 15 minutes, you may wish to note the time and estimate a time of call-back. If a call-back does not occur, this should be noted for evaluation purposes.

The top and bottom header information is the same as on the previous form. You may wish to consider adding a block entitled "Category," to identify the type of message being passed (i.e., environmental, safety, operations, etc.)

For tabletop and orientation types of drills, I like to use the following form entitled *Tabletop Problem Input Form.* I have found it provides a good working tool for data input as well as a player worksheet. An explanation of the form follows:

1. *Information.* This section contains the information available to the participants at the time. Considerations are weather, operational, response, personnel, and community impact information.

2. *Issues.* Here the facilitator will list issues that the participants should identify. The participant will have a blank form and will fill in this block.

3. *Priority.*   Here the facilitator asks the participants to prioritize the issues identified. This generally get the participants involved in a lot of discussion.

4. *Action.*   Here the participants indicate what action should or would be taken to address identified issues.

5. *Responsibility.*   This is where you will have the participants indicate who would complete the action steps. If you note, as has happened, that one name consistently comes up, that may be an indication of potential bottlenecks in the response or problems with the emergency management plan.

As with the previous forms, the header and footer information stays the same.

The evaluator checklist is a form that was developed to evaluate specific portions of the EMRO, operations, activities, etc. Depending on the scope of your drill or exercise, this checklist can be one page or several pages. In the attached example, I have provided a snapshot for some of the evaluation activity related to initial activation and response. These are the key points of this form:

1. *Evaluator assignment.*   The evaluator fills in the location, group, and function that she or he was assigned to evaluate, for example, logistics section, command post.

2. *Evaluation objective.*   This indicates the activity or exercise objective you wish to evaluate, for example, initial activation/response, communications, command post adequacy, etc.

3. *Evaluation item.*   The specific item being evaluated is indicated.

4. *Achieved.*   This indicates how well the item was achieved.

5. *Evaluator's comments.*   This space is for noting only comments, points, etc. related to the item being evaluated. This section is especially helpful when you are working on the drill or exercise report.

You will note the use of a sliding scale for determining the degree to which the item being evaluated was satisfactorily addressed. You may wish to consider a number scale or some other form of sliding scale of effectiveness.

Audit and Evaluation Considerations

All too often we overlook the significance of having an adequate program for the evaluation of emergency preparedness. Within your program, you have made commitments. In many instances, you have made significant commitments, with regard to regulatory compliance and noncompliance-related matters. You and those who have a role in your program need to be aware of and prepared to address the assessment and evaluation of the emergency management system (EMS). For our purposes, we will refer to the evaluation component of the system as the *audit program*. This chapter will provide an overview of an approach to developing and implementing a workable audit program.

> *Audit and evaluation* constitute the means established to periodically verify, document, and ensure emergency preparedness capabilities. It is also the mechanism for change within the system, since the results should reflect current capabilities, hazards, and program orientation.

The relationship between safety audits, job hazard identification, risk assessment, business impact analysis, and your EMS audit program should be clearly established and coordinated to ensure appropriate inputs to the system.

Chapter organizer: What this chapter is about

What are the audit program considerations for the EMS? Nine key elements constitute the scope or focus for the all-hazards EMS audit program structure. By establishing a program that effectively evaluates these nine components, you can begin to develop an effective foundation for making emergency preparedness a part of the way you do business, not an adjunct function of the business you do.

The nine components are (1) program administration, (2) emergency management/response organization, (3) training and retraining, (4) emergency facilities and equipment, (5) coordination with external entities (agencies, mutual aid, corporate, etc.), (6) validation programs: drills and exercises, (7) communications, (8) hazard analysis, and (9) program certification.

You may have noted a similarity to the essential nine elements of analysis presented in Chap. 3. This similarity is not a chance occurrence. Your audit program components should reflect the scope of your initial and ongoing planning and preparedness efforts.

Audit Program Guidelines

The first step in developing an effective audit program is to get all personnel to realize that they have a vested interest in the outcome of every audit. You will also have to convince people that it is acceptable to identify inadequacies, discover new hazards, and challenge the effectiveness of various system components. In fact, it is quite healthy to find issues that need to be resolved.

Unlike a standard project, emergency preparedness is an unending code of activity. You are never truly finished with the development of your program.

The second step has two parts. First, you must develop a policy statement regarding emergency preparedness. Second, you must reflect the policy statement in your plan and supporting documentation.

You might be scratching your head at this point, saying to yourself, "What's he talking about? I've written the plan, appendices, and procedures. Now you're telling me that I need a policy statement. Shouldn't that have been the first task I undertook?"

Many would agree, yes, that is the first task you should have accomplished. I would say, not necessarily. First, you have to know what you are faced with, then have somewhat of a plan in mind to deal with situations, and finally develop and implement an effective policy to ensure concurrence with your program commitments. In this way, you can develop a checks-and-balances system for addressing the commitments you will make in your plan and supporting materials.

The third step is to have management—and by this I mean at the highest levels—sign off on the policy statement. You accomplish several things by doing this. First, you make management part of the process. Second, you establish the importance of the program. And third, you ensure continued interest in and support of the program.

A typical policy statement should contain the following:

- A statement that provides the foundation for overall emergency preparedness
- Reference to your program implementation guidance (if any)
- A listing of the minimum acceptable standards for program implementation and acceptability
- Reference to regulatory compliance and any related programs
- A statement as to management's commitment to the program
- Signature blocks for appropriate levels of management

You should not take the policy development step lightly. It can become one of the most incriminating documents you'll ever have to deal with. Be assured, it will be one of the first that opposing attorneys will seek when conducting discovery after you've had an incident.

Audit Program Components: Overview

In this section, I will not attempt to provide a detailed discussion of all the elements that constitute the audit program. I will provide an overview of the key considerations for the nine program components, with examples of each. At the end of this chapter is a sample of a typical section from an emergency management plan (EMP), addressing the evaluation system.

Program administration

This component consists of all items related to the development and ongoing maintenance of your emergency management system (EMS). Six measures of effectiveness help define the component: assignment of responsibility, authority, coordination, selection and qualification, management guidelines, and reference library. Key issues to be audited include, but are not necessarily limited to, the policy statement, program scope, regulatory compliance initiatives, program authority, assignment of responsibility, program maintenance, reporting and documentation, safety and environmental audits, and other sources of information.

An example of a typical audit question might be:

Are there selection criteria established for those personnel responsible for emergency/crisis management planning?   Yes/No _____

A yes answer would have to be backed up with the appropriate citation to documentation on selection criteria. A no would indicate an area where further development may be required.

Emergency management/response organization

This consists of four elements: organizational structure, organizational composition, position qualifications, and augmentation. Typical issues to be audited include incident command system, concept of operations, capability to carry out assigned functions, long-term continuity of operations, certification of position holders.

Here is an example of a typical audit question:

> Are personnel who may be assigned to the functional area *management selection* specified by position or title and name, in the plan and supporting documentation, throughout all levels of the company? Yes/No _____

The answer at a minimum should include a response to each of the following:

Emergency management functions

- Overall incident management
- Safety
- Legal
- Medical
- Crisis communications
- Liaison

Business management functions

- Normal business operations
- Management interface
- Community interface
- Legal
- Medical

Training and retraining

The audit area provides information on the type of instruction system(s) employed, various training programs (in-house and external), certification and accreditation, documentation, and recordkeeping. Key issues focus on the adequacy of the training and retraining program.

For instance, if you state that all personnel who will assume overall management for an incident will be trained in accordance with applicable regulatory guidance, can you prove it? Are your senior managers going to attend the 40-hour OSHA 1910.120, HAZWOPER, incident commander-designated training sessions? If so, what is the minimum acceptable grade for passing? How are incorrect responses to questions addressed, by retesting or some other means?

Emergency facilities and equipment

Three areas are of interest: emergency facilities, emergency equipment, and expanded support facilities. The type, adequacy, inventory, design, availability, operability, and maintenance of designated emergency facilities and equipment should be assessed. If you list it in your plan and supporting documentation, be sure that it is where it is supposed to be, and, that it works like it's supposed to.

A sample question might be, Is emergency instrumentation periodically calibrated in accordance with approved procedures?

Coordination with external entities

Any entity not within the confines of your location should be considered external. This includes company assets not associated with your operation, for example, corporate augmentation staff or a nonassociated operation such as a pipeline terminal or marketing and transportation operations colocated with your operation. Obviously, any local, federal, and state response agencies as well as contractors are included under this category. And do not forget the news media!

Validation programs

Drills and exercises constitute one of the most visual means of assessing preparedness. However, most drill and exercise programs tend to focus on the response aspects of an incident. You will want to assess your organization's ability to perform at all levels of management and under a variety of conditions. For example, does the drill and exercise program provide for off-hours drills and exercises?

Communications

Four areas should be addressed in this component: crisis communications program, training in personal communication techniques, community outreach, and program monitoring. Notice that there is nothing on communications equipment. Communications equipment is audited under the emergency facilities and equipment component. As with the other components, any yes answer should elicit a documentation trail. Any no answer should elicit a "to be done" response or a "not applicable" response, and any reasons for the response.

Hazard analysis

Three areas are covered: hazard identification and analysis, evaluation of compliance, and commitment identification, resolution, and tracking. A comprehensive audit cannot overlook the hazard analysis. The hazard analysis is one of the most crucial parts of your emergency management system. It must be dynamic, and it must be structured to readily accept change. So you have to periodically audit the results to ensure they are current. The audit program should also have a built-in mechanism that allows for resolution of identified deficiencies.

Program certification

This final component of the audit program focuses on program certification. Certifying your EMP and associated materials will also validate the program. But what do we mean by certification? Certification of your program means that you can comfortably say, "I can produce all the associated documentation to support the commitments made in our program, both regulatory and nonregulatory." It also means that you and your management are willing to sign the appropriate documents to verify the adequacy of the program.

The certification component consists of a document or series of documents verifying program components as adequate. This may include reports, checklists, audit statements, and other official program documents. I would recommend that any certification be accompanied by a notarization of signatures and application of the corporate seal where appropriate.

Good examples of program certification can be found in the nuclear industry emergency preparedness programs, spill prevention control and countermeasures (SPCC) requirements, OSHA 29 CFR 1910, accreditation of training programs for hazardous waste operations, Oil Pollution Act of 1990, and the national preparedness for response exercise program (PREP) guidelines.

As you can see, your audit program brings you back to the beginning, to the point where you take the next step toward upgrading and enhancing the program. Much has been written on continuous improvement processes, total quality management, quality assurance, and quality control. Your audit program must incorporate these features to keep your EMS viable.

Sample

ALL-HAZARDS EMERGENCY MANAGEMENT PLAN SECTION __: EVALUATION

Sample

Plan Development and Maintenance

The emergency management plan (EMP) and supporting material will be reviewed and updated at such times as may be necessary, but in no case less than annually. Updating of the EMP will be preceded by an appraisal of its contents and/or validation critique. Implementation of the EMP in response to an actual emergency will be considered a validation and will require a critique, after-action report, and appropriate follow-up.

Items which are subject to frequent change and will be reviewed annually for possible updating include, but are not limited to, the following:

- Notification and alerting lists, including identity and phone numbers of response personnel
- Off-site response organizations, mutual aid agreements, LEPC committee membership, and EMRO personnel staffing
- Hazard analyses and maps
- Transportation routes for hazardous materials
- Inventories of critical equipment, supplies, and other resources
- Appendices
- Emergency plan implementing procedures (EPIPs)

Update Policy

The following policies apply to the appraisal and updating of the EMP:

- It is the responsibility of the [POSITION, TITLE] to coordinate the update of the plan. Support will be provided by all departments and outside groups which have a role in emergency response under the plan.
- The EMP will be updated as necessary and on an annual basis. This update will be preceded by a thorough review of the plan's contents. A written report on this review will be prepared. The report will highlight significant changes, deficiencies, and other data relevant to an update of the plan.
- In conducting the plan review, input from all departments, local agencies, and other parties will be sought.
- The [DEPARTMENT] will serve as the office of record for the plan and supporting materials. [DEPARTMENT] will maintain files rel-

ative to the planning effort and will keep an inventory of emergency public information and other planning and training materials.

- The [POSITION, TITLE] will maintain a list of controlled copies of the plan and plan holders to ensure appropriate changes are received by all parties.

Purpose of the Audit

The emergency preparedness audit program has been designed to establish a standard means for evaluating the overall adequacy and effectiveness of the emergency response program. The audit program has been designed to evaluate the capability to provide appropriate response and protective action recommendations in the event of an emergency. Any deficiencies are to be reported to [POSITION TITLE].

The audit program has also been designed to facilitate an integrated look at the overall emergency response program. By the very nature of its goal—the evaluation of overall effectiveness and adequacy of the emergency plan implementation—an audit may delve into areas for which there are no explicit regulatory requirements. The audit is not specifically geared toward finding areas of noncompliance, however.

Elements of the Audit

The audit is designed to assess the ability of emergency response personnel to complete the sequence of critical tasks, under emergency conditions, using resources available at the site. Assessment of the organization's ability to provide desired emergency response is based upon an audit of nine essential elements of analysis (EEA):

1. Program administration
2. Emergency management/response organization (EMRO)
3. Emergency response training and recurrent training
4. Emergency response facilities and equipment
5. Coordination with off-site agencies
6. Drills and exercises
7. Communications
8. Hazard evaluation
9. Program certification

Benefits to be gained from the audit program include assurances of adequate emergency planning and preparedness for employees and the general public.

Annual audits will encompass

- General information (site history)
- Management awareness and control programs
- Identification of hazardous materials
- Hazardous materials handling, collection, and storage
- Record keeping and regulatory compliance
- Site characterization

The approach will typically be to conduct

- Personnel interviews
- Overview of written procedures
- Site analysis

Conducting this type of audit will generally identify areas in need of attention, establish a list of compliance commitments that have to be met, and document current efforts to those ends.

Audit Planning Guidelines

In planning the annual emergency preparedness audit, three elements should be taken into consideration:

- What goals does the emergency response program set?
- What goals does the audit have?
- What actions will be taken to resolve audit-identified deficiencies?

The planning procedures for each of these areas should include a review of the areas cited in the emergency management plan. The review will consist of a narrative or statistical report. By looking at the answers to the questions for each area, an overall view of the emergency response program will be developed. The results will help improve the emergency management/response program.

15

Public Outreach Program Considerations

How do you plan to explain to the public, your community leaders, activists, and interested others that your company can respond effectively and manage during an incident? This chapter will provide an overview of various public outreach considerations. Note that often there is a very fine dividing line between public outreach and public outrage. *Public outreach,* as described in the all-hazards emergency management system (EMS), addresses all means that you make available for the public to access information, clarify concerns, and establish a framework for cooperation prior to and during an incident. This includes, but is not limited to, information programs, facility tours, assistance in emergency preparedness activities beyond your plant boundaries, and other forms of community cooperation.

Chapter organizer: What this chapter is about

What are the considerations for an effective public outreach program? Management is never more severely tested than during a crisis. The decision making is immediate, and so are the results. Public outrage can be equated to perception of hazards and understanding of hazards. In most instances, outrage values are high because the general perception is low, combined with either a lack of understanding or a failure to believe (perhaps resistance in some cases) the information provided. How you overcome this resistance and reluctance is important. You must bring the community to a level of understanding that ensures their comfort with your capabilities.

Your company's relationship with the communities in which you operate will have a dramatic influence on your ability to successfully manage a crisis and then return to normal operations.

Community Involvement

Establishing and maintaining a relationship with community leaders, regulatory and nonregulatory agencies, response organizations (public and private), and organizations that support your area's infrastructure (utilities, banks, financial services, churches, and other organizations) can lead to the development of a better emergency management system for all parties. There are several reasons for this. First, only a common terminology can be developed. This allows for improved communications. Improved communications mean everyone has a universal understanding of terms. This leads to efficiency, which, we all know, can lead to reduced response time and reduced operations time. Second, information sharing enhances the planning process. By sharing information, you can evaluate hazards, vulnerabilities, and risks with more confidence and greater understanding. You may even be able to reduce hazards by finding alternatives and/or eliminating sources. Elimination of hazards reduces vulnerability and risk, thereby making the community safer.

It sounds simple, right? Well, you are going to have to overcome some hurdles. The first hurdle is to overcome the public's general distrust of business.

That's why your company should develop and implement a public outreach program as a component of the emergency management plan (EMP) and as part of your normal preparation for handling emergencies. The public outreach program should offer guidelines for ongoing, effective, and responsible communications with the community. Such effective communications can help establish and maintain your company's integrity and credibility.

Business simply must devote sufficient resources to communicate effectively, accurately, and often, in order to gain the public's trust and confidence. When routine incidents are treated as front-page news by the media, you cannot afford to have a skeptical public scrutinize your operations. We must be prepared to deal with public perception as well as reality. You cannot allow the community outreach function to be a "bit player" and then expect a stellar performance when the going gets tough. Your staff will not be ready, and the public is not likely to accept their information as valid and truthful.

As you begin to formulate your public outreach program, you need to understand and assess risk. Risk is an everyday part of life in today's business environment. However, many affected entities view risk differently. The company engineer may view risk as the probability of something happening. Basically, this is an analytical view using numbers to reflect the probability. The company's environmental staff may view risk in terms of the probable health effects related to exposure.

The public, however, views risk in an entirely different fashion. The public response to risk is generally emotional. That is, the public perception of risk may not be in harmony with the results of the engineer or the environmental staff's models of risk. The public, for example, uses many factors in addition to numbers in deciding whether something is risky. That is why an effective public outreach program depends heavily on educating the public. We often think facts and numbers associated with our risk assessments will convince the public to accept risk associated with our operations. Instead, the public generally uses other factors to develop its perceptions and acceptance of the perceived risks involved.

You may be tempted to dismiss the public's emotional reactions to the risks associated with your operations or their tendency to disregard numbers in favor of other considerations. But remember this: *Although the public perception of risk may not bear much resemblance to risk assessment, when it comes to people accepting the risk, perception is reality.*

In order for your public outreach program to be successful, you need to change the public's perception. Having regular meetings with community leaders to review your operations, discuss emergency management plans, and talk about options for assisting the community can lead to building a base of trust within the community.

One area of focus for these community meetings should be to identify ways in which your business can assist the community. This assistance should not be limited to emergency situations. By identifying opportunities for sharing information and resources, you can further reduce hazards, lessen vulnerability, and reduce risk.

In Chap. 4, we discussed mutual aid agreements and other forms of information sharing as an administrative function of the EMS. Mutual aid agreements should be an integral part of your public outreach strategy. They should not be limited to emergency response considerations. Your agreements should define

- The type of assistance to be provided
- Communication protocols
- Activation protocols and chain-of-command considerations
- Humanitarian assistance protocols
- Public information protocols
- Media relations protocols

The last area, media relations, is important. As much as possible you (and your community) should attempt to get the media working for the common interest of all parties. Too often the media are viewed as adversaries. Positive news reporting can have just as big an impact as negative news reporting.

In the following sections of this chapter, we have outlined some examples and thoughts for an effective public outreach program.

Public Outreach Program

The following outline can be used to develop your public outreach program. Consideration should be given, when this program is developed, to your biggest audience—your employees and their families. Make employees an integral part of the program. They can be some of your most effective spokespersons, or they can, if neglected, be one of your biggest critics.

1. *Employee information network.* Establish an employee information network. This can be accomplished in several ways, e.g., employee newsletters, communiqués, periodic meetings with management, and functions such as picnics. All are effective means of getting information communicated to the employees and receiving information and ideas from the employees. One thing is important: Make the information network a means for *two-way* communications. And keep it focused on information sharing, not gripe airing.

2. *Community advisory panel.* Establish a community advisory panel with local community leaders. The Chemical Manufacturers Association (CMA) has developed a *community advisory panel (CAP)* handbook that is designed to facilitate putting a community advisory panel together. Again, the focus of the panel should be communication—information sharing, not confrontation.

3. *Internal audits.* Internal audits ensure that the organization maintains compliance and meets corporate policy goals. Audits also identify areas where increased information sharing can diffuse potential concerns. You can use the audit results for employee and community education. In this way, you provide an opportunity for dialogue, feedback, and community participation.

4. *Product stewardship.* The American Petroleum Institute (API) through its program Strategies for Today's Environmental Partnership (STEP) and the Chemical Manufacturers Association (CMA) Responsible Care Program both provide excellent guidance on product stewardship. Your program should seek inputs from not only the community but also customers, shareholders, suppliers, and others, such as the Securities and Exchange Commission (SEC), which has established requirements for disclosures of environmental liability.

5. *Community service.* Establish a program for community service. This can include training, involvement as a sponsor for various community activities, and nonemergency services such as funding for

community projects. This funding can be in the form of donations of equipment, time, heavy equipment use, etc. During an incident, you can assist the community with personnel, equipment, shelter, feeding facilities, food, clothing, building materials, emergency operations centers, transportation, and other services. Your aim should be active involvement in the community so that both the industry and the community benefit from the relationship.

6. *Public information.* Establish a program for ongoing public information. When an incident expands beyond the facility boundaries, it's too late to build a public information program. The community will want to know the nature and extent of the incident. People will want to know how safe they are, where injuries are being treated, and a host of other humanitarian assistance issues. The goal of the public information component of your outreach program should be to establish an ongoing dialogue with the audience that may be affected by an incident and/or the results of your operations. These may include, but are not limited to, employees and retirees, unions, contractors, suppliers, customers, shareholders, regulatory agencies, appointed and elected officials, special interest groups, industrial neighbors, and the media.

Once you have established the parameters of your program, you should develop a kit that contains readily accessible information which can be easily distributed prior to and/or during an incident. The kit should include background information on your organization, company, and operations. It should also include information on emergency contacts, notification procedures, instructions for sheltering and evacuation assembly, accountability, and key community services. One thing I've found very useful is to develop a calendar with emergency information and other facts on it. These calendars are practical and useful. I don't know anyone who doesn't need a calendar. Hang it over or near the telephone, and you have quick access to important information in an emergency.

Conclusion

The public outreach program should be developed to inform and educate the public. This program can be very effective when it is coordinated with the EMP and local response agencies and authorities. An information package should be developed and distributed at least annually to the affected population. This package should contain generic information about the company, the emergency management/response program, and where to call for more information.

It is prudent to prepare a fact sheet on your facility and have it available for reporters. It is an important hedge against inaccurate news stories and increases the "comfort index" of reporters. Reporters need the correct names of chemicals and processes, the size of the operation, the number of employees, and perhaps even the company's accurate name.

The fact sheet—prepared *before* a crisis happens—helps you avoid answering the simplest questions.

The public outreach program should also contain specific information regarding protective action and what actions the public should take in the event of notification of an emergency situation. Information on sheltering and other protective actions, evacuation maps, and lists of radio and television stations to listen to in an emergency should be included. A list of telephone numbers to call for information, such as the sheriff's department or rumor control, may be included in this package.

Self-addressed mailers for the handicapped or special care facilities should be developed and distributed. This subsection should describe the plan and procedures for maintaining the documentation in a secure and restricted access location.

Revisions to the public outreach packages should be made as often as needed. An annual mailing of the information should be conducted. Mailing lists can be coordinated with the telephone company, electric utility office, and local authorities.

Transient populations in the affected area should be addressed in this chapter also. Plans should be described for the posting of information in public areas, such as the post office, telephone booths, telephone books, and recreation areas.

A description of the evacuation routes and the posting of signs indicating these routes should be part of the public information packages. Occasional public meetings designed to answer questions of the local residents should be planned for and encouraged.

If you take the time to develop and implement an effective public outreach program, using the suggestions just discussed, you will go a long way toward success when a crisis occurs. Then it's up to you, your employees, and the community to implement and maintain the program.

Bibliography

A Conceptual Approach to State and Local Exercises. Civil Preparedness Circular 84-2, Federal Emergency Management Agency, 1984.

Bean, M. (1987): "Tools for Environmental Professionals Involved in Risk Communication at Hazardous Waste Facilities Undergoing Siting, Permitting, or Remediation," Rep. 8730.8. Reston, VA: Air Pollution Control Association.

Bomb and Physical Security Planning, Department of the Treasury, Bureau of Alcohol, Tobacco, and Firearms, July 1987.

Brown, Michael H. (1987): *The Toxic Cloud,* New York: Harper & Row.

Cairncross, Frances (1991): *Costing the Earth.* Cambridge, MA: Harvard Business School Press.

Chemical Emergencies: Guidance for the Management of Chemically Contaminated Patients in the Pre-Hospital Setting, Agency for Toxic Substances and Disease Registry.

Chemical Emergencies: Hospital Emergency Department Guidelines, U.S. Department of Health and Human Services.

Commanding the Initial Response, National Fire Academy, Boston.

Community Emergency Response Exercises, Washington: Chemical Manufacturers Association, 1986.

Construction of Written Achievement Tests, 2d ed., Detroit Edison Company, Employee Training Division, October 1972.

Covello, V. T. (1983): "The Perception of Technological Risks: A Literature Review." *Technological Forecasting and Social Change,* 23:285–297.

Covello, V. T. (1988): "Informing the Public about Health and Environmental Risks: Problems and Opportunities for Effective Risk Communication," in N. Lind, ed., *Risk Communication: A Symposium.* Waterloo: University of Waterloo, Iowa.

Covello, V., and F. Allen (1988): *Seven Cardinal Rules of Risk Communications.* Washington: U.S. Environmental Protection Agency, Office of Policy Analysis.

Covello, V., D. McCallum, and M. Pavlova, eds. (1988): *Effective Risk Communications: The Role and Responsibility of Government.* New York: Plenum.

Covello, V., D. von Winterfeldt, and P. Slovic (1987): "Communicating Risk Information to the Public," in J. C. Davies, V. Covello, and F. Allen, eds., *Risk Communication.* Washington: Conservation Foundation.

Criteria for Review of Hazardous Materials Emergency Plans, National Response Team, May 1988.

Davidow, William H., and Uttal Bro (1989): *Total Customer Service.* New York: Harper Perennial.

Davies, J. C., V. T. Covello, and F. W. Allen, eds. (1987): *Risk Communications.* Washington: Conservation Foundation.

Developing a Hazardous Materials Exercise Program: A Handbook for State and Local Officials, National Response Team, September 1990.

Development of a Checklist for Evaluating Emergency Procedures Used in Nuclear Power Plants, Nuclear Regulatory Commission, NUREG/CR-1970 SAND81-7070.

Egan, Gerard (1993): *Adding Value.* Jossey-Bass Publishers, San Francisco, CA.

Emergency Operating Procedures Writing Guidelines, Institute for Nuclear Power Operations, INPO 82-017, July 1982.

Exercise Design Course, Federal Emergency Management Agency, 1984.

Exercise Design Course: Exercise Scenarios, SM-170.3, Federal Emergency Management Agency, January 1989.

Exercise Design Course: Guide to Emergency Management Exercises, Federal Emergency Management Agency, January 1989.

Exercising Emergency Plans under Title III, SM-305.4, Federal Emergency Management Agency, September 1990.

Fessenden-Raden, J., J. Fitchen, and J. Heath (1987): "Risk Communication at the Local Level: A Complex Interactive Process," *Science, Technology and Human Values,* December.

Fire Command, National Fire Protection Association, Boston.

Fire Protection Guide on Hazardous Materials, 7th ed., National Fire Protection Association, April 1981.

Fire Service Supervision: Increasing Personal Effectiveness, National Fire Academy.

Fischhoff, B. (1985a), "Managing Risk Perception," *Issues in Science and Technology,* 2:83–96.

Fischhoff, B. (1985b): "Protocols for Environmental Reporting: What to Ask the Experts," *The Journalist,* winter, pp. 11–15.

Fischhoff, B., P. Slovic, and S. Lichtenstein (1979): "Weighing the Risks," *Environment,* vol. 21.

Fischhoff, B., S. Lichtenstein, P. Slovic, S. L. Derbe, and R. L. Keeney (1981): *Acceptable Risk.* New York: Cambridge University Press.

George R. Herzog: *Management of Flammable Liquid Storage Tank Fires.*

Guide to Exercises in Chemical Emergency Preparedness Programs. Washington: Environmental Protection Agency, May 1988.

Guidelines on Biological Impacts of Oil Pollution, International Petroleum Industry Environmental Conservation Association.

Hance, B., C. Chess, and P. Sandman (1987): *Improving Dialogue with Communities: A Risk Communication Manual for Government.* Trenton, NJ: Office of Science and Research, New Jersey Department of Environmental Protection, December.

Handbook of Chemical Hazard Analysis Procedures. Washington: Environmental Protection Agency, Federal Emergency Management Agency, Department of Transportation.

HAZ-MAT Response Team Leak and Spill Guide, Fire Protection Publications, Oklahoma State University.

Hazardous Chemical Safety, J. T. Baker Chemical Company, prod. no. 3-4525.

Hazardous Materials Emergency Planning Guide (NRT-1), National Response Team, May 1988.

Hazardous Materials Exercise Evaluation Methodology (HM-EEM) and Manual, Federal Emergency Management Agency, October 1989.

Hydrorefining Process Units: Loss Causes and Guidelines for Loss Prevention, Oil Insurance Association.

Incident Command System and Structural Firefighting, National Fire Academy, Boston.

Incident Command System, Fire Protection Publications, Oklahoma State University.

Interservice Procedures for Instructional Systems Development, Washington: Government Printing Office, TRADOC Pamphlet 350-30.

Johnson, B., and V. Covello, eds. (1987): *The Social and Cultural Construction of Risk: Essays on Risk Selection and Perception.* Boston: Reidel.

Kahneman, D., P. Slovic, and A. Tversky, eds. (1982): *Judgment under Uncertainty: Heuristics and Biases.* New York: Cambridge University Press.

Kasperson, R. (1986): "Six Propositions on Public Participation and Their Relevance to Rick Communication," *Risk Analysis,* 6:275–282.

Kasperson, R., and J. Kasperson (1983): "Determining the Acceptability of Risk: Ethical and Policy Issues," in J. Rogers and D. Bates, eds., *Risk: A Symposium.* Ottawa: The Royal Society of Canada.

Klaidman, S. (1985): *Health Risk Reporting.* Washington: Institute for Health Policy Analysis, Georgetown University.

Major Transportation Carrier Disasters: Improving Response and Coordination, American Hospital Association.

Management of Process Hazards, American Petroleum Institute Recommended Practice 750, January 1990.

Mazur, A. (1981): "Media Coverage and Public Opinion on Scientific Controversies," *Journal of Communication,* pp. 106–115.

Nelkin, D. (1984): *Science in the Streets.* New York: Twentieth Century Fund.

Oil Spill Prevention—Marine Terminals, Management Guidelines, March 27, 1990, American Petroleum Institute.

Oil Spill Response Guide, Pollution Technology Review 174, Robert J. Meyers & Associates, Research Planning Institute, Inc., 1989.

On Scene Coordinator/Regional Response Team, Oil and Hazardous substances discharge simulation, Planning Manual; U.S. Department of Transportation, United States Coast Guard.

Operational Safety Program, Union Carbide Company.

Porter, Michael E. (1980): *Competitive Strategy.* New York: Free Press.

Pre-Fire Planning, Lamar University, Boston.

Preparing for Incident Command, National Fire Academy, Boston.

President's Commission on the Accident at Three Mile Island (1979): *Report of the Public's Right to Information Task Force.* Washington: U.S. Government Printing Office.

Press, F. (1987): "Science and Risk Communication," pp. 11–17 in J. C. Davies, V. T. Covello, and F. W. Allen, eds., *Risk Communication.* Washington: Conservation Foundation.

Radiological Series (Train the Trainer) for Radiological Instructors III in Emergency Management Institute, National Emergency Training Center 1985-1986 Course Catalog; Federal Emergency Management Agency, 1985.

Ruckelshaus, W. D. (1983): "Science, Risk, and Public Policy," *Science,* 221: 1026–1028.

Ruckelshaus, W. D. (1984): "Risk in a Free Society," *Risk Analysis,* September, pp. 157–163.

Ruckelshaus, W. D. (1987): "Communicating about Risk," pp. 3–9 in J. C. Davies, V. T. Covello, and F. W. Allen, eds., *Risk Communication.* Washington: Conservation Foundation.

Sandman, P. M. (1986a): "Getting to Maybe: Some Communications Aspects of Hazardous Waste Facility Siting," *Seton Hall Legislative Journal,* spring.

Sandman, P. M. (1986b): *Explaining Environmental Risk.* Washington: Environmental Protection Agency, Office of Toxic Substances.

Sandman, P., D. Sachsman, and M. Greenberg (1987): *Risk Communication for Environmental News Sources.* New Brunswick, NJ: Industry/University Cooperative Center for Research in Hazardous and Toxic Substances.

Sandman, P., D. Sachsman, M. Greenberg, and M. Gotchfeld (1987): *Environmental Risk and the Press.* New Brunswick, NJ: Transaction Books.

Scenario Development Manual: Exercise Development, Federal Emergency Management Agency, 1985.

Sharlin, H. (1987): "EDB: A Case Study in the Communication of Health Risk," in B. Johnson and V. Covello, eds., *The Social and Cultural Construction of Risk: Essays on Risk Selection and Perception.* Boston: Reidel.

Sikich, Geary W. (1987): "Overview of Emergency Planning under SARA Title III," Chicago Bar Association, Continuing Legal Education Seminar, April 18, 1989.

Sikich, Geary W. (1987): "Overview of Emergency Planning," Emergency Planning Workshop, October 5–6.

Sikich, Geary W. (1993): *It Can't Happen Here: All Hazards Crisis Management Planning.* Tulsa, PennWell Books.

Sikich, Geary W. (1994): *"All Hazards" Crisis Management Planning, International Review for Chief Executive Officers.* London: Sterling Publications.

Sikich, Geary W. (1994): *Multimedia Strategies for Asset Management: Framework for Emergency Management Planning,* American Institute of Chemical Engineers, Denver, Colorado.

Sikich, Geary W., "A Strategic Approach to Reducing Vulnerability for Industries Covered under CERCLA, RCRA, SARA, OSHA," Chicago Bar Association, Continuing Legal Education Seminar, April 18, 1989.

Sikich, Geary W., "Buyer Beware," *Perspective,* 15(1), 1989.

Sikich, Geary W., "Cleaning Up Our Act: Accounting for Environmental and Safety Issues," *1994 Midwest Accounting and Business Show,* Chicago, Illinois CPA Foundation.

Sikich, Geary W., "Crisis Communications Planning," Emergency Planning Workshop, *Hazwaste Expo Chicago '89,* October 16, 1989.

Sikich, Geary W., "Crisis Communications Planning," *Hazwaste Expo Atlanta '89,* Emergency Planning Workshop, May 1–4, 1989.

Sikich, Geary W., "Current Environmental Issues," Illinois CPA Foundation Agribusiness Conference, September 20, 1991.

Sikich, Geary W., "Emergency Planning and Preparedness: The Planning Function," *Hazwaste Expo Chicago '89,* Emergency Planning Workshop, October 16, 1989.

Sikich, Geary W., "Emergency Planning and Preparedness: The Planning Function," Emergency Planning Workshop, October 5 and 6, 1987.

Sikich, Geary W., "Emergency Planning: Managing Compliance with Overlapping Environmental, Health and Safety Regulations," Institute of Business Law Seminar, Chicago, October 16, 1991.

Sikich, Geary W., "Environmental Laws Hold Hospitals Liable for-Wastes," *Hospital Materials Management,* October 1988.

Sikich, Geary W., "Environmental Risks Can Be Made Acceptable through Awareness and Careful Management," *Midwest Real Estate News,* January 1989.

Sikich, Geary W., "Evaluating Compliance," *Hazwaste Expo Chicago '89,* Emergency Planning Workshop, October 16, 1989.

Sikich, Geary W., "Evaluating Compliance," Emergency Planning Workshop, October 5 and 6, 1987; presented at *Financial Reporting of Environmental Exposures,* Washington, December 5 and 6, 1988.

Sikich, Geary W., "Overview of Emergency Planning," *Hazwaste Expo Chicago '89,* Emergency Planning Workshop, October 16, 1989.

Sikich, Geary W., "Reducing Environmental Vulnerability," *New Accountant,* March 1991.

Sikich, Geary W., "Reducing Vulnerability: Accountants and Environmental Regulations in the 90's," 1990 Midwest Accounting and Business Management Show, August 31, 1990.

Sikich, Geary W., "Regulatory Compliance," *Hazwaste Expo Atlanta '89,* May 1–4, 1989.

Sikich, Geary W., "Regulatory Compliance," *Hazwaste Expo Chicago '89,* October 16–19, 1989.

Sikich, Geary W., "Regulatory Compliance," Abbott Laboratories Corporate Environmental Conference; October 24–25, 1989, Abbott Laboratories, Northbrook, IL.

Sikich, Geary W., "The Accountant's Role in Environmental Liability," *Insight,* 4(1), June 1991.

Sikich, Geary W., "What a CPA Needs to Know about Environmental, Health and Safety Regulations," Business Valuation Curriculum Series, Illinois CPA Foundation. Presented as a continuing education course, July 1991 and December 1991.

Sikich, Geary W., "What if...., Corporate Responsibility and Shareholder Rights: The Impact of Environmental Legislation on Shareholders," March 1988; presented at Financial Reporting of Environmental Exposures, Washington, December 5 and 6, 1988.

Sikich, Geary W., "What You *Can* Do: Ways to Assess and Mitigate Your Company's Environmental Risks," Home Center Industry Presidents Council, National Hardware Show, Chicago, August 13, 1989.

Sikich, Geary W., "You Can Lose at Regulatory Roulette," *Safety and Health Magazine,* August 1989.

Sikich, Geary W., *Management's Challenge: Environmental Disclosure Considerations,* Air & Waste Management Association, Chicago, Illinois, 1994.

Sikich, Geary W., and Nelson S. Slavik, "Industry Expectations concerning Healthcare Response to OSHA 1910.120 `Hazardous Waste Operations and Emergency Response'"; *Environmental Health Manager,* 4(1), spring 1990.

Sikich, Geary W., Seminar on Emergency Planning: An Introduction to Emergency Planning; Emergency Plan Development Communicating Emergency Information; Evaluating Regulatory Compliance; Indiana Civil Defense Council, April 27, 1990.

Slovic, P. (1986): "Informing and Educating the Public about Risk," *Risk Analysis,* 4:403–415.

Slovic, P. (1987): "Perception of Risk," *Science,* 236:280–285.

Slovic, P., and B. Fischhoff (1982): "How Safe Is Safe Enough? Determinants of Perceived and Acceptable Risk," in L. Gould and C. Walker, eds., *Too Hot to Handle.* New Haven, CT: Yale University Press.

Slovic, P., B. Fischhoff, and S. Lichtenstein (1982): "Facts versus Fears: Understanding Perceived Risk," in D. Kahneman, P. Slovic, and A. Tversky, eds., *Judgment under Uncertainty: Heuristics and Biases.* Cambridge: Cambridge University Press.

Smart, Bruce (1992): *Beyond Compliance.* World Resources Institute, Harvard Book Review.

Steven Fink (1986): American Management Association, *Crisis Management: Planning for the Inevitable.*

Technical Guidance for Hazard Analysis Emergency Planning for Extremely Hazardous Substances, Washington: Government Printing Office, December 1987.

Thomas, L. M. (1987): "Why We Must Talk about Risk," pp. 19–25 in J. C. Davies, V. T. Covello, and F. W. Allen, eds., *Risk Communication.* Washington: Conservation Foundation.

Transportation of Hazardous Materials: State and Local Activities, Office of Technology Assessment, March 1986.

Truck Loading Rack Safety, Industrial Risk Insurers.

Webster, Charles L. (1993): *Taking Control of Crisis Interviews,* Cleveland, Charle L. Webster & Associates, Inc.Wilson, R., and E. Crouch (1987): "Risk Assessment and Comparisons: An Introduction," *Science,* 236:267–270, April 17.When Every Second Counts...Crisis Communications Planning, Western Union IDP01000754.

YOUR COMPANY

EMERGENCY MANAGEMENT
PLAN MANUAL

REVISION, APPROVAL, AND
CONTROL OF THE EMERGENCY
MANAGEMENT PLAN AND PLAN
IMPLEMENTING PROCEDURES
EPIP-110

REVISION 0

DATE

SUBMITTED BY: _____ DATE: _____
                    TITLE

APPROVED BY: _____ DATE: _____
                   TITLE

1.0 Purpose

This procedure provides guidance and instructions for the preparation, revision, review, approval, and control of *emergency plan implementing procedures* (EPIPs), and revision and approval of the [NAME] emergency management plan.

2.0 Applicability

This procedure applies to the NAME, TITLE, ORGANIZATION, for the maintenance of the plan, appendices, and EPIPs.

3.0 Definitions

3.1 *Emergency plan implementing procedures (EPIPs).*   These are written instructions specifying the actions to be taken by the emergency management/response organization (EMRO) in the event of an emergency condition.

3.2 *Annual review.*   This is an assessment of the emergency management plan and appendices, emergency plan implementing procedures and practices, training, emergency equipment and supplies, government interfaces, and other emergency planning functions.

3.3 *Standard corporatewide policy language.*   This language describes corporate policy and the systemwide emergency organizational structure. This element is known as the *plan standard* and is the basic foundation of each facility plan.

3.4 *Location-specific procedures and information.*   These are specific techniques, procedures, and training materials related to the mitigation of hazards of the SITE-SPECIFIC LOCATION.

3.5 *Facility-specific information.*   This is information specific to the facility. Such information includes facility personnel names, phone numbers, maps, and information related to local outside agencies, including fire and police departments, hospitals, mutual assistance organizations, and news media.

4.0 Instructions

4.1 Responsibilities

4.1.1 *Facility manager.*   The facility manager is responsible for review and updating of the facility-specific information in this plan. He or she is also responsible for maintaining a list of local outside agencies that have a copy of the plan and for updating those outside copies whenever this plan is updated in accordance with this EPIP.

4.1.2 *TITLE.* This person is responsible for the review and updating of the corporation-specific procedures and information in this plan and for managing the facility plan reviews from a corporate standpoint for all facilities of the corporation.

4.1.3 *TITLE.* This person is responsible for the review and updating of the standard corporatewide policy language of the plan; initiating, coordinating, and issuing the final report on annual systemwide reviews; and coordinating the review of actual responses and drills. This person is responsible for the distribution of all revisions to corporate holders of affected plans.

4.2 General information

Except as indicated below, plan modifications and new and modified EPIPs will be developed and processed for approval in accordance with procedures established as part of the emergency management plan policy management system.

Each EPIP will be sufficiently detailed so as to guide designated individuals or groups during emergencies or potential emergencies. These procedures will be written so that these individuals or groups will know in advance the expected course of events that identifies an emergency condition and the actions that should be taken immediately.

Since emergencies may not follow anticipated patterns, these procedures will provide sufficient flexibility to accommodate variations inherent in the incident. These procedures should include the following provisions:

Detailed instructions to cover step-by-step actions to be taken by designated individuals or groups for the implementation of, and subsequent use of, the EPIP(s)

Supplemental background information to further aid designated individuals or groups in the implementation of the EPIP(s)

4.3 EPIP format

All EPIPs will contain the following elements:

- A title descriptive of the emergency task to which the procedure applies.
- An EPIP identifying number.

- The EPIP revision number.
- A brief statement of the purpose or intent of the EPIP.
- A description of the individuals and/or groups to which the EPIP applies.
- A definitions section in which any applicable item or condition clarifying the EPIP will be described.
- An instructions section that provides guidance to initiate or complete the activity and may include precautions, initial actions, and subsequent actions as applicable.
- A list of applicable references.
- A list of any attachments, if applicable.
- The attachments themselves, which contain information pertinent to the accomplishment of the function or task described in the EPIP. This information may include drawings, telephone lists, data sheets or forms, checklists, flowcharts, and maps. If there are none, the EPIP will so state.

Each page of an EPIP will contain the following information:

- Title or EPIP identifying number
- Revision number
- Issue date
- Page number as part of the entire procedure

The attachments contained in each EPIP will contain the following information:

- EPIP identifying number the first time an attachment is used. This will be the same number if the attachment is used in multiple EPIPs (i.e., log or record-keeping forms) so as to prevent duplication of forms, flowcharts, etc.
- Attachment number.
- Revision number.
- Issue date.
- Attachment page number as part of the entire attachment.

4.4   Review, revision, and approval of the plan and EPIPs

4.4.1   **Annual systemwide review.**   In January of each year, the

TITLE will request each facility manager and TITLE to review the elements of the EMP that they have update responsibility for.

No element of any facility's plan may be modified except by the office of the TITLE. All requests to incorporate changes into this plan shall be transmitted to that office by using the following procedures. Updated pages of the plan will be distributed to holders of affected plans by that office.

Facility-level annual review. Upon receiving notification that the annual systemwide review has been initiated, the facility manager shall review her or his facility's plan and check the accuracy of facility personnel titles; facility personnel names and phone numbers; main contacts, phone numbers, and addresses of all outside agencies mentioned in the plan; all maps contained in the plan; and a controlled copy list.

Next the facility manager shall review each of the following items and determine if they are current, are still applicable to facility operations, and contain no inaccurate information:

- Letters of agreement
- Applicable EPIPs and attachments

The facility manager shall then complete the *plan review report form* within 3 workweeks of receiving notification that the annual systemwide review has been initiated, indicating any changes that need to be made and suggestions for improvements of any elements of the plan. If there are no changes, the facility manager shall so certify on the form. The form shall be submitted to the TITLE.

Corporate-level annual review. Upon receiving notification that the annual systemwide review has been initiated, the TITLE shall

Review all LOCATION-specific plan standards, specifically

Emergency response team member information (names, phone numbers, locations, team leader designation) shall be checked for accuracy.

All EPIPs that were developed specifically for LOCATION operations shall be reviewed for relevance and accuracy.

Other elements of the plan standards shall be reviewed to see if there might be any suggestions for improvements in light of corporate experiences during the previous year.

Process all LOCATION facility plan review reports:

Gather all reports from the field.

Determine a corporate consensus on necessary non-facility-specific changes.

Organize and list necessary non-facility-specific changes.

Within 45 calendar days of receiving notification that the annual systemwide review has been initiated, the TITLE shall submit in writing any changes that need to be made and suggestions for improvements of any elements of the plan. A copy of each facility's plan review report shall be attached. If there are no changes, the TITLE shall so certify on the form. The TITLE shall indicate by signature on each facility's form her or his approval of any indicated changes in facility-specific information. The entire package of forms shall be submitted to TITLE (corporate headquarters).

System-level annual review. The TITLE shall conduct a review of the corporation plan standard. Specifically, the TITLE shall review the plan standard for compliance with applicable federal regulations, gather and process all plan review reports from the TITLE as described above, and issue revised pages to all corporate holders of affected plans.

The TITLE will issue a final report to the TITLE within 60 days of initiating the annual review process. The report shall indicate changes that have been made and a schedule for processing any other changes yet to be made.

4.4.2 Requesting plan modifications outside the annual review. When information or procedures need to be updated or modified, the facility manager shall send a written request to the TITLE. The TITLE shall approve and forward the request to the TITLE. All other processing shall be in accordance with section 4.4.3.

4.4.3 Approval authority for plan modifications. Changes to LOCATION information and procedures unique to the LOCATION may be incorporated into the EMS database files upon receiving the request from the TITLE.

4.5 Control and distribution of the plan and EPIPs

No changes are permitted to any facility EMPs within the EMS except by the office of the TITLE.

All revised pages will be printed and distributed to holders of affected plans by the office of the TITLE.

The facility manager will send copies of the revised pages to all local outside holders of the plan as listed on the current controlled copy list (see EPIP-130, Plan Distribution).

5.0 References

LOCATION emergency management plan

EPIP-130, Plan Distribution

EPIP-920, Incident Investigation

Corporate administrative support manual

6.0 Attachments

Include the plan review report form.

YOUR COMPANY
EMERGENCY MANAGEMENT
PLAN MANUAL

MAINTENANCE AND INVENTORY
OF EMERGENCY EQUIPMENT
AND SUPPLIES
EPIP-120

REVISION 0

DATE

SUBMITTED BY: _____   DATE: _____
              TITLE

APPROVED BY: _____   DATE: _____
              TITLE

1.0 Purpose

This procedure provides guidance and describes methods for periodic verification of availability and operability of dedicated emergency response equipment.

2.0 Applicability

This procedure applies to personnel assigned the responsibility of ensuring the availability and operability of dedicated emergency response equipment.

3.0 Definitions

Emergency response equipment (or just *emergency equipment*) is any item that is dedicated to emergency response use. Examples of emergency equipment include fire extinguishers and self-contained breathing apparatus (SCBA) that is maintained *solely* for response to emergency or potential emergency incidents. First aid cabinets are *not* considered emergency equipment if they are used for routine first aid injuries (i.e., not solely dedicated to emergency response activities). Likewise, SCBA that is occasionally used during maintenance operations shall not be considered emergency equipment and shall not be labeled as such.

Emergency equipment is divided into two general categories: *facility emergency equipment* (listed in attachment 1) that is dedicated for use in facility incidents by facility personnel and *emergency response team emergency equipment* that is designated exclusively for the use of emergency response team members. Although primarily intended to respond to transportation and customer incidents, emergency response teams may be called upon to respond to facility incidents and may use emergency response team emergency equipment in those instances.

4.0 Instructions

4.1 Precautions

All emergency equipment will be inventoried monthly or after each use.

Where applicable, all emergency equipment will have operability tests performed in accordance with the manufacturer's recommendations or after each use.

Where applicable, all emergency equipment will have routine maintenance performed as prescribed by the manufacturer at recommended intervals.

Where applicable, all emergency equipment will be cleaned as prescribed by the manufacturer at manufacturer-recommended intervals or after each use.

Survey instruments and respiratory protection equipment will have a current calibration or inspection tag as applicable.

Any emergency equipment removed from its designated storage area will be replaced.

Any emergency equipment which is found to be inoperable or out of calibration will be removed from service immediately and replaced within 24 hours.

Emergency kits and/or cabinets will not be resealed until the applicable inventory list has been satisfied.

Materials having a fixed shelf life will be dated to ensure appropriate cycling.

All batteries dedicated for use in emergency equipment will be cycled semiannually.

All procedures and forms required to be available to facility personnel will be the current revision at the time the inventory sheet is completed.

All quantities specified in equipment lists shall be minimums.

Emergency equipment will not be used for routine work or non-emergency duties and functions without permission from the facility manager.

4.2 Verification procedures

The facility manager is responsible for ensuring that inventory and operability verifications are carried out as prescribed above. Such verifications may be performed by properly trained facility personnel, outside contractors, or a combination of the two.

Designated personnel will inventory all items, using the appropriate inventory list included in the attachments.

Designated personnel will perform operability tests for equipment as indicated on the appropriate inventory list included in the attachments.

When all requirements of an inventory list have been satisfied, the inspecting individual will sign off that sheet. Completed sheets will be reviewed by the facility manager and kept on file for not less than 2 years.

All dedicated emergency kits or cabinets in which the contents have been verified, and are complete, will be sealed.

5.0 References

LOCATION emergency management plan.

6.0 Attachments

1. Emergency equipment inventory list

(INSERT YOUR EMERGENCY EQUIPMENT
INVENTORY LIST HERE)

YOUR COMPANY
EMERGENCY MANAGEMENT
PLAN MANUAL

EMERGENCY MANAGEMENT
PLAN DISTRIBUTION
EPIP-130

REVISION 0

DATE

SUBMITTED BY: _____ **DATE:** _____
                        TITLE

APPROVED BY: _____ **DATE:** _____
                        TITLE

1.0 Purpose

An executive summary of the plan, appendices, and emergency plan implementing procedures (EPIPs) contained in this *Emergency Management Manual* will be distributed to specific individuals of off-site organizations in accordance with all applicable federal, state, and local regulations. Distribution of this material must be carefully controlled so that all distributed material is kept current and up to date as changes are made to the manual. This procedure provides guidance for the distribution of such material and for maintenance of a controlled copy list.

2.0 Applicability

The facility manager is responsible for the proper execution of this procedure.

3.0 Definitions

Controlled copies are numbered copies of this manual's executive summary (as defined below) that have been issued to specific individuals. These individuals have signed for the numbered copy of the executive summary. Such distribution is documented so that future revisions may be transmitted to these individuals in order to keep distributed material current.

The *executive summary* consists of the following:

1. Letter of transmittal and return acknowledgment request (see attachment 2 of this EPIP)

2. The section of this manual entitled *Executive Summary*

3. A copy of the following appendices:
   Appendix D, Technical and Chemical Library
   Appendix F, Maps and Evacuation Routes

4. A copy of the following attachments of EPIP-410:
   Attachment 1, COMPANY Emergency Phone Numbers
   Attachment 2, Government Notification Agencies
   Attachment 4, Cleanup Contractors

4.0 Instructions

4.1 Materials to be distributed

Each external organization or agency requiring information contained in the EMP will be sent an executive summary as defined above.

Upon request and internal approval, COMPANY will provide additional information from the EMP.

No off-site organization or agency will be sent a copy of any other part of the nine-section plan, appendices, or EPIPs unless specifically requested by that off-site organization or agency, and only after the individual who is to receive these materials has signed the nondisclosure agreement on behalf of the organization or agency (see attachment 3).

This manual will be readily accessible for inspection by employees, their representatives, and regulating agencies. *No individuals from outside the company shall copy any part of this manual until they have signed the nondisclosure agreement (see attachment 3).*

4.2 Precautions

No changes are permitted to any elements of this Emergency Management Manual except by the office of the TITLE.

Any modifications to this plan may be initiated by the facility manager by following EPIP-110, Revision, Approval, and Control of the Emergency Plan and Plan Implementing Procedures, subsection 4.4.2.

All revised pages will be printed by the office of the TITLE. These revisions will be forwarded to the facility manager for local distribution.

All copies of original and revised plan elements of the executive summary (as defined above) shall be sent to outside agencies by certified mail, return receipt requested, or registered mail.

4.3 Controlled copy list

The facility manager shall establish and maintain an official list of outside agencies that hold controlled copies of the executive summary (herein referred to as the *controlled copy list*). The controlled copy list shall include the following information for each entity listed:

Name, address, and phone number of receiving entity

Name and title of person taking possession of the executive summary

Date of original transmittal of the executive summary

A copy of the controlled copy list shall be sent to the TITLE whenever an entity is added or subtracted from the list. The most current revision of the controlled copy list shall be placed at the front of this Emergency Management Manual.

4.4 Distribution procedures

When revised plan elements are received from the office of the TITLE, the facility manager will sign and return the receipt acknowledgment cover letter to the TITLE, generate cover letters of transmittal, make copies of the revised pages as needed, send copies to all currently listed entities on the controlled copy list by registered mail, and maintain copies of mail receipts in files for not less than 5 years.

5.0 References

EPIP-110, Revision, Approval, and Control of the Emergency Plan and Plan Implementing Procedures

6.0 Attachments

1. Sample letter of transmittal for plan revisions
2. Sample letter of transmittal and return acknowledgment request
3. Nondisclosure agreement

Date

Person's name

Person's title

Organization name

Organization address

Dear _____:

Please find enclosed the following revised sections of the emergency management plan for LOCATION:

Section name	Revision no.	Revision date

Please remove and destroy prior versions of these sections from your copy of our plan and insert these new pages.

If there are any questions concerning this revision, please do not hesitate to call me at this number:

Sincerely,

Date

Person's name

Person's title

Organization name

Organization address

Dear _____:

Please find enclosed an executive summary of the emergency management plan for LOCATION. This consists of:

An executive summary of the facility plan, appendices, and emergency plan implementing procedures (EPIPs)

A copy of the following appendices: .

Appendix D, Technical and Chemical Library

Appendix F, Maps and Evacuation Routes

Corporate and local emergency phone numbers (EPIP-410, attachment 1)

Government notification agencies (EPIP-410, attachment 2)

Cleanup contractors (EPIP-410, attachment 4)

The complete Emergency Management Manual for this facility is available at the facility during normal operating hours for your inspection or as needed in the event of an emergency.

Please sign and return a copy of this letter to acknowledge receipt of this transmittal. If there are any questions concerning this revision, please do not hesitate to call me.

Sincerely,

I hereby acknowledge receipt of the materials described above.

Signed:_____ Date: _____ / _____ / _____

Nondisclosure Agreement   DATE

In the course of performing emergency response service in accordance with this emergency management plan dated _____, or in connection with such services, ENTITY will receive from COMPANY data, information, documents, and other materials belonging to, prepared by and for, or concerning COMPANY and its customers, employees, software, and trade secret licensors.

For purposes of this agreement all such data, information, documents, and other material, including all summaries, extracts, copies, compilations, analyses, interpretations, presentations, and other materials derived therefrom, shall be called *information*. CRI agrees that until such time as any such information becomes a part of the public domain without breach of this agreement by any agent or employee of ENTITY, and in any event for at least five (5) years after the termination of this agreement, ENTITY shall:

1. Treat, and obligate ENTITY's employees (if any) to treat, as secret and confidential all such information, whether or not it be identified by COMPANY as confidential

2. Not disclose any such information or make available any reports, recommendations, and/or conclusions which ENTITY may make for COMPANY to any person, firm, or corporation or use it in any manner whatsoever without first obtaining the written approval of COMPANY

3. Reveal the information only to such of ENTITY's employees who require access to such information in order to perform the services hereunder

4. Not employ the information to ENTITY's advantage, other than as herein provided.

This agreement shall become effective on the date written below and shall continue until terminated in writing by either party. The obligation to protect the confidentiality of information received prior to such termination shall survive the termination of this agreement.

ENTITY   COMPANY

DATE: _____   DATE: _____

BY: _____   BY: _____

TITLE: _____   TITLE: _____

COMPANY

LOCATION

EMERGENCY MANAGEMENT PLAN MANUAL

DUTIES OF THE EMERGENCY MANAGER EPIP-210

REVISION 0

DATE

SUBMITTED BY: _____ DATE: _____
                  TITLE

APPROVED BY: _____ DATE: _____
                TITLE

1.0 Purpose

The purpose of this procedure is to identify the required actions, responsibilities, authorities, and interfaces of the emergency manager relative to the overall direction and control of emergency management and response efforts.

2.0 Applicability

This procedure applies to the emergency manager in the event that an emergency condition at the LOCATION requires the activation of the emergency management plan (EMP).

3.0 Definitions

None.

4.0 Instructions

4.1 Precautions

4.1.1 The emergency manager has ultimate authority for declaring an emergency classification, implementing the EMP, and approving public information and news media releases.

4.1.2 The emergency manager may designate a communicator to handle the notification to the various off-site agencies in accordance with EPIP-410, Emergency External Notification.

4.1.3 *Primary position holders.* The individuals designated to assume this position are (in descending order of succession):

- TITLE (primary)
- TITLE (alternate)
- TITLE (alternate)

4.2 Major functions, duties, and tasks (initial activities)

The following responsibilities apply to all personnel who may assume the role of emergency manager (see emergency manager's checklist, attachment 2 to this EPIP):

If the incident occurs off shift, upon arrival, get a thorough briefing on the incident and current conditions from the TITLE.

Review the assessment of the emergency condition. Confirm that the appropriate emergency classification has been made.

Ensure that proper notification of emergency organization personnel has been done, that all personnel have reported to their assigned locations, and that the emergency management response organization (EMRO) is adequately staffed.

Establish communications with key on-site and off-site emergency personnel.

Assemble the management team (EMRO) and conduct initial and updated briefings periodically and when dictated by circumstance.

Review and approve all public information and news media releases.

Authorize the procurement of equipment, materials, and other resources, as necessary.

Ensure (24-hour) operations capability of the EMRO. Designate personnel to interface with federal, state, and local officials.

Approve the protective action recommendations that are made to off-site officials (EPIP-510).

Evaluate, coordinate, and control all COMPANY response activities until the event is closed out or the COMPANY recovery organization is formed.

If the event is to be terminated and a recovery effort initiated, obtain guidance from EPIP-820, Reentry and Recovery Operations.

Maintain a log, using form EPIP-210-1, Activities Record Sheet.

4.3 Subsequent activities

Transfer of the responsibilities of emergency manager is formally accomplished when the following steps have been completed:

- The current emergency manager is assured that her or his successor has been fully briefed on the current status of the incident and response activities.

- The necessary off-site organizations have been notified of the turnover.

- The turnover is documented on form EPIP-210-1, Activities Record Sheet, and attachment 2, Emergency Manager's Checklist.

5.0 References

Emergency management plan, sections 2, 4, 5, 8

EPIP-240, Duties of the Emergency Management/Response Organization during Emergencies

EPIP-410, Emergency External Notification

EPIP-510, Assessment of Emergency Conditions, Emergency Classification, and Protective Action Recommendation Guides

EPIP-711-YKT, Managing Public Information

EPIP-820, Reentry and Recovery Operations

6.0 Attachments

Attachment 1, form EPIP-210-1, Activities Record Sheet

Attachment 2, Emergency Manager's Checklist

CONFIDENTIAL - WORK PRODUCT

ACTIVITIES RECORD SHEET

DATE:

EMERGENCY TITLE: _____ NAME: _____ PAGE ___ of ___ PAGES

TIME:	SUMMARY OF ACTIVITIES

CONFIDENTIAL WORK PRODUCT

SIGNATURE: _____

ATTACHMENT 2
PAGE   of   PAGES

Emergency Manager's Checklist

Primary: TITLE

Alternates: TITLE

              TITLE

_____ Confirm proper classification of the emergency per EPIP-510.

_____ Contact National Response Center.

_____ Approve press releases (EPIP-710).

_____ Give situation updates to the EMRO and NRC (National Response Center).

_____ Ensure proper notification is ongoing per EPIP-410.

_____ Assess environmental response.

_____ Initiate evacuation, assembly, accountability (EPIP-511).

_____ Recommend protective action (EPIP-510).

_____ Activate emergency facilities (EPIP 620-630).

_____ Responsibility/authority transferred to:

    1. Emergency manager   _____

    2. Recovery manager   _____

_____ Initiate postincident sampling (EPIP-820).

_____ Initiate reentry/recovery (EPIP-820).

_____ Close out emergency.

COMPANY

LOCATION

EMERGENCY MANAGEMENT PLAN MANUAL

DUTIES OF THE INCIDENT SUPPORT DIRECTOR EPIP-220

REVISION 0

DATE

SUBMITTED BY: _____ DATE: _____
                    TITLE

APPROVED BY: _____ DATE: _____
                  TITLE

1.0 Purpose

This procedure provides guidance regarding the required actions, responsibilities, authorities, and interfaces of the *incident support director (ISD)* relative to the overall direction and control of emergency response efforts at the LOCATION.

2.0 Applicability

This procedure applies to the incident support director in the event that an emergency condition at the LOCATION requires the activation of the EMP.

3.0 Definitions

None.

4.0 Instructions

4.1 Precautions

The incident support director may designate a communicator to handle the notification to the various agencies in accordance with EPIP-410, Emergency External Notification.

4.1.1 Primary position holders. The individuals designated to assume this position are

- TITLE (primary)
- TITLE (alternate)
- TITLE (alternate)

4.2 Major functions, duties, and tasks

Ensure that communications with the field incident commander (FIC) are established and maintained, per EPIP-410.

Coordinate requests from the field incident commander.

Review and evaluate all available environmental release data to assess the on-site and off-site consequences of any releases of hazardous materials from the LOCATION.

Ensure that current and forecasted meteorological data are obtained and their effect upon any hazardous material releases and dose projections is determined.

Ensure that appropriate records of hazardous materials monitoring activities are maintained.

Coordinate the COMPANY on-site hazardous materials assessment activities with those of the state and federal agencies.

Provide the emergency manager (EM) with hazardous materials data to be used in formulating protective action recommendations for off-site agencies.

Advise the EM on matters involving hazardous materials safety.

Send requests for support personnel, material, and equipment through the logistics director.

Direct requests for engineering evaluations of special tools and equipment to the maintenance and engineering manager.

Provide the public affairs director with accurate hazardous materials data for release to the public and the news media.

5.0 References

Emergency management plan, sections 2, 4, 5, 7, 8

EPIP-250, Activation of the Emergency Management/Response Organization

EPIP-350, Bomb Incident Response

EPIP-410, Emergency External Notification

EPIP-420, Emergency Communications

EPIP-510, Assessment of Emergency Conditions, Emergency Classification, and Protective Action Recomendation Guides

EPIP-511, Evacuation, Sheltering, and Accountability

EPIP-630, Activation of the Emergency Operations Center and Personnel Duties

EPIP-820, Reentry and Recovery Operations

6.0 Attachments

Attachment 1, form EPIP-210-1, Activities Record Sheet

Attachment 2, Incident Support Director's Checklist

CONFIDENTIAL — WORK PRODUCT

ACTIVITIES RECORD SHEET

DATE:

EMERGENCY TITLE: _____ NAME: _____ PAGE ___ of ___ PAGES

TIME:	SUMMARY OF ACTIVITIES

CONFIDENTIAL WORK PRODUCT

SIGNATURE: _____

ATTACHMENT 2
PAGE   of   PAGES

Incident Support Director's Checklist

Primary: TITLE

Alternates: TITLE

             TITLE

_____ Establish communications with the FIC.

_____ Provide all available environmental and meteorological data as requested by the FIC or EM.

_____ Support the FIC with personnel, materials, and equipment through the logistics director as requested.

_____ Coordinate activities with the security officer.

_____ Ensure that adequate exposure monitoring is being performed and protective actions are taken.

_____ Provide the EM with protective action recommendations for off-site agencies.

_____ Ensure that all records of hazardous materials monitoring activities are being maintained.

_____ Ensure notification procedures are activated per EPIP-410, Emergency External Notification.

_____ Provide the public affairs director with accurate environmental data for press releases.

_____ Coordinate on-site hazardous materials activities with outside agencies.

_____ Brief the security officer as needed.

COMPANY

LOCATION

EMERGENCY MANAGEMENT PLAN MANUAL

DUTIES OF THE FIELD INCIDENT COMMANDER
EPIP-230

REVISION 0

DATE

SUBMITTED BY: _____ DATE: _____
                        TITLE

APPROVED BY: _____ DATE: _____
                       TITLE

1.0 Purpose

The purpose of this procedure is to identify the required actions, responsibilities, authorities, and interfaces of the field incident commander (FIC) relative to the overall direction and control of emergency response efforts at the LOCATION.

2.0 Applicability

This procedure applies to the field incident commander in the event that an emergency condition at the LOCATION requires activation of the emergency management plan (EMP).

3.0 Definitions

None.

4.0 Instructions

4.1 Precautions

4.1.1 The FIC will not delegate the decision-making authority for implementing the EMP.

4.1.2 *Primary position holders.* The individuals designated to assume this position are (in descending order of succession):

- TITLE (primary)
- TITLE (alternate)
- TITLE (alternate)

4.2 Major functions, duties, and tasks

The following responsibilities apply to all personnel who may assume the role of FIC. The incumbent will be responsible for the management of emergency response at the incident scene at the LOCATION during an emergency.

During an emergency, the field incident commander will:

- Assess the incident situation.
- Assist the affected area supervisor in incident classification (EPIP-510).

- Ensure necessary elements of the EMP are activated.
- Brief, or designate a person to brief, personnel at the scene.
- Determine information needs and request them from emergency response personnel, affected unit supervision, and emergency operations center (if activated).
- Coordinate mobile command center (MCC) activity.
- Manage incident operations.
- Coordinate search and rescue activities.
- Coordinate requests for additional resources.
- Conduct periodic tactical and logistics briefings.
- Coordinate incident termination activities.

4.2.1 Transfer of responsibility to the FIC. This is formally accomplished when the following steps have been completed:

1. The most senior available TITLE has arrived at the scene and has been fully briefed on the current emergency status and the overall status of emergency response activities.
2. Off-site emergency response organizations have been notified of the turnover.
3. The turnover is documented.

The FIC will retain her or his respective responsibilities and authority until such time that either the event is terminated or the recovery organization is formed.

5.0 References

Emergency management plan, sections 4, 5, 6, 8

EPIP-410, Emergency External Notification

EPIP-420, Emergency Communications

EPIP-510, Assessment of Emergency Conditions, Emergency Classification, and Protective Action Recommendation Guides

EPIP-820, Reentry and Recovery Operations

6.0 Attachments

Attachment 1, form EPIP-210-1, Activities Record Sheet

Attachment 2, Field Incident Commander Checklist

CONFIDENTIAL — WORK PRODUCT

ACTIVITIES RECORD SHEET

DATE:

EMERGENCY TITLE: _____ NAME: _____ PAGE ___ of ___ PAGES

TIME:	SUMMARY OF ACTIVITIES

CONFIDENTIAL WORK PRODUCT

SIGNATURE: _____

LOCATION

Emergency Plan Manual

Issue Date

_/_/_

Procedure No.

EPIP-230

Duties of the Field
Incident Commander

Rev. Date

_/_/_

Revision No.

0

Page __ of __ Pages

ATTACHMENT 2
PAGE of PAGES

Field Incident Commander Checklist

Primary: TITLE

Alternates: TITLE

             TITLE

_____ Size up the incident and initiate the proper response. Are additional resources necessary? Have they been notified?

_____ Assess possible hazards to human health and to the environment that may result from any release.

_____ Classify incident (EPIP-510). Notify main gate as follows: "This is the FIC, we have an (*unusual event, alert, site area emergency, general emergency*)."

_____ If release or potential release could threaten human health outside the facility, notify LOCATION county officials immediately.

_____ Provide field incident command and stabilize the scene as soon as possible. Take all reasonable measures necessary to ensure that fires, explosions, and releases do not occur, recur, or spread to other facilities.

_____ Coordinate emergency response activities with the affected area supervisor of the affected facility.

_____ Coordinate emergency response and search-and-rescue activities with outside responders.

_____ Provide for personnel exposure monitoring to ensure and document that safe exposure levels are not exceeded.

_____ Initiate activities to limit or mitigate the impact of either the incident or response activities. (Build dikes, dams, or berms to limit spread of contamination, etc.)

_____ Keep the incident support director informed of needs and the status of response activities.

_____ Initiate activities to ensure the proper handling, treating, storing, or disposal of waste, contaminated soil or surface water, or any other material that results from a release, fire, or explosion at the facility.

_____ Sector incident as needed.

_____ Assign safety officer as needed.

COMPANY

LOCATION

EMERGENCY MANAGEMENT
PLAN MANUAL

DUTIES OF THE EMERGENCY
MANAGEMENT/RESPONSE
ORGANIZATION DURING
EMERGENCIES
EPIP-240

REVISION 0

DATE

SUBMITTED BY: _____ DATE: _____
              TITLE

APPROVED BY: _____ DATE: _____
             TITLE

1.0 Purpose

The purpose of this procedure is to identify the responsibilities, authorities, and interfaces of various emergency management and response personnel during emergencies.

2.0 Applicability

This procedure applies to all personnel assigned emergency management responsibilities if an emergency condition requires the activation of the emergency management plan (EMP).

3.0 Definitions

The *designee* is an individual assigned to act in the capacity of a position holder (primary, alternate) during the position holder's absence or as delegated by an EMRO member with proper authority.

4.0 Instructions

4.1 Precautions

None.

4.1.1 Table of contents. Use this to quickly locate EMRO positions discussed in this EPIP:

| LOCATION | Issue Date | Procedure No. |
| Emergency Plan Manual | _/_/_ | EPIP-240 |

Duties of the LOCATION	Rev. Date	Revision No.
Emergency Management/Response	_/_/_	0
Organization During Emergencies		Page __ of __ Pages

Medical representative	Section 4.13
Accounting director	Section 4.14
News center staff	Section 4.15
Radio operator	Section 4.16
Recorder	Section 4.17
Engineering and inspection	Section 4.18
Incident investigation coordinator	Section 4.19
Administrative support	Section 4.20

4.2 Emergency manager

4.2.1 Primary position holders

- TITLE
- TITLE
- TITLE

4.2.2 Major functions, duties, and tasks. The emergency manager will function in accordance with EPIP-210, Duties of the Emergency Manager.

4.3 Assistant emergency manager

4.3.1 Primary position holders

- TITLE
- TITLE
- TITLE

4.3.2 Major functions, duties, and tasks. Assist emergency manager as needed. Assume decision-making role for emergency manager if the EM is temporarily unavailable. Manage the EOC. The assistant emergency manager will also function in accordance with EPIP-210, Duties of the Emergency Manager.

| LOCATION | Issue Date | Procedure No. |
| Emergency Plan Manual | _/_/_ | EPIP-240 |

Duties of the LOCATION	Rev. Date	Revision No.
Emergency Management/Response	_/_/_	0
Organization During Emergencies		Page __ of __ Pages

4.4 Incident support director (ISD)

4.4.1 Primary position holders

- TITLE
- TITLE
- TITLE

4.4.2 Major functions, duties, and tasks. The incident support director will function in accordance with EPIP-220, Duties of the Incident Support Director.

4.5 Field incident commander (FIC)

4.5.1 Primary position holders

- TITLE
- TITLE
- TITLE

4.5.2 Major functions, duties, and tasks. The FIC will function in accordance with EPIP-230, Duties of the Field Incident Commander.

4.6 Operations coordinator

4.6.1 Primary position holders

- TITLE
- TITLE

See attachment 1 for checklist.

4.6.2 Major functions, duties, and tasks

Develop operations plans for, and manage, the unaffected areas.

Coordinate operations with the affected area.

Obtain briefings from the emergency manager.

| LOCATION | Issue Date | Procedure No. |
| Emergency Plan Manual | _/_/_ | EPIP-240 |

Duties of the LOCATION	Rev. Date	Revision No.
Emergency Management/Response	_/_/_	0
Organization During Emergencies		Page __ of __ Pages

Determine needs and request additional resources.

Coordinate personnel assigned to unaffected area operations.

Report information about special operational activities and occurrences to the emergency manager.

4.6.3 Primary EPIPs used during emergencies

Emergency Communications	EPIP-420
Assessment of Emergency Conditions, Emergency Classification, and Protective Action Recommendation Guides	EPIP-510
Reentry and Recovery Operations	EPIP-820

4.6.4 Position-specific references.
Emergency management plan, sections 2, 3, and 5; appendices G, H, K, P, R, and S.

4.7 Logistics director [emergency damage control (EDC) function]

4.7.1 Primary position holders

- TITLE
- TITLE
- TITLE

See attachment 2 for checklist.

4.7.2 Major functions, duties, and tasks

Expedite logistical assistance provided in support of emergency response and recovery efforts, as appropriate to incident severity.

Coordinate and respond to requests from the emergency management/response organization (EMRO) for logistical assistance.

Ensure the general needs of all on-site emergency response personnel (including state, local, and federal personnel) are met with regard to food, communications, equipment repair, supplies, etc.

Assist in the acquisition of additional equipment and supplies, as required.

Coordinate emergency damage control activities. Advise the EM and other LOCATION personnel regarding the status of on-site emergency damage control activities.

Advise maintenance personnel regarding any changes in LOCATION conditions that may impact emergency damage control activities.

Coordinate the requisitioning and ordering of emergency equipment and supplies.

4.7.3 Primary EPIPs used during emergencies

Emergency Communications	EPIP-420
Assessment of Emergency Conditions, Emergency Classification, and Protective Action Recommendation Guides	EPIP-510
Activation of the Incident Support Center and Personnel Duties	EPIP-620
Reentry and Recovery Operations	EPIP-820

4.7.4 Position-specific references. Emergency management plan, sections 2, 3, 4, 5, and 6; appendices G, H, K, and P.

4.8 Public affairs director and human resources function

4.8.1 Primary position holders

- TITLE
- TITLE
- TITLE

See attachment 3 for checklist.

4.8.2 Major functions, duties, and tasks

Formulate company news releases concerning the incident.

Ensure news releases are up to date and technically accurate.

Assist the emergency manager or designated LOCATION spokesperson in news release briefings and presentations.

Obtain approval for all news releases from the EM.

Establish a rumor control hotline, and keep message up to date.

Coordinate news releases, rumor control, and public information activities with county, state, and local personnel, if available.

Make arrangements for and coordinate any press conferences or joint press conferences to be conducted.

Act as a liaison between the LOCATION and COMPANY.

Establish a single news center near the EOC when possible.

The human resources director will also function in accordance with procedures outlined in EPIP-830, Humanitarian Assistance.

4.8.3 Primary EPIPs used during emergencies

Emergency Communications	EPIP-420
Activation of the Emergency Operations Center and Personnel Duties	EPIP-630
Managing Public Information	EPIP-711
Humanitarian Assistance	EPIP-830

4.8.4 Position-specific references. Emergency management plan, sections 2, 3, 7, and 8; appendices I, J, and N; Human Resources Department procedures; Employee Assistance Program manual; humanitarian assistance plan (HAP).

4.9 Security officer

4.9.1 Primary position holders

- TITLE
- TITLE
- TITLE

See attachment 4 for checklist.

4.9.2 Major functions, duties, and tasks

Ensure the security of the entire site.

Coordinate the movement and badging (as required) of personnel entering the site to provide emergency response support.

LOCATION	Issue Date	Procedure No.
Emergency Plan Manual	_/_/_	EPIP-240

Duties of the LOCATION	Rev. Date	Revision No.
Emergency Management/Response	_/_/_	0
Organization During Emergencies		Page __ of __ Pages

Ensure that unauthorized personnel cannot enter the site.

Assist off-site support agencies with security requirements as needed.

Initiate personnel accountability procedures, and maintain accountability records during the emergency condition.

Obtain briefings from the incident support director (ISD).

Request required personnel support to accomplish work assignments.

Coordinate security activities with appropriate personnel.

Keep the peace; settle disputes through coordination with agency representatives.

Prevent theft of company property.

Demobilize in accordance with the EMP and security operating procedures.

Maintain a log of all activities and complaints, significant events, and suspicious occurrences.

4.9.3 Primary EPIPs used during emergencies

Duties of the Emergency Management/Response Organization during Emergencies	EPIP-240
Activation of the Emergency Management/Response Organization	EPIP-250
Transporting Contaminated Injured Personnel	EPIP-340
Bomb Incident Response	EPIP-350
Emergency External Notification	EPIP-410
Emergency Communications	EPIP-420
Evacuation, Sheltering, and Personnel Assembly and Accountability	EPIP-511
Activation of the Emergency Operations Center and Personnel Duties	EPIP-630

4.9.4 Position-specific references.   Emergency management plan, sections 2, 3, and 4; appendices I, J, L, M, and P; and security plan.

4.10 Communications coordinator

| LOCATION | Issue Date | Procedure No. |
| Emergency Plan Manual | _/_/_ | EPIP-240 |

Duties of the LOCATION	Rev. Date	Revision No.
Emergency Management/Response	_/_/_	0
Organization During Emergencies		Page __ of __ Pages

4.10.1 Primary position holders

- TITLE
- TITLE
- TITLE

See attachment 5 for checklist.

4.10.2 Major functions, duties, and tasks

Coordinate and direct the activities of those communicators stationed at the EOC.

Ensure that a radio operator monitors radio traffic and maintains contact with the mobile command center (MCC), incident support center (ISC), and other emergency personnel.

Coordinate the recall and deployment of administrative support personnel in response to the incident.

Ensure that communications procedures are being properly implemented and that records of incoming and outgoing messages are being properly maintained by the EMRO personnel.

Contact the security officer (main gate), and verify that a security officer has been dispatched to the administration building.

Initiate requests through the logistics director for assistance required for the repair and maintenance of communications equipment or for additional communications equipment, if it is needed.

Provide general support and assistance to the EM.

Respond to clerical requests from the EM and other EMO members.

Obtain briefings from the EM.

Add, delete, or modify communications structure requirement and/or linkages for personnel, equipment changes, and releases.

Coordinate communications activities with appropriate personnel.

Maintain a log of all activities and significant events.

4.10.3 Primary EPIPs used during emergencies

Activation of the Emergency Management/Response   EPIP-250
Organization

Emergency External Notification   EPIP-410

Emergency Communications   EPIP-420

Activation of the Emergency Operations Center and   EPIP-630
Personnel Duties

4.10.4 Position-specific references. Emergency management plan, sections 2, 3, and 4; appendices I, J, L, M, and P.

4.11 Environmental coordinator

4.11.1 Primary position holders

- TITLE
- TITLE
- TITLE

See attachment 6 for checklist.

4.11.2 Major functions, duties, and tasks

Advise the ISD and EM on environmental matters.

Provide environmental support to the affected areas and FIC.

Identify the need for and coordinate any corporate or outside environmental assistance.

Review news releases prior to their issuance, to ensure technical accuracy.

Ensure that emergency sampling and environmental survey procedures are being properly implemented and that the resultant information is available to the EOC and at the incident scene.

Accumulate, tabulate, and evaluate data regarding incident conditions, such as meteorological data, monitor readings, and environmental survey results.

Ensure personnel are properly decontaminated, if necessary, by involving industrial hygienists, medical personnel, and any appropriate outside support.

Review and evaluate all on-site environmental data, including appropriate chemical analysis results.

Ensure reports are filed with regulatory agencies as necessary.

| LOCATION | Issue Date | Procedure No. |
| Emergency Plan Manual | _/_/_ | EPIP-240 |

Duties of the LOCATION	Rev. Date	Revision No.
Emergency Management/Response	_/_/_	0
Organization During Emergencies		Page __ of __ Pages

4.11.3 Primary EPIPs used during emergencies

Oil Spill Response	EPIP-380
Emergency External Notification	EPIP-410
Emergency Communications	EPIP-420
Assessment of Emergency Conditions, Emergency Classification, and Protective Action Recommendation Guides	EPIP-510
Activation of the Emergency Operations Center and Personnel Duties	EPIP-630
Reentry and Recovery Operations	EPIP-820

4.11.4 Position-specific references. Emergency management plan, sections 2, 3, 5, and 6; appendices G, H, and K.

4.12 Safety officer

4.12.1 Primary position holders

- TITLE
- TITLE
- TITLE

See attachment 7 for checklist.

4.12.2 Major functions, duties, and tasks. Assess hazardous or unsafe situations, and develop measures for ensuring personnel safety at the incident scene. Coordinate use of protective clothing, respiratory protection, and access control at the incident scene. Coordinate all safety matters with the FIC.

4.12.3 Primary EPIPs used during emergencies

Transporting Contaminated Injured Personnel	EPIP-340
Bomb Incident Response	EPIP-350
Emergency Communications	EPIP-420
Evacuation, Sheltering, and Accountability	EPIP-511
Reentry and Recovery Operations	EPIP-820

4.12.4 Position-specific references. Emergency management plan; appendices H, I, J, and K.

| LOCATION | Issue Date | Procedure No. |
| Emergency Plan Manual | _/_/_ | EPIP-240 |

Duties of the LOCATION	Rev. Date	Revision No.
Emergency Management/Response	_/_/_	0
Organization During Emergencies		Page __ of __ Pages

4.13 Medical representative

4.13.1 Primary position holders

- TITLE
- TITLE
- TITLE

4.13.2 Major functions, duties, and tasks

Coordinate all activities with local medical facilities.

Provide personnel medical records.

Provide medical assistance and first aid as needed.

Provide medical supplies to the triage area as needed.

4.13.3 Primary EPIPs used during emergencies

Transporting Contaminated Injured Personnel	EPIP-340
Emergency Communications	EPIP-420
Managing Public Information	EPIP-711

4.13.4 Position-specific references. Emergency management plan; appendices K and O; medical department procedures.

4.14 Accounting director

4.14.1 Primary position holders

- TITLE
- TITLE
- TITLE

See attachment 8 for checklist.

4.14.2 Major functions, duties, and tasks

Coordinate and provide accounting services to the purchasing department for supplying equipment and materials.

Ensure all accounting records are being tracked, logged, and filed.

Arrange transportation and temporary housing for off-site emergency response personnel as needed.

Maintain status of all expenditures.

Supply information to the EMRO as requested.

4.14.3 Primary EPIPs used during emergencies

Emergency Communications	EPIP-420
Managing Public Information	EPIP-711

4.14.4 Position-specific references.

Emergency management plan (reference only); accounting procedures; and loss reporting and insurance claims manual.

4.15 News center staff

4.15.1 Primary position holders

- TITLE
- TITLE
- TITLE

See attachment 9 for checklist.

4.15.2 Major functions, duties, and tasks

Activate the news center.

Ensure that the news center is properly arranged per EPIP-711.

Ensure that telephones and communications equipment are properly placed (EPIP-711).

Notify the public affairs director of news center activation.

Assist the public affairs director with coordination of public information releases.

Arrange for and coordinate news conferences.

Ensure that news media representatives receive a copy of "Instructions to the News Media" (attachment to EPIP-711).

LOCATION	Issue Date	Procedure No.
Emergency Plan Manual	_/_/_	EPIP-240

Duties of the LOCATION	Rev. Date	Revision No.
Emergency Management/Response	_/_/_	0
Organization During Emergencies		Page __ of __ Pages

Establish and organize news center files.

File news releases, reports, and forms submitted to news center by public affairs director.

Check the accuracy and completeness of news releases and reports submitted for files.

Keep rumor control hotline message up to date.

Answer news media inquiries by reading the LOCATION official news releases.

Prepare incident documentation when requested.

Maintain, retain, and store incident files for postincident use.

4.15.3 Primary EPIPs used during emergencies. EPIP-711, Managing Public Information.

4.15.4 Position-specific references. Emergency management plan, sections 7 and 8; appendices N and P; public and government affairs guidance.

4.16 Radio operator

4.16.1 Primary position holders

- TITLE
- TITLE
- TITLE

See attachment 10 for checklist.

4.16.2 Major functions, duties, and tasks

Maintain radio communications with mobile command center (MCC), emergency operations center (EOC), and other emergency personnel.

Relay requests and information to the appropriate EMRO members.

Assist activation of the EOC.

Ensure that telephones and communications equipment are properly placed.

LOCATION	Issue Date	Procedure No.
Emergency Plan Manual	_/_/_	EPIP-240

Duties of the LOCATION	Rev. Date	Revision No.
Emergency Management/Response	_/_/_	0
Organization During Emergencies		Page __ of __ Pages

Notify the incident support director of radio communications activation.

Prepare incident documentation when requested.

Maintain, retain, and store incident files for postincident use.

4.16.3 Primary EPIPs used during emergencies. EPIP-420, Emergency Communications.

4.16.4 Position-specific references. Emergency management plan, sections 3 and 4; appendices M and O.

4.17 Recorder

4.17.1 Primary position holders

- TITLE
- TITLE
- TITLE

See attachment 11 for checklist.

4.17.2 Major functions, duties, and tasks

Maintain a log of all pertinent emergency response activities occurring in the EOC, using the Activities Log Sheet, form EPIP-210-1.

Establish and organize incident files.

Retain and file duplicate copies of official forms and reports.

Maintain contact with the communications coordinator to obtain information related to the incident.

Post information related to the incident on the sequence-of-events board, as appropriate.

Maintain, retain, and store incident files for postincident use.

4.17.3 Primary EPIPs used during emergencies

Emergency External Notification	EPIP-410
Emergency Communications	EPIP-420

4.17.4 Position-specific references. Emergency management plan, sections 2, 8, and 10; appendices H and K.

4.18 Engineering and inspection director

4.18.1 Primary position holders

- TITLE
- TITLE
- TITLE

See attachment 12 for checklist.

4.18.2 Major functions, duties, and tasks

Coordinate, direct, and respond to requests from the EMRO for engineering, technical, and inspection assistance.

Coordinate the recall and deployment of engineering personnel to respond to the incident.

Ensure timely completion of technical assistance provided in support of emergency response and recovery efforts.

Supervise and coordinate the retrieval of drawings and documents for the EMRO.

Ensure on-site records management and record-keeping efforts are being carried out.

Assist the logistics director in the acquisition of additional equipment and supplies, as required.

Ensure appropriate radiological actions are taken by the radiological control group (inspection department) when a radiological incident has occurred.

Ensure personnel radiation exposures are maintained in accordance with 10 CFR, part 20, and applicable Department of Transportation regulations. Coordinate this effort with inspection and medical.

4.18.3 Primary EPIPs used during emergencies

Emergency Communications EPIP-420

Incident Investigation EPIP-811

4.18.4 Position-specific references. Emergency management plan, sections 8 and 10; appendix H.

4.19 Incident investigation coordinator

4.19.1 Primary position holders

- TITLE
- TITLE
- TITLE

4.19.2 Major functions, duties, and tasks. Accumulate information and data pertaining to the incident at hand. Conduct incident investigation as needed.

4.19.3 Primary EPIPs used during emergencies

Emergency Communications EPIP-420

Incident Investigation EPIP-811

4.19.4 Position-specific references. Emergency management plan, sections 8 and 10; appendix H; process safety guidelines.

4.20 Administrative staff

4.20.1 Primary position holders

- TITLE
- TITLE
- TITLE

| LOCATION | Issue Date | Procedure No. |
| Emergency Plan Manual | _/_/_ | EPIP-240 |

Duties of the LOCATION	Rev. Date	Revision No.
Emergency Management/Response	_/_/_	0
Organization During Emergencies		Page __ of __ Pages

4.20.2 Major functions, duties, and tasks

Assist in activation of the EOC.

Ensure that telephones and communications equipment are properly placed.

Establish and organize files.

Retain and file duplicate copies of official forms and reports.

Prepare incident documentation when requested.

Maintain, retain, and store incident files for postincident use.

4.20.3 Primary EPIPs used during emergencies. All EPIPs as necessary.

4.20.4 Position-specific references. Emergency management plan, sections 2, 3, and 4; appendices M and O.

5.0 References

Emergency management plan

EPIP-210, Duties of the Emergency Manager

EPIP-230, Duties of the Field Incident Commander

6.0 Attachments

Attachment 1, Operations Coordinator Checklist

Attachment 2, Logistics Director Checklist

Attachment 3, Public Affairs Director Checklist

Attachment 4, Security Officer Checklist

Attachment 5, Communications Coordinator Checklist

Attachment 6, Environmental Coordinator Checklist

Attachment 7, Safety Officer Checklist

Attachment 8, Accounting Director Checklist

Attachment 9, News Center Staff Checklist

Attachment 10, Radio Operator Checklist

Attachment 11, Recorder Checklist

Attachment 12, Engineering and Inspection Director Checklist

ATTACHMENT 1
PAGE   of   PAGES

Operations Coordinator Checklist

Primary: TITLE

Alternate: TITLE

_____ Establish status of all operating facilities.

_____ Stabilize facility operations for the safety of personnel and equipment.

_____ Coordinate orderly shutdown of any process facilities as required.

_____ Communicate LOCATION status to emergency operations center (EOC).

_____ Ensure adequate work force is maintained to continue safe operations.

_____ Communicate LOCATION status to the appropriate personnel.

_____ Coordinate facility process interactions with emergency management/response organization (operations managers).

_____ Coordinate safe operation of unaffected facilities.

LOCATION	Issue Date	Procedure No.
Emergency Plan Manual	_/_/_	EPIP-240

Duties of the LOCATION	Rev. Date	Revision No.
Emergency Management/Response	_/_/_	0
Organization During Emergencies		Page _ of _ Pages

ATTACHMENT 2
PAGE   of   PAGES

Logistics Director Checklist

Primary: TITLE

Alternates: TITLE

TITLE

_____ Stand by the phone when you hear the siren or are informed of the emergency.

_____ If activated, report to the incident support center.

_____ Inform emergency operations center that incident support center is operational.

_____ Confirm accounting of all central and contractor personnel on site.

_____ Inform emergency manager or utilities shift supervisor that you are now assuming responsibility for calling additional mechanical personnel.

_____ Keep unassigned personnel in a designated area until they are needed.

_____ Maintain and execute plans to ensure that adequate electric power and communications are maintained.

_____ Provide mobile equipment and operators as needed.

_____ Maintain list of outside firms for access to additional equipment (i.e., cranes, VAC trucks, portable generators, portable lighting, portable toilets, radios).

_____ Procure materials and supplies as needed for both emergency operations and initial repairs. This will include providing for emergency response personnel.

LOCATION	Issue Date	Procedure No.
Emergency Plan Manual	_/_/_	EPIP-240

Duties of the LOCATION	Rev. Date	Revision No.
Emergency Management/Response	_/_/_	0
Organization During Emergencies		Page __ of __ Pages

ATTACHMENT 3
PAGE   of   PAGES

Public Affairs Director Checklist

Primary: TITLE

Alternates: TITLE

             TITLE

_____ Stand by the phone when you hear the siren or are informed of the emergency.

_____ If emergency facilities are activated, report to the emergency operations center (EOC).

_____ Establish status of all operations and facilities.

_____ Collect injury information.

_____ Coordinate informing of family members of injured personnel.

_____ Prepare statements for the press to be approved by the emergency manager.

_____ Prepare statement for rumor control hotline.

_____ Get out press handout on the history of the facility.

_____ Establish press receiving area in the news center (LOCATION).

_____ Establish communications with hospital to determine the extent of employees' injuries.

_____ Coordinate damage and injury claims from the outside public.

_____ Update rumor control hotline as needed.

_____ Update press releases as additional information is available.

ATTACHMENT 4
PAGE   of   PAGES

Security Officer Checklist

Primary: TITLE

Alternate: TITLE

Notifications

_____ If notified of an *alert* or *site area emergency* by the field incident commander during off-hours, contact the following individuals and inform them an alert or site area emergency situation exists in the LOCATION.

Group 1

Title	Name	Home phone
Title	Name	Home phone
Title	Name	Home phone

_____ If notified of a *general emergency* by the field incident commander during off-hours, contact group 1 members (above) and the following individuals, and inform them that a general emergency situation exists in the LOCATION.

Group 2

Title	Name	Home phone
Title	Name	Home phone
Title	Name	Home phone
Title	Name	Home phone

LOCATION	Issue Date	Procedure No.
Emergency Plan Manual	_/_/_	EPIP-240

Duties of the LOCATION	Rev. Date	Revision No.
Emergency Management/Response	_/_/_	0
Organization During Emergencies		Page __ of __ Pages

ATTACHMENT 4
PAGE   of   PAGES

Security Officer Checklist

When members of the emergency organization are notified, the following format will be used by the security officer on duty:

> I am security officer (*give name*). There is a (*fire, release, spill, etc.*) on the (*unit name*) at the LOCATION, an (*alert, site area, or general emergency*) classification has been declared, and the emergency management/response organization is being activated.

Additional actions

_____ Obtain additional staffing as required.

_____ Control access to LOCATION and administration building.

_____ Coordinate traffic control (with outside law enforcement officers if neccessary).

_____ Keep detailed logs of all persons entering the facility.

_____ Supply security personnel for traffic control at the emergency operations center (EOC) and the news center in the administration building.

LOCATION	Issue Date	Procedure No.
Emergency Plan Manual	_/_/_	EPIP-240

Duties of the LOCATION	Rev. Date	Revision No.
Emergency Management/Response	_/_/_	0
Organization During Emergencies		Page __ of __ Pages

ATTACHMENT 5
PAGE of PAGES

Communications Coordinator Checklist

Primary: TITLE

Alternates: TITLE

             TITLE

_____ Report to the emergency operations center (EOC).

_____ Coordinate the setup and activation of the EOC.

_____ Ensure that a radio operator monitors radio traffic and maintains communications with MCC, ISC, and other emergency personnel.

_____ Ensure that a log (including time) of all communications is being kept as accurately as possible.

_____ Verify that a security officer has been dispatched to the administration building.

_____ Coordinate the recall and deployment of any administrative support personnel, as needed.

_____ Ensure that communication procedures are implemented and records of incoming and outgoing messages are properly maintained.

_____ Initiate request through the logistics director for additional communication equipment or the repair and maintenance of the equipment.

_____ Coordinate clerical requests from or for EMO personnel.

_____ Ensure proper adjustments are made for communication personnel and equipment as appropriate.

LOCATION	Issue Date	Procedure No.
Emergency Plan Manual	_/_/_	EPIP-240

Duties of the LOCATION	Rev. Date	Revision No.
Emergency Management/Response	_/_/_	0
Organization During Emergencies		Page _ of _ Pages

ATTACHMENT 6
PAGE   of   PAGES

Environmental Coordinator Checklist

Primary: TITLE

Alternates: TITLE

TITLE

_____ Provide monitoring and sampling support to the FIC and affected or unaffected units as needed.

_____ Keep a log of all data that have been recorded during the incident.

_____ Provide technical information to the FIC, ISD, and/or EOC.

_____ Review all news releases pertaining to environmental matters, to ensure technical accuracy.

_____ Review environmental release information to determine if any reportable quantities (RQs) have been exceeded.

_____ Advise the ISD on all environmental regulations as they pertain to the incident at hand.

_____ Make appropriate notifications to state and federal agencies.

_____ Coordinate necessary assistance with corporate personnel.

| LOCATION | Issue Date | Procedure No. |
| Emergency Plan Manual | _/_/_ | EPIP-240 |

Duties of the LOCATION	Rev. Date	Revision No.
Emergency Management/Response	_/_/_	0
Organization During Emergencies		Page __ of __ Pages

ATTACHMENT 7
PAGE   of   PAGES

Safety Officer Checklist

Primary: TITLE

Alternate: TITLE

_____   Provide safety support to the FIC or affected area supervisor as required.

_____   Ensure all response personnel are equipped with personal protective equipment (SCBA, turnouts, etc.).

_____   Ensure that all nonessential personnel have vacated the incident scene in a safe and efficient manner and remain out.

_____   Alert any and all response personnel to any unsafe situation that may be present.

_____   Brief the outside response personnel of any hazards or dangers that they may encounter.

| LOCATION | Issue Date | Procedure No. |
| Emergency Plan Manual | _/_/_ | EPIP-240 |

Duties of the LOCATION	Rev. Date	Revision No.
Emergency Management/Response	_/_/_	0
Organization During Emergencies		Page _ of _ Pages

ATTACHMENT 8
PAGE   of   PAGES

Accounting Director Checklist

Primary: TITLE

Alternate: TITLE

_____ Set up special charge codes for the purchasing department for supplying equipment and materials.

_____ Log and file all accounting records.

_____ Arrange transportation and temporary housing for outside response personnel as needed.

_____ Supply accounting information and data to the EMO as requested.

_____ Provide support to the logistics director as needed.

ATTACHMENT 9
PAGE   of   PAGES

News Center Staff Checklist

Primary: TITLE

Alternate: TITLE

_____ Verify that a security officer has been dispatched to the administration building.

_____ Ensure that the news center is properly arranged per EPIP-711 (telephones, communications equipment, etc.).

_____ Notify the public affairs director of news center activation.

_____ Arrange for and coordinate news conferences.

_____ Keep the rumor control hotline message up to date.

_____ Hand out copies of "Instructions to the News Media" (attachment to EPIP-711) to all news media representatives.

_____ Keep copies of all official forms and reports.

_____ Check for accuracy and completeness of all news releases and forms.

_____ Answer news media inquiries by reading the official news releases.

_____ Prepare incident documentation when requested.

| LOCATION | Issue Date | Procedure No. |
| Emergency Plan Manual | _/_/_ | EPIP-240 |

Duties of the LOCATION	Rev. Date	Revision No.
Emergency Management/Response	_/_/_	0
Organization During Emergencies		Page _ of _ Pages

ATTACHMENT 10
PAGE   of   PAGES

Radio Operator Checklist

Primary: TITLE

Alternate: TITLE

_____ Report to the emergency operations center (EOC).

_____ Ensure that telephones and communications equipment are properly placed in the EOC.

_____ Announce on radio channel _____ that the EOC has been activated and is standing by.

_____ Notify the ISD of radio communications activation.

_____ Monitor and maintain radio communications with MCC, ISC, and other emergency personnel.

_____ Relay all requests and information to the appropriate EMO personnel.

_____ Set up communications files.

_____ Await field reports. Record the following when reported.*

_____ Rescue ■   Is everyone out?

              ■ Estimate how many unaccounted for. _____

_____ Fire   ■ Where is it? _____

              ■ Is it spreading? _____

              ■ What is burning? _____

_____ Control ■ Can brigade control it? _____

              ■ LOCATION fire department responding _____

---

*Minimize radio calls to the field.

_____

■ Staging location _____

_____ Other needs _____

■ Additional equipment needed? _____

_____

_____

_____

ATTACHMENT 11
PAGE   of   PAGES

Recorder Checklist

Primary: TITLE

Alternate: TITLE

_____ Maintain a log of all pertinent emergency response activities occurring in the EOC, using the Activities Log Sheet, form EPIP-210-1.

_____ Establish and organize incident files.

_____ Retain and file duplicate copies of official forms and reports.

_____ Maintain contact with the communications coordinator to obtain information related to the incident.

_____ Post information related to the incident on the sequence-of-events board.

_____ Maintain, retain, and store incident files for postincident use.

_____ Prepare incident documentation when requested.

_____ Assist EOC personnel as needed.

LOCATION	Issue Date	Procedure No.
Emergency Plan Manual	_/_/_	EPIP-240

Duties of the LOCATION	Rev. Date	Revision No.
Emergency Management/Response	_/_/_	0
Organization During Emergencies		Page __ of __ Pages

ATTACHMENT 12
PAGE   of   PAGES

Engineering and Inspection Director Checklist

Primary: TITLE

Alternate: TITLE

_____ Stand by the phone when you hear the siren or are informed of the emergency.

_____ If command posts are established, report to the emergency operations center.

_____ Call out additional engineering and inspection personnel as needed.

_____ Provide support and engineering data to incident support center.

_____ Assemble drawings and other engineering data to facilitate response and repair planning and execution.

_____ Provide support for safety issues involving radioactive sources.

_____ Prepare and execute a survey of damaged areas once access is approved by the incident support director, field incident commander, and operations personnel.

_____ Specify any nondestructive inspection and/or testing requirements prior to returning equipment to service.

COMPANY

LOCATION

EMERGENCY MANAGEMENT PLAN MANUAL

ACTIVATION OF THE EMERGENCY MANAGEMENT/RESPONSE ORGANIZATION EPIP-250

REVISION 0

DATE

SUBMITTED BY: _____   **DATE:** _____
                         TITLE

APPROVED BY: _____   **DATE:** _____
                        TITLE

1.0 Purpose

This procedure provides guidance and instructions for the activation of the emergency management/response organization (EMRO).

2.0 Applicability

This procedure is applicable to field incident commander, LOCATION security personnel, and EMRO staff.

3.0 Definitions

None.

4.0 Instructions

4.1 Activation

4.1.1 Utilities will receive all emergency calls via telephone or plant radio transmissions. Utilities personnel will sound the appropriate refinery alarm and handle emergency radio transmissions as needed to notify refinery personnel of the situation.

4.1.2 On off-shifts when notified of an emergency, the TITLE becomes field incident commander (FIC), until relieved by the first responding TITLE.

4.1.3 The FIC will activate the mobile command center (MCC) and assist the affected area supervisor in classifying incidents in accordance with EPIP-510, Assessment of Emergency Conditions, Emergency Classification, and Protective Action Recommendation Guides. Once the classification has been determined, the FIC will announce the classification on radio channel _____ .

4.1.4 Plant security personnel will monitor the radio channel. When the emergency classification is announced, security will make the notifications indicated for the given classification. (See EPIP-240, attachment 4.)

4.1.5 For incidents assessed as site area emergency or general emergency, the FIC is responsible for determining whether off-site protective actions are warranted. If so, utilities will notify the LOCATION public safety agency with a recommendation to take such protective actions as specified by the FIC or affected area supervisor. In this situation, the FIC may use EPIP-510, Assessment of Emergency Conditions, Emergency Classification, and Protective Action Recommendation Guides for guidance. *Do not wait for higher authority if you believe the public is in danger. Take immediate action to notify those downwind or in the danger zone that they should protect themselves.*

4.1.6 After taking action to warn the public, if necessary, the utilities shift supervisor will contact security to ensure that notification of EMRO personnel has been initiated.

5.0 References

Emergency management plan, sections 2, 4, and 5

EPIP-410, Emergency External Notification

EPIP-420, Emergency Communications

EPIP-510, Assessment of Emergency Conditions, Emergency Classification, and Protective Action Recommendation Guides

6.0 Attachments

None.

COMPANY

LOCATION

EMERGENCY MANAGEMENT PLAN MANUAL

FIRE OR EXPLOSION
EPIP-311

REVISION 0

DATE

SUBMITTED BY: _____   DATE:_____
                  TITLE

APPROVED BY: _____   DATE:_____
                  TITLE

1.0 Purpose

The purpose of this procedure is to provide guidance and to initiate actions necessary for evaluation, isolation, and mitigation in the event of a fire, explosion, or release (with the potential of ignition).

2.0 Applicability

This procedure is applicable to all personnel at the LOCATION.

3.0 Definitions

Release—any spilling, leaking, pumping, pouring, emitting, emptying, discharging, injecting, escaping, leaching, dumping, or disposing into the environment.

Incipient-stage fire—in the first stage of existence, just beginning to exist or to come to notice.

Explosion—detonation of any form due to friction, impact (blows), shock, and/or heat. Detonation generally results in a very rapid release of energy that usually creates very high pressures.

4.0 Instructions

4.1 Precautions

4.1.1 In the event of a release (with the potential of ignition), fire, or explosion which creates an immediate operational or personnel hazard, the person discovering the condition will promptly notify the shift supervisor of the affected unit or notify utilities via plant phone.

Make sure you tell someone to get help before you attempt to extinguish a fire!

4.1.2 Internal facility alarms will be activated, personnel notified, and all nonessential personnel evacuated, if necessary, from the affected area, as detailed in EPIP-511, Evacuation, Sheltering, and Accountability.

4.1.3 Personal protective clothing and respiratory requirements will be determined, based upon the type and magnitude of the situation, prior to deploying personnel for response activities.

4.1.4 The field incident commander (FIC) or emergency manager may receive advice on protective actions from the incident support director, safety coordinator, or environmental health and safety department.

4.2 Initial actions

These include but are not limited to the following:

On-scene observer

- Notify affected area shift supervisor or call utilities.
- Take appropriate action to mitigate the incident, if this can be done safely.

Affected area supervisor

- Assess the situation. If necessary, call to request assistance.
- Sound unit emergency alarm.
- Initiate appropriate actions as indicated by the situation and standard operating instructions.
- Assist FIC in incident classification per EPIP-510.
- Coordinate any activities which might impact response efforts with the FIC.

Field incident commander

- Activate mobile command center (MCC).
- With input from the affected area supervisor, classify the incident per EPIP-510.
- Announce incident classification over plant radio channel.
- Ensure response teams (LOCATION, TYPE, NAME) and EMO have been activated, if required.
- Coordinate activities with arriving response personnel.
- Keep log.
- On off-shifts, when relieved of FIC duties, the TITLE shall proceed to the emergency operations center (EOC) and brief the emergency manager (EM) or first arriving alternate emergency manager on the current conditions of the incident.

Utilities, on days

- Sound LOCATION fire alarm (three 10-second blasts on the siren at 5-second intervals).
- If call was not from the affected area, notify the affected area.
- Notify the FIC of the emergency, and carry out notification procedures of the response teams as directed by the FIC.
- Activate in-plant radio alert system, giving location of fire or emergency, per utilities standard operating procedure (portable radios will activate automatically).
- Dial emergency contact phone numbers, giving location and nature of emergency.
- Request assistance from (OFF-SITE AGENCIES), as instructed by the FIC.
- Account for all utilities operations personnel.
- Keep a log of all activities.
- Alert the community, if necessary, to take protective actions (EPIP-510), at the direction of the FIC or affected area supervisor.
- Obtain additional personnel as instructed by the FIC.
- Sound *All Clear* as instructed by the FIC.

Utilities, off-shift (nights, holidays, and weekends)

- Sound fire alarm.
- If the call was not from the affected area, notify the affected area.
- Notify (OFF-SITE AGENCIES) and give location of the fire and/ or emergency, at the direction of the affected area supervisor or the FIC.
- Activate volunteer radio alert per utilities standard operating procedure. If acknowledgment call is not received from one of the brigade officers in 2 or 3 minutes, notify operations to activate the backup radio alert system. If no acknowledgment call is received from the backup system either, start phone procedures to obtain volunteers as listed in the standard operating instructions.
- Dial emergency contact telephone number, giving location and nature of the emergency.

- Notify the FIC of the emergency, and continue notification procedures of the response teams as directed by the FIC.
- Account for all utilities operations personnel.
- Keep a log of all activities.
- Obtain additional operators or mechanics as needed or per instructions by the FIC. The utilities supervisor shall use the overtime call-out procedures located in the supervisor's office.
- Should a potential problem arise (such as a release without ignition), the utilities supervisor or the affected area supervisor may choose to call the TITLE at home to seek instruction on tone-out and alarm procedures as necessary.
- Sound *All Clear* as instructed by the FIC.

Operations, unaffected areas

- Release one fire brigade member, if one is on shift, at the discretion of the supervisor.
- Account for all unit operations personnel.

Fire brigade

- Report to fire station.
- Suit up and report status to FIC.
- First arriving officer will assume the role of the FIC.
- No members (except officers) or equipment will leave the fire station until so instructed by the FIC.
- In the event a release occurs with the potential of ignition, brigade members will be staged at the fire station in a standby mode, awaiting instructions from the FIC.

Incident support director

- Ensure EMRO activation is adequate.
- Review incident for reportable quantity (RQ) issues, as appropriate.
- Call appropriate agencies.
- Monitor incident.
- Support FIC as needed.

- Keep a log.
- Prepare follow-up report (postincident investigation).

Operations managers

- Coordinate and communicate with EMRO.
- Support supervisors as needed.
- Coordinate LOCATION operations.
- Keep a log.

Maintenance

- If on the affected unit, report to the supervisor at the predesignated muster area.
- If not on the affected unit, check in with the supervisor to be accounted for; then continue with daily assignment until instructed otherwise.
- On nights, holidays, and weekends, report to the utilities supervisor to be accounted for and then go to the mechanical shop to wait for further instructions.*

Mechanical Department

- If on the affected facility, report back to the supervisor at the central shop. If not on the affected facility, check in with the supervisor to be accounted for, then continue with daily assignment until instructed otherwise.
- On nights, holidays, and weekends, report to the utilities supervisor to be accounted for; then go to the mechanical shop and wait for further instructions.*

Security

- If on patrol or dock run, return immediately to the main gate.
- Activate EMRO per EPIP-250 and the incident classification announced by the FIC.

---

*During an emergency incident, if an individual is called upon to assist at the firehouse, here are a few tasks that she or he may be asked to perform: transport hose, foam, equipment, air bottles, and drinks; obtain drinking water, food, and other supplies.

- Regulate the flow of gate traffic.
- During an emergency, the guards *will not* permit any unauthorized personnel through the gate at any time.

Construction gate guard

- In the event that a construction gate is being used or has to be opened for an emergency, the guard shall regulate traffic from the construction parking lot or from the LOCATION as an exit only. This gate will not be used as an entrance gate during an emergency unless the main gate is inaccessible or at the direction of the FIC.

Outside contractors

- If on the affected unit, contractors shall report promptly to the gate where they entered, to be accounted for, and stand by in the parking area designated by the security officer, until instructed otherwise.

Secretaries and office assistants

- Notify their respective manager and/or superintendent of the emergency.

Materials management

- Upon hearing the radio alert, notify shop personnel of fire and location, using shop loudspeaker system.

Technical and supervisory personnel

- Assist as instructed by EMO personnel.*

4.3 Subsequent actions

The incident support director will prepare a written report to the appropriate regulatory agencies in accordance with COMPANY reporting guidelines.

5.0 References

Emergency management plan, sections 3, 4, and 5

EPIP-410, Emergency External Notification

EPIP-510, Assessment of Emergency Conditions, Emergency Classification, and Protective Action Recommendation Guides

EPIP-511, Evacuation, Sheltering, and Accountability

6.0 Attachments

None.

COMPANY

LOCATION

EMERGENCY MANAGEMENT PLAN MANUAL

TRANSPORTING CONTAMINATED INJURED PERSONNEL EPIP-340

REVISION 0

DATE

SUBMITTED BY: _____ DATE: _____
               TITLE

APPROVED BY: _____ DATE: _____
               TITLE

1.0 Purpose

This procedure provides guidance for the handling and transporting of contaminated injured personnel from the LOCATION to area hospitals.

2.0 Applicability

This procedure applies to potentially contaminated individuals whose injuries may require off-site emergency medical care. In the absence of any other emergency considerations, implementation of this procedure will be considered cause for declaring an *unusual event* and activating the emergency management plan accordingly.

3.0 Definitions

Minor injury—an injury that does not endanger the life of an individual; basic emergency care is generally sufficient treatment. Decontamination should be completed prior to treating the injury.

Serious injury—an injury or condition including unconsciousness, profuse bleeding, extensive burns, severe pain without an obvious injury, an obvious fracture, or any other injury that requires medical treatment as soon as possible. Contamination is of less concern than the serious injury.

4.0 Instructions

4.1 Precautions

4.1.1 Medical assistance rendered will be within the scope of the rescuer's qualifications.

4.1.2 Contaminated individuals transported to the hospital will be accompanied by emergency medical personnel.

4.1.3 If any individual is suspected of being exposed to a hazardous material, the LOCATION county medical technician on the transporting medical unit will be notified so that arrangements can be made for any needed decontamination procedures.

LOCATION	Issue Date	Procedure No.
Emergency Plan Manual	_/_/_	EPIP-340

Transporting Contaminated	Rev. Date	Revision No.
Injured Personnel	_/_/_	0
		Page __ of __ Pages

4.1.4 If the victim's condition is complicated by hazardous material contamination, either suspected or confirmed, the victim will be transported to a hospital facility for medical evaluation and required treatment.

4.1.5 The medical technician will ensure notification of the medical facility that a contaminated injured person is coming.

4.1.6 As required, communications should be maintained between the hospital, the medical unit, and the LOCATION. Available communication options include telephone between the LOCATION and the hospital and two-way radio between the medical unit and the hospital.

4.1.7 Protective clothing will be worn by personnel attending the victim(s) per previous training instructions. Treatment personnel should exercise caution when handling a victim to minimize the spread of contamination.

4.2 Initial actions

4.2.1 The individual who discovers an injured or contaminated person will briefly assess the situation, report the injury and request emergency assistance, and for injuries provide the number of victims, present location of the victims, and type of injury.

4.2.2 The affected area supervisor will initiate medical treatment of obvious injuries in accordance with standard operating procedures. The supervisor will also assist in moving victim(s) to a safe area, provided that they can be moved without incurring further injury.

   The affected area supervisor will remain with the victim until released by emergency medical personnel, unless this poses a safety hazard for the responder.

   Note: On off-shifts, anyone discovering a contaminated individual should initiate decontamination as quickly as possible, but only if it can be accomplished without aggravating or extending further injury to the individual. If at all possible, keep the injury itself covered while decontamination procedures are being administered.

4.3 Responsibilities

4.3.1 Field incident commander, incident support director, and/or emergency manager. The FIC, ISD, or EM will:

Declare an *unusual event* if the injured individual is contaminated and requires off-site medical treatment and if an emergency condition does not already exist.

Initiate notification and communication procedures EPIP-410 and EPIP-420, if an emergency condition has not already initiated them.

Ensure that emergency medical technicians, hazardous materials personnel, and emergency response personnel, as needed, are alerted to the situation and informed of the location of the victim(s).

Ensure that the ambulance service is informed of the following:

- Number of victim(s)
- Extent of their injuries (if known)
- Contamination level of the victim(s)
- Destination of the medical unit
- Final destination of the medical unit

Notify the security coordinator of the pending arrival of the emergency vehicle and where it is to be taken.

Note: Situation updates should be made to the appropriate individuals as soon as possible.

4.3.2 Emergency medical response. The first responder will be in charge of the medical response activities at the scene until relieved by a higher-level emergency medical responder.

The first responder will document all decontamination efforts and fill out the appropriate form for each victim transported from the LOCATION for treatment.

Note: If time permits, efforts should be made to remove as much of the contamination as possible without aggravating the injuries, before transportation is effected.

The first responder will establish and maintain contamination controls, as appropriate, and ensure that emergency medical personnel are equipped with appropriate personal protective equipment before they accompany the victim(s) to the hospital.

4.4 Subsequent actions

4.4.1 The FIC, ISD, EM, or designee will ensure that all follow-up actions are accomplished in accordance with approved procedures. Some guidance may be obtained from EPIP-830, Humanitarian Assistance, which discusses operation of the injury/fatality tracking center.

4.4.2 All swabs, rags, and flushing solutions used for treating injuries will be packaged into containers labeled *Biohazard* and disposed of as medical waste. Individuals exposed to blood must follow the LOCATION's blood-borne pathogen plan.

4.4.3 If more definitive medical care is required, the FIC, ISD, or designee may contact CHEMTREC to determine which facilities are available. Transportation and conditions of transfer will be arranged as agreed between the ISD and the destination facility.

5.0 References

Emergency management plan, sections 5, 7, and 8

Standard operating procedures

EPIP-410, Emergency External Notification

EPIP-420, Emergency Communications

EPIP-830, Humanitarian Assistance

Blood-borne pathogen plan

6.0 Attachments

Attachment 1, List of Associated Hazardous Materials

Attachment 1

List of
Associated Hazardous Materials
(insert data specific
to facility or operation)

COMPANY

LOCATION

EMERGENCY MANAGEMENT
PLAN MANUAL

BOMB INCIDENT RESPONSE
EPIP-350

REVISION 0

DATE

SUBMITTED BY: _____ DATE: _____
              TITLE

APPROVED BY: _____ DATE: _____
              TITLE

1.0 Purpose

This procedure provides guidance and describes the actions, responsibilities, authorities, and interfaces for responding to a bomb threat at the LOCATION.

   This procedure provides suggested guidelines for incident mitigation and organizational control. The actions described herein may be altered, depending on the situation, by the personnel responsible for implementing the procedure.

2.0 Applicability

This procedure applies to all personnel in the event that a bomb incident or threat at the LOCATION requires the activation of the emergency management plan (EMP).

3.0 Definitions

   Bomb threat—any threat received regarding the potential use of an explosive or incendiary device against the LOCATION, administrative buildings, or personnel.

   Critical areas—list those for your facility.

4.0 Instructions

4.1 Precautions

4.1.1 *Telephone procedure:*   Remain calm, and try to keep the caller on the line. Ask the caller to repeat the message. Record the information verbatim. Listen carefully for any background noises, speech mannerisms, accents, etc.

4.1.2 Complete the bomb threat checklist (attachment 1 to this EPIP). Notify security by dialing extension _____ . Relay all information regarding the call, including your name and telephone number.

4.1.3 When a bomb threat is received, the emergency manager (EM) or incident support director (ISD) will declare an *alert* emergency classification.

4.1.4 The affected area supervisor and/or ISD may designate a communicator to handle notification of the various government agencies in accordance with EPIP-410, Emergency External Notification.

4.1.5 The EM will not delegate approval authority for public information and news media releases.

4.2 Responsibilities

The following responsibilities apply to all personnel who may assume the role of EM or ISD in response to a bomb threat:

- Declare an alert emergency classification in accordance with EPIP-510, Assessment of Emergency Conditions, Emergency Classification, and Protective Action Recommendation Guides. Initiate appropriate provisions of the EMP.

- Initiate notification of EPIP-410, Emergency External Notification, to the emergency management/response organization (EMRO).

- Initiate actions as defined in EPIP-210, Emergency Manager, as appropriate.

4.3 Specific actions

4.3.1 **Call-out procedure.** Twenty-four hours a day, on normal working days, nights, weekends, and holidays, call plant security at extension _____ . Inform the on-duty security officer of what you have received or found.

Security personnel will notify:

- TITLE
- TITLE
- TITLE

The LOCATION manager or a designee will determine if and when the LOCATION management should be notified.

If the LOCATION manager or a designee determines that the emergency operations center (EOC) should be activated, all entrance to the LOCATION shall be halted by security. Only operators and other LOCATION employees necessary for the bomb threat emergency will be allowed to enter.

4.4 Bomb search

Should a bomb search be conducted in the LOCATION, a specific, orderly, and thorough plan must be carefully followed to ensure a thorough search and to minimize harm to employees and damage to the LOCATION.

An explosives ordinance disposal team does not conduct bomb searches. Team members only disarm and remove a bomb after it has been located; therefore, LOCATION employees will have to conduct all searches. Our employees know the LOCATION better than anyone from the outside. Their concern for their own safety will contribute to a more thorough search than would be conducted by any outside search team.

As a member of a search team, an employee's responsibility will be only to *look* for a bomb, *not to touch it or attempt to disarm it. The handling of a bomb or suspected bomb will be performed by a professional bomb squad.*

All information and findings from the search shall be phoned in immediately to the EOC at the administration building, extension _____ , as the searches progress. Plant security will coordinate all searches from the EOC. *Do not use the location radio systems or cellular phones to communicate on the units or areas where a search is being conducted.*

Do not use the location radio systems to call in information or results of a search.

In the EOC, a large LOCATION plot plan will be utilized to mark off the areas that have been searched and cleared.

Anything unusual discovered during a search must be reported immediately to the EOC. Do not halt a search because one suspicious object has been found. If there is the possibility of one bomb being placed, then there could be other bombs. *You may have found a decoy.*

When any suspicious or unusual object (or obvious bomb) is located, plant security will respond to evaluate the situation. Security will report back to the EOC with any findings. All personnel in the area will follow the instructions of security personnel.

Each manager will conduct searches of his or her area and control areas, using the staff from those locations. It shall be the manager's responsibility to assign search team leaders and areas to search.

- A plot plan of each area will be available at the control room to mark off each section of the area as it is cleared.

- Areas and locations other than a unit shall be marked off on a LOCATION map as being cleared.

- A record will be kept of members of search teams. The record shall include the name of each search team member, the area she or he searched, the time and date of search, and the name of the search team leader.

- The record of this team will be submitted by the individual managers to the TITLE so that it may become part of the investigative report.

The TITLE will have fire crew members available to assist in the searches, as authorized by the TITLE.

Whenever a security team is dispatched to the scene of a possible bomb finding, team members will direct all actions relating to the possible bomb. Security teams will be the liaison between the bomb location and the EOC.

4.4.1 Room search technique. Each bomb search team will be composed of at least two individuals, qualified to perform bomb search operations. Bomb search team personnel should minimize their own exposure(s) consistent with the needs of the activity to be performed.

First team action: Listening. When the first team enters the room to be searched, team members will first move to the center of the room and stand quietly, with their eyes shut, and listen for any clockwork device. The team should move to various areas in the room in a clockwise fashion, repeating this action to listen for any clockwork device sounds.

Second team action: Division of room and selection of search height. The room should be divided into two equal parts, if possible. This equal division should be based on the number and type of objects in the room to be searched, not on the size of the room.

The first searching height will be from the floor level to approximately waist height. The search will cover all items in the search area at the selected level.

The second searching height will be from the waist to the top of the head.

The third searching height will be from the top of the head to the ceiling and will include all ducts, hanging light fixtures, etc.

The fourth searching height will be the suspended- or false-ceiling area.

Room sweep. With the room divided and the first searching height selected, the team will go to one end of the room and start from a back-to-back position. This is the starting point, and the same point will be used for each successive searching sweep.

Each team member will start searching her or his way around the room, working toward the other person. Check items resting on the floor around the wall area of the room. The team will continue the search, checking items in the middle of the room. The team will continue this technique until the entire room, at all search heights, has been searched.

Restated, these are the basics of the search technique:

- Divide the area.
- Select search heights.
- Start from bottom and work up.
- Start back to back and work toward each other.
- Go around the walls, working into the center of the room.
- Do not touch or remove any foreign or strange-looking materials.

Marking of searched rooms. Each room will be marked after completion of its search with a small piece of tape, approximately 1 inch square, which is placed on the lower corner of the door or door frame on the side opposite of the door knob.

4.4.2 General building search. The general building search will be conducted as follows:

Personnel will be evacuated from the building in accordance with EPIP-511, Evacuation, Sheltering, and Accountability. All electric plug-in equipment should be unplugged prior to the evacuation.

The EM or ISD will notify the appropriate off-site agencies for support as necessary. This may include, but is not limited to, establishment of law enforcement safety lines and traffic and access control in and around the affected area.

If a radio-controlled device is suspected, a rooftop search by law enforcement personnel may be requested.

The building search will be conducted as the room search with the following exception: *All outside areas around the building extending from the building to 25 feet from the building will be searched.*

Note: When the search is conducted of outside areas, pay particular attention to street drainage systems, manholes, trash receptacles, parked vehicles, mailboxes, etc.

Once inside, the search team will start at the bottom and work its way up. The team will employ the same techniques as for the room search. This will include subbasement and basement areas.

4.4.3 Discovery of suspicious object. If a suspicious object is found, the search will continue until the premises of the entire refinery are covered, because there may be additional suspicious objects. *Do not touch.* Leave this to the professionals.

A. Immediate precautions. Notify the EOC.

- Rope off the area.

- Post search personnel to guard the area.

- No one is to enter until authorized by the EOC.

B. Evacuation procedures. No one is to leave unless instructed to do so by the EOC.

C. Disarmament procedures. The emergency operations center will

- Notify the LOCATION sheriff's office emergency number _____.

- Notify corporate security at the 24-hour number _____.

Professional bomb disposal technicians will be dispatched and take custody of the bomb.

Do not touch, jar, move, or attempt to pull on any object or device suspected as a bomb.

Your responsibility as a search team member is only to look for a bomb, not to handle it or try to be a hero.

LOCATION personnel perform only those duties agreed to by both the bomb disposal unit and the emergency operations center. LOCATION employees do not touch the suspicious object under any conditions.

4.5 Search responsibilities

4.5.1 The first person to arrive at each unit command center will assume command of the area until relieved by the FIC or EM. As each command center is established, the EOC will be contacted.

4.5.2 Each command center will have a detailed search checklist for the area.

4.5.3 Search priorities and work force distribution will be assigned by the person in charge of the command center until the security coordinator and/or FIC arrives.

4.5.4 The security coordinator and/or FIC will remain in close contact with security.

4.5.5 Upon completion of the unit and area search, search leaders will report results to the security coordinator and/or FIC. These results will then be relayed to the EM. The EM will announce *All Clear* or order an evacuation in accordance with EPIP-511.

4.5.6 In the event of a site evacuation, the EM will declare a *site area emergency* in accordance with EPIP-510 and notify the appropriate off-site agencies, recommending that a general emergency be declared and appropriate protective actions taken.

4.6 Subsequent actions

4.6.1 Brief personnel at frequent intervals to ensure that the latest conditions at the LOCATION are understood and potential problems are considered.

4.6.2 Ensure that the off-site agencies are apprised of any changes in the situation at least every 60 minutes or as conditions warrant or until the emergency is terminated.

4.6.3 *Return to normal operation.* Return all borrowed items to their owners. Forward the logbook to the TITLE, along with comments, so a final report can be submitted to the LOCATION manager. A report is also needed for critique purposes. The security coordinator will complete and submit a security incident report on the appropriate form.

5.0 References

Emergency management plan, section 5

EPIP-210, Duties of the Emergency Manager

EPIP-230, Duties of the Field Incident Commander

EPIP-410, Emergency External Notification

EPIP-420, Emergency Communications

EPIP-510, Assessment of Emergency Conditions, Emergency Classification, and Protective Action Recommendation Guides

EPIP-820, Reentry and Recovery Operations

6.0 Attachments

Attachment 1, checklist for bomb threat telephone call.

LOCATION
Emergency Plan Manual

Bomb Incident Response

Issue Date
_/_/_

Rev. Date
_/_/_

Procedure No.
EPIP-350

Revision No.
0

Page __ of __ Pages

CHECKLIST FOR BOMB THREAT

TELEPHONE CALL

DIVISION_____ DATE_____

TIME OF CALL _____ OUTSIDE/INSIDE CALL_____

PHONE NUMBER CALL RECEIVED ON_____

EXACT WORDS OF CALLER (use back of sheet if necessary):

_____

_____

_____

_____

DESCRIPTION OF CALLER'S VOICE AND CALL:_____

Male, Female, Young, Middle Age, Old, Child_____

_____

Tone of Voice:_____

Accent, speech impediment, oddities of voice:_____

_____

Is the voice familiar? How so?_____

Background noises of any type:_____

Time caller hung up:_____

What questions did you ask?_____

_____

Person receiving the call:_____

Supervisor notified and time notified:_____

COMPANY

LOCATION

EMERGENCY MANAGEMENT
PLAN MANUAL

OIL SPILL RESPONSE
EPIP-380

REVISION 0

DATE

SUBMITTED BY: _____ DATE: _____
                  TITLE

APPROVED BY: _____ DATE: _____
                  TITLE

1.0 Purpose

The purpose of this procedure is to provide guidance and to establish the actions necessary for evaluation, isolation, and mitigation of an oil spill on navigable waters or land.

2.0 Applicability

This procedure is applicable to all personnel at the LOCATION.

3.0 Definitions

Oil is any petroleum-based material that does not have a reportable quantity (RQ) assigned to it (e.g., slop oil, fuel oil, crude oil). For spills of materials that do have an RQ, refer also to the Department of Transportation guidebook and MSDS information.

Oil spill classifications are as follows:

- *Minor oil spill:* less than 10,000 gallons (up to 240 barrels)
- *Moderate oil spill:* 10,000 gallons (240 barrels) up to 100,000 gallons (2400 barrels)
- *Major oil spill:* more than 100,000 gallons (2400 barrels)

4.0 Instructions

4.1 Precautions

4.1.1 This procedure is limited to oil spills that can be safely controlled by using the methods listed in attachments 1 to 9.

4.1.2 Typically, major oil spills to navigable waters will be classified as either a site area emergency or a general emergency. Major oil spill cleanup efforts will be directed by COMPANY, when they arrive on the scene, and will be governed by the U.S. Coast Guard upon arrival.

4.1.3 Internal facility alarms may be activated, if necessary, to notify personnel and evacuate nonessential personnel from the affected area, as detailed in EPIP-511.

4.1.4 Personal protective clothing and respiratory protection needs will be determined, according to the type and magnitude of the spill, before response personnel are dispatched.

4.1.5 The emergency manager may receive advice on protective measures from the incident support director or environmental health and safety department.

> *Note:* For full protection, personnel should use a self-contained breathing apparatus, protective clothing as specified by the nature of the release, hard hat, neoprene rubber gloves, goggles, and rubber boots.

4.2 Initial actions

Personnel at the scene (on-scene commander). Upon arrival at the scene, and if the spill is of sufficient magnitude to warrant help, the supervisor will immediately call in the outside spill contractor(s). In most cases the initial response efforts will be to

1. Stop the release.

2. Initiate the LOCATION response plan [notify spill contractor(s) and designated personnel].

3. Contain oil at the source while the spill area is relatively small.

4. Notify appropriate federal and state agencies.

If the spill is originating from a vessel, notify the vessel master that you are initiating spill containment and cleanup activities on the vessel's behalf. If the master states that he or she will call his or her own contractor, explain that due to the quick response capability of our contractor, we are initiating containment procedures with our contractor. We will consider having our contractor stand down when other forces are on site and ready to begin work.

To stop spillage from a vessel, it may be necessary for the vessel to transfer cargo from a damaged compartment. If the vessel does not have available capacity onboard, the vessel master may request to discharge cargo to shore. Work with the vessel in any way possible to stop the flow of oil into the environment.

4.2.1 Call _____ and report the incident.

4.2.2 Call out the emergency cleanup contractor, using the phone list from attachment 5.

4.2.3 Notify the U.S. Coast Guard of the nature and magnitude of the spill. The local phone number is (_____)-_____-_____.

4.2.4 Notify the National Response Center by calling the tollfree number (800) 424-8802.

4.2.5 Notify the marine superintendent.

4.2.6 Notify Environmental Health and Safety by calling extension _____ or using the call-out list from attachment 1.

4.2.7 Notify security to secure the leak site area.

4.2.8 Follow the spill response actions outlined in attachment 2 to this EPIP.

Marine superintendent (on-scene commander)

4.2.9 Assume responsibility for managing or otherwise supporting cleanup efforts by contractors until (or unless) relieved of this duty by COMPANY personnel.

4.2.10 Assist the field incident commander (FIC) with assessment of the incident, per EPIP-510, Assessment of Emergency Conditions, Emergency Classification, and Protective Action Recommendation Guides.

4.2.11 Contact the following:

- COMPANY personnel (if warranted)
- TITLE

Note: The emergency manager (EM), incident support director (ISD), and/or the FIC will evaluate the situation and make a protective action recommendation (if necessary) in accordance with EPIP-510.

Incident support director (for water or land spills)

4.2.12 Ensure notification of off-site authorities as required (EPIP-410), e.g., National Response Center, state, and company.

4.2.13 *Emergency damage control (EDC)* teams will be dispatched as required to assess the extent of the spill and perform mitigation operations as necessary. EDC teams will dress in appropriate protective clothing and respiratory protection equipment as specified by the safety coordinator.

4.2.14 Containment of the affected area will be in accordance with attachment 2 for water spills and attachment 3 for land spills.

4.3 Subsequent actions

4.3.1 After the environmental incident has been stopped, the EM or the assistant emergency manager may close out or deescalate the emergency as detailed in EPIP-510.

4.3.2 The FIC, oil movements shift supervisor, and/or ISD will complete a spill incident report form (attachment 7 to this EPIP).

4.3.3 The environmental health group will prepare a written report to the EPA in accordance with the LOCATION reporting guidelines and will submit it within 15 days. It must include

- Date, time, and type of incident
- Name and quantity of materials
- Extent of any contaminated injuries and assessment of actual or potential health hazards
- Quantity and disposition of recovered material

4.3.4 The following are accountable for oil spill prevention in their respective areas of responsibility:

- TITLE, area
- TITLE, area
- TITLE, area

5.0 References

Emergency management plan, sections 3, 4, and 5

EPIP-420, Emergency Communications

EPIP-510, Assessment of Emergency Conditions, Emergency Classification, and Protective Action Recommendation Guides

EPIP-511, Evacuation, Sheltering, and Accountability

EPIP-620, Activation of the Incident Support Center and Personnel Duties

6.0 Attachments

Attachment 1, Environmental Health and Safety Call-Out List

Attachment 2, Spill Response Actions

Attachment 3, Land Spill or Seepage

Attachment 4, Oil Spill Contractors

Attachment 5, Oil Spill Containment Equipment

Attachment 6, Emergency Cleanup Contractors

Attachment 7, Spill Incident Report Form

Attachment 8, Incident-Reporting Flowchart

ATTACHMENT 1
PAGE   of   PAGES

Environmental Health and Safety Call-Out List

Name	Home phone	Extension	Cellular phone	Plant radio

ATTACHMENT 2
PAGE   of   PAGES

Spill Response Actions

It is not possible or practical to prepare detailed procedures that address all possible oil spill scenarios. There are too many variables involved, from the type of product spilled to the tide and weather conditions. Therefore, the following discussion will outline various considerations in determining the appropriate response to a given spill.

The following priorities shall be used while you are evaluating an emergency and developing strategies for dealing with emergencies:

1. Protect human health and safety.
2. Prevent or minimize the release of pollution to the environment.
3. Protect the dock facilities, the vessel, and its cargo.
4. Mitigate the impact of pollution on sensitive environmental areas.
5. Cooperate fully with local, state, and federal agencies having jurisdiction over the affected site.
6. Keep the public informed.

In most cases the initial response efforts will be to:

1. Stop the release.
2. Contain oil at the source while the spill area is relatively small.
3. Initiate the EMP.
4. Notify appropriate federal and state agencies.

The following comments expand on these activities. Some of these items may seem obvious, but they are included for less experienced personnel.

Stop the release

Spills will be from one (or both) of two sources, a vessel or dockside equipment. In the event the spill is found to originate from a vessel, notify the vessel immediately. Assist the vessel in any way possible to

LOCATION	Issue Date	Procedure No.
Emergency Plan Manual	_/_/_	EPIP-380
Oil Spill Response	Rev. Date	Revision No.
	_/_/_	0
		Page _ of _ Pages

ATTACHMENT 2
PAGE   of   PAGES

safely stop the flow of oil into the environment. It may be necessary for the vessel to transfer cargo from a damaged compartment to stop a release. If the vessel does not have available capacity onboard, it may request to discharge cargo to shore.

A spill from damaged or faulty dockside equipment may also occur. In most cases, initial actions will be to stop a transfer, if one is in progress, and depressurize the system involved.

Containment at the source

If a spill is originating from a vessel, notify the vessel master that you are initiating spill containment and cleanup activity on the vessel's behalf. If the master states that she or he will call her or his own contractor, explain that due to our contractor's quick response capability, we are going ahead with containment activities. We will consider having our contractor stand down when other forces are on site, ready to begin work.

Our primary spill contractor is NAME. NAME should be called immediately to boom the source of any spill and will clean up minor spills in the immediate dock area. NAME should be on scene within 15 to 20 minutes during working hours and about 30 minutes to 1 hour during off-hours. NAME is equipped to deploy COMPANY's boom which is stored at three locations on site. NAME also maintains a stock of sorbents and other supplies to clean up minor spills.

The LOCATION also retains a spill contractor from LOCATION, NAME. The spill contractor should be called in also to attack major spills that will have impacts well beyond our dock facilities.

NAME maintains a variety of equipment including trailers ready to respond to different spill emergencies, for example,

- Six quick-response trailers, preloaded with 1500 feet of boom, boat, sorbents, drums, and filter fence material

- Five containment trailers, preloaded with 5000 feet of boom and a boat for quick deployment.

- Five spill equipment trailers, preloaded with sorbents, hose, pumps, tools, etc.

ATTACHMENT 2
PAGE   of   PAGES

Therefore, you must be prepared to give NAME sufficient information to respond with the proper resources. A detailed list of NAME's equipment is included in this section.

Clearly, having two contractors available may lead to some confusion. However, proper planning, training, and some forethought should eliminate any problems. NAME gives us a quick response to contain and clean up relatively small spills. NAME is a large company which can provide additional workers and equipment to address a major emergency.

It is impossible to detail specific guidelines for when NAME should be called out; that judgment will have to be made given the specifics of an event. If a spill is significant or has the potential to have impacts beyond our immediate dock area, call NAME. It is better to overreact initially and be able to scale back than to have a situation get out of control.

ATTACHMENT 3
PAGE   of   PAGES

Land Spill or Seepage

Responsibilities of on-scene personnel

1. Report the spill or seepage to the affected area supervisor so that an appropriate response can be made.

2. If you are contaminated by the leaking substance, use the nearest safety shower and then report to medical for further treatment.

Responsibilities of affected area personnel

1. Take any safety control steps needed to abate the ongoing leak or seepage. This action may entail calling out emergency damage control support from central maintenance. In any case, the material leaking or seeping should be clearly identified so appropriate protective clothing and equipment are employed.

2. Notify the TITLE of the spill or seepage and assist that person in classifying the incident per EPIP-510, Assessment of Emergency Conditions, Emergency Classification, and Protective Action Recommendation Guides.

3. The TITLE and/or FIC may implement the EMP in support of the unit or area with the problem.

4. The incident support director (if activated) will notify the appropriate agencies or corporate groups (EPIP-420):

   - National Response Center (800) 424-8802
   - State (###) ###-####
   - Company (###) ###-####.

Note: Land spills or seepage which require cleanup of potentially hazardous materials will require the use of cleanup contractors trained and appropriately equipped per HAZWOPER guidelines approved by the LOCATION. Attachment 5 to this EPIP gives call-out instructions for cleanup contractors.

ATTACHMENT 3
PAGE   of   PAGES

5. The incident support director will report the following:

- Company name and site location
- When and where the spill occurred
- What was spilled
- How much was spilled
- What is being done to contain and clean up the spill

The ISD will also log the time the call was made and ask the name of the individual receiving the call.

6. The FIC and/or ISD will complete a spill incident report form (attachment 7 to this EPIP) or delegate this responsibility to the appropriate party.

7. If COMPANY personnel are involved in cleanup activities, they will clean up all response equipment and return it to the proper storage area when done. They will wear safety equipment and protective clothing approved for the job by the safety coordinator.

ATTACHMENT 4
PAGE   of   PAGES

Oil Spill Contractors

NAME maintains and deploys the LOCATION-owned oil spill response equipment. NAME keeps LIST EQUIPMENT to facilitate the deployment of this equipment.

NAME employees and their supervisor live nearby and are on call 24 hours a day. Their response time is approximately _____ minutes during normal business hours and 1 hour during weekends and evenings.

The second tier of contractor resources upon which LOCATION relies is NAME. The LOCATION subscribes to the AREA OIL SPILL CONSORTIUM offered by NAME. As such, we have access to NAME's personnel and spill response equipment. Through NAME, the LOCATION also has access to the personnel and equipment of NAMEs.

The LOCATION also maintains an inventory of oil spill response equipment for use in responding to both small spills, which do not have the potential to affect surface waters, and larger spills in which the services of NAME and other contractors are required. A revolving inventory of absorbent pads and hay bales is carried at LOCATION. Mobile spill response equipment located within the LOCATION includes

- List equipment.

This equipment is immediately available to the affected area supervisor. The affected area supervisors and operators are trained in the use of this equipment.

ATTACHMENT 5
PAGE   of   PAGES

Oil Spill Containment Equipment: Spill Response Trailer

Inventory, date

Sorbents

List

Containment boom and accessories

List

Pumps and accessories

List

Hand tools

List

Miscellaneous

List

Inventory of boom on dock

List

Inventory of sorbent

List

ATTACHMENT 6
PAGE   of   PAGES

Emergency Cleanup Contractors

Land Spills:

Marine Spills:

NAME
ADDRESS
PHONE NUMBERS

PHONE LIST

Name	Home	Beeper	Mobile	Portable

Land Spills: The field incident commander (FIC) will call for outside assistance via the security coordinator, if necessary. Telephone lists are maintained in EPIP-420, Emergency Communications.

Marine Spills: NAME handles marine spill and cleanup for the LOCATION. Its phone list is shown in attachment 5 of this EPIP.

If outside assistance is required from NAME members for a marine spill, the shift supervisor should notify the FIC.

```
              EPIP-380  ATTACHMENT 7
              SPILL INCIDENT REPORT FORM

Location_____  Date_____
Affected Waterway_____  Tide Stage_____
Time Spill Occurred_____  Time Observed_____
Wind Direction_____ Wind Speed_____  Wave Action_____
                                         (calm, mod., light)
Weather_____  Temperature_____
       (fair, showers, cloudy, etc.)
Area Likely to be Affected_____
Nature of Spill, Including Cause of Spill/Related Danger:
_____
_____
_____
_____

Action Being Taken, Including Agencies Involved, Methods:
_____
_____
_____

Persons and Agencies Notified:_____
_____
Agencies Conducting Investigation of Spill:_____
_____
Legal Action Taken or Contemplated:_____
_____
Known Publicity, Including Statements Made to News Media,
Agencies, or Others Outside the Company:_____
_____

Give the Following Information if Vessel or Barge Involved:
Name of Craft:_____  Barge Number:_____
Owner:_____  Owners Phone No._____
Address:_____  Zip Code:_____
Product:_____
Vessel Tank(s) Involved:_____
Volume in Vessel or Barge:_____  Draft:_____
Location of Vessel or Barge:_____  Position:_____
                          (dock no.,etc)        (spot no.)
Additional Comments:_____
_____
_____
_____

cc: TITLE
    TITLE
    Incident Support Director

SIGNATURE_____  TIME:_____
```

Attachment 8

Incident-Reporting Flowchart
(Insert Incident-Reporting
Flowchart here)

COMPANY
LOCATION

EMERGENCY MANAGEMENT
PLAN MANUAL

EMERGENCY
EXTERNAL NOTIFICATION
EPIP-410

REVISION 0

DATE

SUBMITTED BY: _____ DATE: _____
TITLE

APPROVED BY: _____ DATE: _____
TITLE

1.0 Purpose

This procedure provides guidance and instructions for notifying off-site company, corporate, federal, state, and local authorities in the event of a declared emergency.

2.0 Applicability

This procedure applies to designated emergency management/response organization (EMRO) personnel with emergency notification responsibilities.

3.0 Definitions

None.

4.0 Instructions

4.1 Precautions

4.1.1 For emergency notifications outside the LOCATION, the initial message will be transmitted by voice communications. Follow-up messages should be sent by telecopier (facsimile) for legal records; however, voice communications are acceptable if it is impractical to use fax for any reason.

4.1.2 An emergency message form is found as attachment 4 to this EPIP, Telephone Incident Report. When you are using voice communications to transmit emergency message form information, cover each paragraph, in sequential order, with specific, concise diction.

4.1.3 Each message form transmitted verbally should be completed in its entirety by using current information or the phrase *not applicable*.

4.1.4 In drill and exercise situations, initial communications related to an event should be *preceded and followed* by *"This is a drill."*

4.1.5 All bracketed information on a message form is considered proprietary data and is not to be released.

4.2 Initial actions

4.2.1 Notification and reporting. The affected area supervisor is responsible for making the required notifications for all incidents meeting the classification criteria for declared emergencies. Required notifications include

- National Response Center (NRC)
- LIST STATE AGENCIES
- LIST COUNTY AGENCIES

See attachments to this section for phone numbers and associated report forms.

For all other environmental and/or safety incidents requiring off-site agency notification, the incident support director (ISD) or a qualified representative will be responsible for ensuring proper notification is accomplished. This includes responsibility for making the required notifications for oil spills that do not have the potential to reach surface waters.

Required notifications include:

- List those applicable
- SARA reportable release: NRC, state, county
- CERCLA reportable release: NRC
- Fatality and/or multiple hospitalizations: Occupational Safety and Health Administration (OSHA)

4.3 Subsequent actions

4.3.1 Record-keeping requirements. All personnel with assigned communication responsibility, once in position, will maintain a communication log, using form EPIP-210-1, Activities Record Sheet.

Upon termination of the emergency, the affected area supervisor, the incident support director, and the communications coordinator will ensure that all communication records are filed in accordance with standard operating procedures.

5.0 References

Emergency management plan, section 4

EPIP-240, Duties of the Emergency Management/Response Organization during Emergencies

EPIP-420, Emergency Communications

EPIP-510, Assessment of Emergency Conditions, Emergency Classification, and Protective Action Recommendation Guides

EPIP-711, Managing Public Information

6.0 Attachments

Attachment 1, Notification Instructions

Attachment 2, Telephone Numbers

Attachment 3, Incident Report Forms

Attachment 1: Notification Instructions

Emergency message format

When off-site emergency organizations are to be notified, the following format will be used:

1. Assess and classify the incident (EPIP-510).

2. Determine if an off-site *protective action recommendation* (*PAR*) is required. If PAR is necessary, contact TITLE to notify local authorities.

3. Ensure appropriate activation of the EMRO.

4. Maintain a log of all incoming and outgoing communications, using form EPIP-210-1.

5. Record the times that notification calls are placed.

Upon contact with off-site entities:

6. Give your name and title.

7. Briefly inform them of the situation.

8. Where appropriate, note which individual was contacted.

9. During the notification process, depending on the time of day, make no more than two attempts at contacting the external organization.

Attachment 2: Telephone Numbers

National Response Center	1-800-424-8802
Environmental Protection Agency (EPA), region	1-###-###-####
EPA emergency spill phone	1-###-###-####
National Chemical Transportation Emergency Center (CHEMTREC), Washington, D.C.	1-800-424-9300
Poison Control Center	###-####
State hazardous waste emergency response team	###-####

Attachment 3: Incident Report Forms

Telephone incident report

1. Caller: _____ Phone number: _____

2. Call received by: _____ Date: _____ Time: _____

3. Date of incident: _____ Time of incident: _____

4. Location of incident: _____
   _____

5. General description of incident: _____
   _____
   _____

6. Identify all hazardous materials (including products and feed-stocks) involved:
   _____
   _____
   _____
   _____

7. If spill or leak, estimate gallons spilled: _____

   Estimate gallons recovered: _____

   Net gallons lost: _____

8. Names of injured (employees and others): _____
   _____
   _____

9. Names of fatalities (employees and others): _____
   _____
   _____

10. Estimate value of loss to company property: $_____

11. Estimate value of loss to property of others: $_____

12. Action taken to mitigate incident: _____

_____

13. Circle those of the following that have already been notified by reporting party:

- TITLE
- TITLE
- TITLE

14. This report relayed to:

Date:

Time:

TITLE   _____

TITLE   _____

TITLE   _____

TITLE   _____

TITLE   _____

Other   _____   _____ _____

_____   _____ _____

15. Remind caller to follow up in writing as appropriate.

Form 1: Emergency Reporting

The NRC Watchstanders will need concise and accurate information. Be prepared to report as much of the following information as possible:

1. Your name: _____

   Address: _____

   Phone Number: _____

2. Party or individual responsible for the incident

   Name: _____

   Mailing address: _____

   Phone number: _____

3. The incident occurred or was discovered

   Date: _____

   Time: _____

4. Specific location of incident: _____
   _____

5. Name of material spilled and/or released: _____

6. Source of spilled material: _____

7. Cause of release: _____

8. Total quantity discharged: _____

9. Material release to air, ground, water, or subsurface: _____
   _____

10. Amount spilled to water: _____

11. Weather conditions: _____

12. Vessel name, railcar number: _____

13. Name of carrier: _____

14. Number and type of injuries and fatalities: _____
    _____

15. Have evacuations occurred? _____

16. Estimated dollar value of property damage: _____

17. Description of cleanup actions taken and future plans: _____

_____

18. Other agencies you have notified or plan to immediately notify:

_____

_____

COMPANY

LOCATION

EMERGENCY MANAGEMENT
PLAN MANUAL
EMERGENCY COMMUNICATIONS
EPIP-420

REVISION 0

DATE

SUBMITTED BY: _____ DATE: _____
                 TITLE

APPROVED BY: _____ DATE: _____
                 TITLE

1.0 Purpose

This procedure provides a description of the LOCATION communications equipment, guidance for its use during emergencies, and an emergency telephone directory which may be useful in contacting outside agencies.

2.0 Applicability

This procedure applies specifically to EMRO personnel who have been assigned communication responsibilities; however, it may be used by any personnel with the need to communicate outside the LOCATION during emergencies.

3.0 Definitions

None.

4.0 Instructions

4.1 Precautions

4.1.1 Outside communications are to be carefully controlled during emergencies. Do not give out information to unidentified personnel. If you receive a call from someone you do not know, log the concern, using form EPIP-210-1, and refer any questions to TITLE, as appropriate.

4.1.2 In the event this procedure is initiated as part of an emergency preparedness drill or exercise, initial radio and telephone communications will be *preceded and followed* by the statement *"This is a drill."*

4.2 General information

The emergency management/response organization uses the following voice communications systems during an emergency at the LOCATION:

- Communications carriers and cellular telephone service outside the LOCATION. The wire line systems can also carry data from facsimile machines and computers.

- *Private branch exchange (PBX) systems.* Wire line telephone service within the LOCATION is carried by a pair of local switches which link "extensions" to one another and interconnect to outside services via communications carriers.

- *Two-way radio communication systems.* The LOCATION has EQUIPMENT and several smaller, conventional two-way radio systems which are used for emergency and normal operations.

4.3 Initial actions

4.3.1 Emergency manager. After assuming the role of emergency manager, in accordance with EPIP-220, the emergency manager will

- Ensure that communications with the incident support director, field incident commander, and affected area manager are established and maintained.

- Ensure appropriate activation of the EMRO per instructions in EPIP-250, Activation of the Emergency Management/Response Organization.

4.3.2 Emergency management/response organization. Personnel assigned to the EMRO should try to keep all communications formal, accurate, and timely and should make only those calls that are necessary for mitigation of the emergency condition, since communications resources can become overloaded and adversely impact the emergency response.

4.4 Communications instructions

4.4.1 Telephone dialing instructions. [Insert dialing instructions for your location.]

4.4.2 Computer system. [Insert computer instructions for your location.]

4.4.3 Radio communications. [Insert radio instructions for your location.] For example:

Radio call names

FIC	Command
Fire station	Base
EOC	Administration
ISC	Support
ISD	Unit 1
Main gate	Main gate

4.5 Subsequent actions

4.5.1 All personnel should ensure that records of significant communications are maintained, using form EPIP-210-1, Activities Record Sheet, and/or the Telephone Incident Report form (attachment 4 to EPIP-410).

4.5.2 The communications coordinator will ensure that the records of incoming and outgoing emergency response communications are properly entered in the communication logbook in the EOC.

4.5.3 Upon termination of the incident, designated communications personnel will ensure that all communication records are sent to the incident support director.

5.0 References

Emergency management plan, section 4

EPIP-410, Emergency Notification

6.0 Attachments

Attachment 1, Emergency Telephone Directory.

Attachment 1: Emergency Telephone Directory

Contents

Emergency telephone list

COMPANY environmental health and safety contacts

COMPANY emergency management/response organization

COMPANY emergency contact list

COMPANY emergency assistance roster

COMPANY cellular phones

Emergency telephone list

Off-site Department of Public Safety	XXX-XXXX
Off-site fire department	XXX-XXXX
Hospital	XXX-XXXX

Environmental health and safety

Name	Home phone	Work extension	Cellular phone	Plant radio

Security

| | Home | Work | Plant |
| Name | phone | extension | radio |

Medical department

| | Home | Work | Cellular | Plant |
| Name | phone | extension | phone | radio |

Emergency management/response organization

Emergency title	Name	Home phone

Power-fail phones

Location	Extension	Trunk number	Phone number

Cellular phones

Name   Number

Emergency phone numbers

National Response Center   1-800-424-8802
U.S. Coast Guard Marine Safety Office
State
Contractor
U.S. Fish and Wildlife Service
National Oceanic and Atmospheric Administration (NOAA)
Company contacts

COMPANY

LOCATION

EMERGENCY MANAGEMENT PLAN MANUAL

ASSESSMENT OF EMERGENCY CONDITIONS, EMERGENCY CLASSIFICATION, AND PROTECTIVE ACTION RECOMMENDATION GUIDES EPIP-510

REVISION 0

DATE

SUBMITTED BY: _____ **DATE:** _____
                  TITLE

APPROVED BY: _____ **DATE:** _____
               TITLE

1.0 Purpose

This procedure provides guidelines for initial incident assessment and subsequent emergency classification, and it delineates responsibilities for the activation of the emergency management plan (EMP).

2.0 Applicability

This procedure applies to the affected unit shift supervisor, field incident commander, and emergency manager. This procedure also serves as a reference for all personnel assigned to the LOCATION emergency management/response organization.

3.0 Definitions

3.1 Emergency conditions

These are situations occurring which cause or threaten to cause hazards affecting the health and safety of employees or the public, or which may result in damage to property.

3.2 Emergency classification

This is a classification system of emergency severity based on operational and monitored conditions at or near the LOCATION.

3.3 Internally reportable event

An *internally reportable event* is a minor incident or problem such as a small, localized fire, minor material release, equipment malfunction, unit upset, or other internal event which can be handled by unit personnel using standard operating procedures. It is not visible off site, requires no emergency response team, and requires no report to local, state, or federal regulatory agencies. This includes "Near Miss" situations as defined by OSHA in 29CFR1910.119, "Process Safety Management of Highly Hazardous Materials."

3.4 Unusual event (level 1)

An *unusual event (level 1)* is a minor emergency or problem such as a fire, material release, major equipment malfunction, unusual noise, unusual odor, abnormal and/or extended flaring activity, or other internal event which may be visible or detectable off site which may require a report to outside agencies, but which presents no off-site threat and requires no assistance or protective actions by off-site persons. *The situation is under control; however, response by in-plant personnel may be required.*

3.5 Alert (level 2)

An *alert* (*level 2*) is an emergency such as a fire, explosion, material release, major equipment malfunction, or other event which has the potential to escalate to a more serious emergency and/or affects plant operations. *The emergency is not under control but poses no threat to off-site areas; however, response by off-site personnel may be required.*

3.6 Site area emergency (level 3)

A *site area emergency* (*level 3*) is a serious emergency such as a fire, explosion, material release, major equipment malfunction, or other event that has occurred or is imminent which poses a threat to residents in the immediate vicinity and/or seriously affects plant operations. Response by off-site personnel is required. *The emergency is not under control, and protective actions by off-site persons may be necessary.*

3.7 General emergency (level 4)

A *general emergency* (*level 4*) is a severe emergency such as a fire, explosion, material release, major equipment malfunction, or other event that has occurred or is imminent which seriously affects off-site areas well beyond site boundaries and/or plant operations. Response by off-site personnel is required. *The emergency is not under control, and protective actions by off-site entities are necessary.*

4.0 Instructions

4.1 Precautions

4.1.1 Unit-specific operator actions required to mitigate the emergency condition are prescribed in standard operating procedures and are independent of any actions outlined in this procedure.

LOCATION	Issue Date	Procedure No.
Emergency Plan Manual	_/_/_	EPIP-510

Assessment of Emergency	Rev. Date	Revision No.
Conditions and Emergency	_/_/_	0
Classification		Page __ of __ Pages

4.1.2 Emergency management personnel classifying the event should consider the effect that combinations of events have upon the emergency classification; i.e., events taken individually would constitute a lower emergency classification, but collectively may dictate the need for a higher emergency classification.

4.2 Initial actions

4.2.1 Upon recognition that an abnormal or emergency condition exists, the affected area supervisor should be notified. Recognition of the event can occur as a result of either process operations or other personnel observing the abnormal or emergency condition.

4.2.2 The affected area supervisor should make an initial evaluation of conditions and request any needed assistance.

4.2.3 Process operators should initiate actions called for based upon the indicated symptoms and appropriate emergency operating procedures.

4.2.4 Upon notification of an emergency, the field incident commander (FIC), with input from the affected area supervisor, shall evaluate the event to determine the appropriate emergency classification level.

4.2.5 The FIC or affected area supervisor shall activate the EMRO as required for the type and classification of emergency.

4.2.6 The supervisor, emergency manager, and FIC may use attachments 1 and 3 of this EPIP to help classify the incident.

4.3 Protective action recommendation guides

4.3.1 The emergency manager or field incident commander is responsible for selecting and ensuring that the protective action recommendations are communicated to the county and state authorities in a timely manner.

The protective action recommendations generally concern the _____-mile EPZ. Protective action recommendations may be provided to county and state authorities for any potentially affected areas outside that EPZ.

LOCATION	Issue Date	Procedure No.
Emergency Plan Manual	_/_/_	EPIP-510

Assessment of Emergency	Rev. Date	Revision No.
Conditions and Emergency	_/_/_	0
Classification		Page __ of __ Pages

4.3.2 The LOCATION has no authority with respect to imposing protective action response options beyond the boundaries of the site.

4.3.3 Recommendations to the county will be made as appropriate to achieve the desired degree of protection for the public.

4.4 Protective actions: Initial actions

The initial protective action recommendation by the emergency manager or FIC to the county department will be based upon LOCATION conditions, meteorological data, and any exposure projection data available at the time.

The following factors will also be considered when a protective action recommendation is made:

4.4.1 *Population at risk,* including special concerns in the area of release

4.4.2 *Response time,* including the time to assemble needed resources in order to implement the recommendation

4.4.3 *Weather,* current conditions, short-term and long-term forecasts, and changes in wind direction

4.4.4 *Physical and environmental conditions*—limiting factors which will affect the response time of the off-site agencies

Note: All precautionary considerations to ensure safety of the public will be based upon available data to ensure the safety of the population at risk. The emergency manager/OEM and/or FIC will recommend the action to be taken, how much time is available to take the action, and the potential effects of the recommended action.

4.5 Responsibilities

The emergency manager and/or FIC is responsible for making protective action recommendations to off-site authorities and ensuring that personnel are properly protected. Information on LOCATION conditions to be considered concerning protective action recommendations is provided to the emergency manager by the field incident commander, incident support director, affected area personnel, and emergency operations center (EOC) personnel.

4.6 Subsequent actions

4.6.1 The FIC or emergency manager will continue to evaluate the incident and the potential of actual off-site consequences associated with the incident to determine the need for any change in the emergency classification.

4.6.2 The OSHA standard on process safety management of highly hazardous chemicals (CFR 1910.119) requires that incidents which result, or could have resulted, in a catastrophic release be investigated within 48 hours.

For level 0 and level 1 incidents, the affected area supervisor shall evaluate the incident and determine if it had catastrophic potential. If so, she or he shall notify the TITLE of appropriate responsible person(s) as soon as possible.

4.6.3 As LOCATION conditions change or are projected to change or as additional information becomes available, the protective action recommendations will be reevaluated and any changes will be transmitted to the county department.

4.6.4 Additional information for evaluating subsequent protective action recommendations is located in the last reference listed in this EPIP.

5.0 References

Emergency management plan, section 5, appendices H, I, and J

EPIP-210, Duties of the Emergency Manager

EPIP-230, Duties of the Field Incident Commander

EPIP-410, Emergency External Notification

EPA-520/1-75-001, *Manual of Protective Action Guides and Protective Actions for Nuclear Incidents,* Environmental Protection Agency, September 1975 (revised June 1980)

6.0 Attachments

Insert flowchart for classification of emergencies for your operations.

(Insert Flowchart for Specific Operation)

COMPANY

LOCATION

EMERGENCY MANAGEMENT PLAN MANUAL

EVACUATION, SHELTERING, AND ACCOUNTABILITY
EPIP-520

REVISION 0

DATE

SUBMITTED BY: _____ DATE: _____
TITLE

APPROVED BY: _____ DATE: _____
TITLE

1.0 Purpose

This procedure provides guidelines for evacuation, sheltering, assembly, and accountability.

2.0 Applicability

This procedure is applicable to LOCATION employees, contractor personnel, security personnel, and visitors.

This procedure is effective during any emergency condition requiring evacuation and/or sheltering.

3.0 Definitions

3.1 Nonessential personnel

Nonessential personnel fall into one of the following categories:

- Employees not having emergency assignments
- Visitors
- Contractor and construction personnel
- Individuals who are involved in nonoperational activities

3.2 Sheltering

Sheltering involves members of the population at risk seeking shelter in designated control rooms and/or buildings that can be made relatively airtight.

3.3 Area or building evacuation

This is the evacuation of specific on-site areas or buildings due to an incident affecting those areas. This evacuation may not affect all personnel or all areas and may be prompted by one of the following conditions:

- Uncontrolled release of toxic materials
- A fire requiring the assistance of the volunteer fire department
- Any incident that, in the opinion of the field incident commander and/or emergency manager, requires evacuation as a protective action measure

3.4 Site evacuation

A partial or total evacuation of all nonessential personnel from the LOCATION may be required if a site area emergency or general emergency is declared.

3.5 Refinery evacuation routes

Evacuation routes in the LOCATION will be determined by incident circumstance, and supervisors will advise evacuees of appropriate egress options. These routes will be assessed to determine a safe route of egress.

3.6 Visitors

Visitors are any personnel requiring an escort and whose safety and conduct are the responsibility of that escort.

3.7 Assembly areas

Assembly areas are locations in and around the LOCATION where personnel will congregate in the event of an evacuation.

4.0 Instructions

4.1 Precautions

Prompt and accurate evaluation of the incident is necessary to determine the need for and extent of evacuation and/or sheltering.

Individuals requiring an escort will remain with an escort at all times until released by EMRO personnel.

LOCATION security will have the authority to direct the activities of contract security during emergency conditions in accordance with security standard operating procedures.

Personnel in an affected area will be alerted promptly to expedite sheltering in the area and to prevent any unnecessary exposure to airborne contamination or other hazards.

Personnel working in the affected area will assemble as directed by the emergency manager or field incident commander.

Upon hearing the sheltering announcement or alarm signal, emergency organization personnel will report to their assigned emergency facility, unless directed otherwise by the emergency manager.

Upon hearing the evacuation announcement or alarm signal, emergency organization personnel will report to their assigned emergency facility and/or areas as directed. Personnel working in the affected area will evacuate the area, observing recognized evacuation routes. Possible routes are shown in appendix I, Evacuation Routes, and are posted throughout the LOCATION. Egress for the LOCATION will normally be via the main roads through the main gate. Alternate routes through the [Insert instructions].

Personnel will not reenter an affected area unless specific authorization has been given by the field incident commander and/or emergency manager.

If time permits, personnel will place their equipment in a safe condition before proceeding to the nearest designated shelter area.

Other personnel should avoid the affected area.

It shall be the responsibility of the supervisor in charge of each operating facility to assess the seriousness of any developing situation and decide whether to shut down and/or sound the alarm to evacuate the immediate area, based on her or his best judgment and training. Examples of situations which might warrant the shutting down and/or evacuation of an area or adjacent areas are listed here:

1. [Insert situation information.]

2. [Insert situation information.]

3. [Insert situation information.]

4. Verified bomb threat

5. Hazardous materials release that poses an imminent threat

6. A situation out of control at an adjacent process unit

4.2 Initial actions

4.2.1 Evacuation. When a site evacuation is ordered, all nonessential personnel will leave the LOCATION in accordance with routine egress procedures as outlined in attachments 1 to 4.

Each manager of an emergency facility (incident support center, emergency operations center), or a representative, will provide a roster of the personnel in the facility to the security shift supervisor within 30 minutes after activation of that facility.

Within 30 minutes after the evacuation has been ordered, the security supervisor will provide the emergency manager with a list of names of personnel unaccounted for in the LOCATION.

The list generated for the emergency manager will be updated until all personnel have been located.

To locate missing individuals, the security supervisor will initiate steps such as reviewing gate logs, interviewing coworkers, and checking sign-in sheets to determine the last known location of the individual. As required, these activities will be coordinated with the security and/or communications coordinator.

After the initial 30-minute accountability period, security will maintain continuous accountability of all individuals within the LOCATION throughout the duration of the emergency condition.

When an evacuation is ordered, personnel in the affected area(s), unless assigned an emergency function, will proceed to a designated assembly area.

Everyone is responsible for the safety of his or her coworker; therefore, absenteeism should be reported to security as soon as possible.

All visitors will be escorted to a designated assembly area at the administration building. *Note:* This may include some individuals who are involved in nonoperational activities.

Local law enforcement agencies responding to an evacuation should assist by providing traffic access control in coordination with the EMRO.

4.2.2 Sheltering. The field incident commander and/or emergency manager will:

- If not already initiated, initiate sheltering if the area cannot be evacuated or if evacuation cannot be accomplished in a timely manner.

- Make a LOCATION-wide radio announcement addressing the nature of the incident and the sheltering procedures to be followed. The radio announcement should include information concerning the area to be sheltered, hazards that should be avoided, and any special instructions to be followed.

- Advise local law enforcement agencies of the site sheltering order, as appropriate.

- Inform county department to notify adjacent facilities in accordance with EPIP-410, Emergency External Notification.

Personnel responding to a sheltering announcement or alarm will:

- Shelter in the areas listed in attachments 1 to 4 unless otherwise directed by the field incident commander and/or emergency manager.

- Remain at the designated assembly area until released by emergency organization personnel or the emergency manager.

In the event that sheltering is ordered, *security* will account for all personnel within the LOCATION in accordance with security standard operating procedures and/or attachment X.

4.3 Subsequent actions

Those who may have been exposed to toxic materials will inform an EMT or medical representative.

Personnel will remain in the assembly area until released by the field incident commander or the emergency manager. Should the safety of a designated assembly area be compromised, personnel at that area will be directed to an alternate assembly area.

Area *supervisors* (including contractors), upon hearing the shelter order, should ensure that personnel in their areas have heard the alarm and are sheltering and then immediately shelter themselves. *Note:* This *does not* mean that supervisors must physically account for all personnel reporting to them. If required, the emergency manager in consultation with the field incident commander will initiate the necessary actions to locate any missing persons.

5.0 References

Emergency management plan, section 5, appendices I and J

EPIP-410, Emergency External Notification

Security standard operating procedures

6.0 Attachments

Attachment 1, Assembly Points

Attachment 2, Accountability Checklist

Attachment 3, Shelter-in-Place Checklist

Attachment 4, Evacuation Checklist

Attachment 1: Assembly Points

Location

Muster/assembly points

Attachment 2: Accountability Checklist

Supervisor or designee

1. Conduct a head count.

2. Determine whether any visitors were at the unit (check unit visitor sign-in log) and the status of visitors.

3. Determine whether any injuries were sustained during movement to the assembly area. If injuries or fatalities occurred, call the field incident commander and/or incident support director for immediate assistance.

4. Coordinate the head count and unit visitor status with the field incident commander and/or incident support director. Identify any missing or unaccounted for personnel.

5. Advise all personnel to remain in the assembly area.

6. Outside operators, dock personnel, and/or other remote-location personnel can be accounted for via radio.

Attachment 3: Shelter-in-Place Checklist

1. Close all doors to the outside, and close and lock all windows (windows sometimes seal better when locked).

2. Set all ventilation systems to 100 percent recirculation so that no outside air is drawn into the structure. Where this is not possible, ventilation systems should be turned off.

3. Turn off all heating systems.

4. Turn off all air conditioners and switch inlets to the closed position. Seal any gaps around window-type air conditioners with tape and plastic sheeting, wax paper, aluminum wrap, or other available materials.

5. Turn off all exhaust fans.

6. Close as many internal doors as possible.

7. Use tape and plastic food wrapping, wax paper, aluminum wrap, or other available material to cover and seal vents and other openings to the outside to the extent possible (including any obvious gaps around external windows and doors).

8. If the gas or vapor is soluble or even partially soluble in water, hold a wet cloth or handkerchief over your nose and mouth if gases start to bother you. For a higher degree of protection, go into a bathroom, close the door, and turn on the shower in a strong spray to "wash" the air. Seal any openings to the outside of the bathroom as best as you can.

9. If an explosion is possible outdoors, close drapes, curtains, and shades over windows. Stay away from external windows to prevent potential injury from flying glass.

10. Minimize the use of elevators in buildings. These tend to "pump" outdoor air in and out of a building as they travel up and down.

11. Await instructions from EMRO personnel, field incident commander, and/or incident support director.

Attachment 4: Evacuation Checklist

1. Sound evacuation alarm.
2. Account for all personnel, and report this information to one of the following:
   - Field incident commander
   - Incident support director
   - Your operations manager
3. Assess safety of primary assembly area.
4. Ensure all personnel remain at designated assembly areas.
5. Ensure accountability of outside operators via radio contact. Maintain radio contact with the outside operators (if not at assembly area) until all personnel are released by the field incident commander and/or incident support director.

Index

Index note: The *f.* after a page number refers to a figure.

ABOUT THE AUTHOR

Geary W. Sikich is the founder of Logical Management Systems, Corp. (LMS). His responsibilities include strategic planning, business development, financial management of corporate assets, and client consultation.

Mr. Sikich is the author of *It Can't Happen Here: All Hazards Crisis Management Planning* (PennWell Books, 1993). He has also written extensively for a variety of business publications.

LMS's clientele includes *Fortune* 1000 companies, representing all facets of industry, health care, and professional service corporations. Internationally the firm is involved in projects for OPEC member countries, as well as European and Asian countries.

Mr. Sikich has developed federally mandated Hazardous Materials Response Plans for clients throughout the United States. He has provided litigation support as an expert witness on emergency planning, training, crisis communications, and information management for the nuclear industry. He has also developed HAZVAL, an environmental assessment program, IPAC, an incident response assistance program, and AUDITRAK, an emergency preparedness evaluation program.